THE STORY OF
ENGLAND

THE STORY OF
ENGLAND

TOM BEAUMONT JAMES

TEMPUS

I dedicate this book to the memory of my father,
James Lyne Beaumont James (1886–1952)
whose Story of France *was completed in Paris, August 1916,*
during the battle of the Somme.

Cover Illustration: Sun shining through Stonehenge. Photograph taken by Harald
Sund. Reproduced courtesy of Getty Images.

First published 2003

Tempus Publishing Limited
The Mill, Brimscombe Port,
Stroud, Gloucestershire, GL5 2QG
www.tempus-publishing.com

© Tom Beaumont James, 2003

The right of Tom Beaumont James to be identified as the Author
of this work has been asserted in accordance with the
Copyrights, Designs and Patents Act 1988.

British Library Cataloguing in Publication Data.
A catalogue record for this book is available from the British Library.

ISBN 0 7524 2578 1

Typesetting and origination by Tempus Publishing Limited.
Printed in Great Britain by Midway Colour Print, Wiltshire.

Contents

England is the single country in the world that, in looking after its own interest with meticulous care, has at the same time something to give others; the single country in the world where patriotism does not represent a threat to the rest of the world...

Wilhelm Dibelius, 1922

The English character is not a removable part of the British Empire; it is the foundation of the whole structure, and the secret strength of the American Republic.

Walter Raleigh, 1918

The full flood of 'England' swept him on from thought to thought. He felt the triumphant helplessness of a lover.

Rupert Brooke, 1914

England, queen of the waves, whose green inviolable girdle enrings thee round.

Algernon Swinburne, 1877

England is a great and powerful nation, foremost in human progress, enemy to despotism, the only safe refuge for the exile, friend of the oppressed.

Giuseppe Garibaldi, 1854

And did those feet in ancient time
Walk upon England's mountains green?
And was the holy Lamb of God
On England's pleasant pastures seen?

William Blake, 1808

An Englishman is content to say nothing when he has nothing to say.

Samuel Johnson, *c.*1750

All the people of Europe are not equally subject to their princes: for instance the impatient humour of the English seldom gives their king the time to make his power heavy.

Baron de Montesquieu, 1721

Walls of Oak. England hath the best in the world, not for fineness but for firmness... our English oak is the substantial outside.

Thomas Fuller, 1662

Preface and
Acknowledgements

It is a commonplace that English is alone in having separate words for 'history' and 'story'. This distinctive feature of the English language has led to the choice of title: *The Story of England*. The text traces the development and inhabitants of England within the borders as we know them today, from 500,000 BC to the present. It begins with a reflection on England and the English. This is a an up-to-the-minute text, taking the longest view, and in so doing considers the past in a new way and raises issues for the future. This short book draws on both archaeology and history, taking evidence and examples from both.

There are no footnotes to impede the flow, and a short bibliography indicates some useful and contrasting approaches to the subject. I believe that individuals are important: Stonehenge (plate 43) was certainly neither conceived nor built by a committee. Someone made it happen, but we shall never know who. In equal measure groups and societies, masters and servants are important, whether as artists, in cemetery groups, entrepreneurs, intellectuals, rulers, soldiers or as subjects. I make no apology for retaining references of kings and queens in the historic period, where they were important; but I hope also to have shown the contribution of their subjects and of the millions of prehistoric occupants who preceded them, and created the English countryside of today.

This book began life as essays for the BBC's prize-winning series *This Sceptred Isle* (Sony 'Talkie' award 1996). That series covered the period from 55 BC to the death of Queen Victoria in 1901. The essays provided continuity of narrative between the episodic sources chosen by Christopher Lee and narrated by Anna Massey, with historical extracts read by the late Paul Eddington and Peter Jeffrey. The essays have been rewritten and extended in chronological scope for this book.

Among the many credits for bringing this to publication, I would like to thank Sue Anstruther of BBC Worldwide who commissioned me to do the original work; Mick Aston, for writing the introduction and for his warm friendship; Timothy Darvill, Stella Fletcher, Jonathan Foyle, and Christopher Gerrard who did his best to keep me outside and not 'on the bus' and provided much archaeological inspiration besides; Jonathan Reeve at Tempus who commissioned this book; Andrew Reynolds, Paul Stamper, John Steane, William Watson (who stuck up for the Scots), Julie Wright and many others, including colleagues at King Alfred's. My extended family have been helpful in many ways in answering detailed queries; my immediate family have been inconvenienced by the presence of my laptop on the corner of the kitchen table from time to time. To them I extend the warmest thanks, for making writing so pleasurable and for their many comments and insights.

Tom Beaumont James
Cheltenham 2003

Foreword

Scrambling through hedges and ditches at Shapwick in the early 1990s to show Tom and his family a Roman excavation of 'bones from Julius Caesar's dinner' we chatted about our mutual interest in the long sweep of English archaeology and history. My Shapwick Project has been looking at the dev-elopment of that Somerset village from prehistory to the present day. Tom is leading a similar, smaller-scale, project at Clarendon in Wiltshire. Likewise *Time Team*, which I have been involved in for over ten years, ranges from antiquity through the Middle Ages to industrial archaeology and the present – and much wider than England, the subject of this book. *Time Team* aims to bring the past to life for a wide spectrum of people. This book paints the story of England on a broad canvas: the development of the built environment, demography, econ-omy and social structure, and religion. It gets to grips with both archaeological and written evidence, while allowing each source to speak for itself from ancient times to now.

I came to archaeology through geography, Tom through history and we both share a common interest in the Middle

Ages. We are among that small group of people for whom 'medieval' is not a term of abuse! So much of England today, from place-names to parish churches, has firm roots in the Middle Ages where England literally began in the centuries following Roman times. Archaeology helps us to see that this naming process was applied to landscapes which were much older. Continuity is as much a theme in the study of England as change is. Above all archaeology and history bring us into contact with people and landscapes at all levels of past society. What is plain from this new study, which incorporates both disciplines, is that the English are not a race but a nation, from earliest times made up of migrant farmers and workers who, then as now, intermingle with those already there.

Mick Aston
4 September 2003
(Translation of St Birinus, Translation of St Cuthbert)

Introduction

In the distant past England was from time to time apparently cleared of settlers, depopulated by ice and victimised by the elements. Not surprisingly the English still worry about the weather. At least twice in the historic period plagues have reduced the population, perhaps to a million or fewer. Communities died out or fled, cultures were extinguished: new peoples arrived on our shores, new groups and priorities emerged. These changes, combined with the constants of the encircling Channel and mountains of Scotland and Wales, have led to the development of the unique identity of England and the English.

In telling the story from Piltdown Man to the pill boxes of the Second World War and beyond, from the invasion by the empire of Rome to the European Union, I have attempted to keep five themes alive: the built environment, population, economy, social structure and religion (details are found in the chronology, p.276). Wherever possible these subjects are illuminated from both the perspective of archaeology and of history, for example the Dissolution of the Monasteries was recorded by eyewitnesses and their ruination by the antiquary John Leland, but the archaeology of the book-clasps in the ashes of the reformers' fires, and the lead melted into ingots and stamped with Henry VIII's royal arms are equally dramatic evocations of religious reform.

Until recent advances in scientific methods it was not possible to closely date much in the prehistoric period. From 500,000 BC to 55 BC we rely almost solely on archaeology and some standing remains; thereafter there are increasing numbers of historical sources. Scientific dating has also transformed our understanding of the historic period, both in its material culture and its ecology. Each discipline tells its own story. Traditionally historians and archaeologists have dealt in different currencies: historians in dates, events and people; archaeologists in groups and societies, periods and phases, artefacts and structures. Archaeologists are now much more precise, both about when events took place (for example, the building of the Sweet Track (plate 42) in 3807 BC and 3806 BC), and about individuals – the ability to trace genetic links between a man of Cheddar today and Cheddar Man (plate 1) over 9,000 years ago, for instance. There are also differences in methods: historians 'go to the library'; archaeologists pull on their boots and go outside to see for themselves.

The quest for Englishness and the roots of our society is never-ending. We all want to know who we are and where we have come from. If we fuse together our historic view of the nation with current archaeological evidence we come ever closer to this discovery. Archaeology has taken this investigation far back into a past which is increasingly charted by accurate chronologies and, where links are made, by DNA. Archaeology can bring us closer to the past through skeletons, through reconstructions of faces and physiques and, on occasion, face-to-face with our English ancestors. The body of John Torrington was excavated in 1984; he had died on the ill-fated Franklin expedition which set out in 1845 searching for a north-west passage. Torrington and his colleagues were found to have traces of pneumonia and tuberculosis in their bodies, but most significantly high, and recent, concentrations of lead which is likely to have contributed to their untimely deaths. This kind of work brings us very close indeed to ordinary members of past times. But archaeology is as much about the lives as the deaths of former inhabitants of England: their homes and settlements, their work and their possessions. Today there is less talk of invasions and more of 'immigration', 'investigations' and 'visits', for example by Julius Caesar, the Anglo-Saxons, Vikings and Normans. To be sure there were elements of invasion, but in all cases strong links existed before the new rulers took over. Archaeology has significantly enhanced the shorthand of the historical date – of the 'Roman invasion AD 43' variety. It has also given us a clearer insight into the people the English once were and the path that led them to who they are today.

Many single words and phrases conjure up images of England and Englishness, past and present: rain (and the weather in general), afternoon tea, Church of England, cricket, football (and football-supporter rioting), the monarchy, the eccentric nobility, individualism, ingenuity as inventors, multiculturalism, National Health, politeness, public schools, reserve, the stiff upper lip and rule by outsiders. It is tempting to think that there is something exceptional and separate about the English and their language, but the truth is that, back as far as 7000 BC the

Indo-European language may have spread westwards into Europe and thence to England across the land-bridge. This group of languages provides common elements in Hindi and Sanskrit, as well as in Romance languages and what was to develop into the English language. Taken together these form as diverse a group of languages as are heard in England today. But the uniqueness of the people who 1,500 years ago became the English comes from the way in which they have drawn from everything they have encountered in the world to give us the England we have today. In this period since the age of Arthur the English have dominated the islands of Great Britain and Ireland. The AD 400s were that cradle of Englishness, when Germanic invaders made their laws in clearings in the forest. Since then the English nation has enjoyed an adolescence of wars with its neighbours in France and Spain, before maturing in the age of empire, thereafter beginning to settle into a grand, if troubled, old age in the twentieth century. The English it is plain to see are not a race but a nation, and always have been.

1

Albion and Britannia
Myth and Reality,
Prehistory and Romans

The Holy Grail of archaeology, the missing link between apes and men, was found, or so it appeared, near a Sussex pub at Piltdown in 1912. Thus as the twentieth-century English fought their way through two world wars, they did so in a spirit of confidence knowing that 'Piltdown Man' demonstrated their unrivalled antiquity as a people. The find was reported at the London Geological Society to a rapturous reception in December 1912, raising spirits at the close of a year of disasters: the loss of the *Titanic* and of Scott in the Antarctic. 'Piltdown Man' appeared to grasp *for England* the clearest evidence for human evolution through the remains of skulls, teeth and a jaw of what became known to contemporaries as the 'Earliest Englishman'. People at home and around the world who loved England embraced Piltdown and the significance of the find was enhanced by an associated find of a large bone shaped like a cricket bat! Surely this showed what had been demonstrated through the empire on which the sun never set: that the English were a chosen people – not merely since the first Elizabethan Age and as the

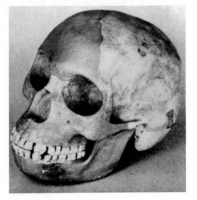

Piltdown Man (1912) was the hoax 'Earliest Englishman') compiled from a human cranium and an ape's jaw, stained to look ancient. The 'discovery' placed England ahead of Germany in the race leading up to the First World War to establish the cradle of Europe. Piltdown demonstrated the potential for the misuse of archaeological evidence before the era of reliable archaeological science.

inventors of cricket, but from earliest prehistory, in which the key artefact of the national sport had appeared in the archaeological record?

It was irritating for the English that their European rivals at that time, the Germans, had found a jaw (without a cranium) dubbed *Homo heidelbergensis* in 1907 which had held the stage as the missing link (stressing the antiquity of the 'new nation' united by Bismarck in 1871) as relations worsened and war loomed. English archaeology had faced a stiff challenge: Piltdown Man, with a 'complete' skull and jawbone put the matter beyond dispute. It not until 1954, as England launched enthusiastically into a new Elizabethan Age, that Piltdown was exposed as a fraud (an ape's jaw and a human cranium, stained to look antique) and discredited by modern scientific archaeology.

The good news is that, so far as the 'missing link' and England were concerned, Piltdown was not the end of the story. In the 1980s the remains of a human shin bone securely, and scientifically, dated to around 500,000 years ago, was found at Boxgrove, also in Sussex. This find restored the country's and the county's prehistoric archaeological reputations, and 'the oldest hominid' title was brought back to our shores. The Boxgrove *Homo erectus* find extended knowledge of humankind in England back far beyond the traditional dates for first colonisation of north-west Europe during the Old Stone Age (300,000–10,000 BC). During that period, between about 120,000 BC and 60,000 BC, for example, people occupied the caves and rock-shelters of the dramatic river-gorge site at Cresswell Crags (Derbyshire/Nottinghamshire). Boxgrove man shows that human communities had moved into England much earlier, indeed about half a million years previously. Unless in the future it is shown that human life developed independently on our island (which even for the most diehard Englishman must be unlikely), it must have been that the first dwellers in England made a short visit to an uninhabited land. As it was at that date merely a peninsula of north-west Europe, the land mass of England looked very different from its familiar island shape today.

The chewed remains of the once-muscular leg of Boxgrove man may yet prove to be a false horizon as it predates by 200,000–300,000 years a proposed parting of the ways between *Homo sapiens* (who developed in Africa and is believed to be our ancestor) and *Homo neanderthalensis* (a Rhenish-Prussian 'cousin' from near Düsseldorf). What remains fiercely debated is whether peoples diffused from Africa or whether there were regional developments as exemplified at Boxgrove and by *Homo neanderthalensis*. However, after the false dawn at Piltdown, Boxgrove has for the present at least given that most English of downland landscapes, Sussex, a secure place as a cradle of humanity. The very

17

A flint knapper at work. Compare this drawing with the knapping evidence from Boxgrove (Sussex), where remains of the oldest English man (or woman) were found in 1994 dating to c.500,000 BC – genuinely the oldest human remains in northern Europe.

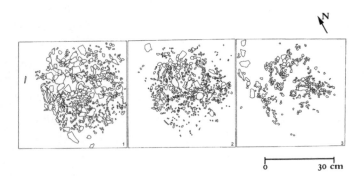

An individual seated on the ground knapped flints 500,000 years ago, the scatter falling around their legs. The quality of recording and the ability to date evidence such as that found at Boxgrove have enabled the establishment of prehistoric chronologies with a precision unimaginable even 50 years ago. Such discoveries have made chronological surveys much more secure.

unromantic Boxgrove quarry-site environment of today was vastly different 500,000 years ago when a sea-side cliff fall buried the bone, which had been gnawed at both ends by a large wolf-like creature. It was some 498,500 years later that the English (Anglo-Saxons, from northern Germany) arrived along the south coast to establish the basis of the English 'nation' as we know it today. Both groups exemplify the migrants who have sustained England since earliest times.

Bridging that gap between Boxgrove and the historic period is the well-tried formula for the prehistoric period of the Palaeolithic (Old Stone Age, 300,000–10,000 BC), Mesolithic (Middle Stone Age, 10,000–4000 BC), Neolithic (New Stone Age, 4000–2000 BC), Bronze Age (2000–700 BC) and Iron Age (700 BC–AD 43) which remain helpful terms, however much they shade into one another and overlap depending on region and people. Each period left its characteristic monuments: Stone Age long barrows, Bronze Age round barrows and Iron Age hill forts with their impressive earthen banks are all easily recognised.

Contemporaries of Boxgrove man occupied England long before the first *Homo sapiens* (modern humans) arrived in England *c.*40,000 BC. But even these settlers were displaced by the later Devensian Ice Age, the last ice sheet to affect England. Stone tools found in river gravels are likely to be cultural remains of the hunter-gatherers who moved around on the ice sheet, leaving their tools to be swept away in the rivers which carried away the melting ice-water. The evidence suggests people made occasional visits to what we know as England until the start of the post-glacial age, about 12,000 years ago when Arctic conditions around the ice-sheet enabled more extended residence in an inhospitable environment.

Street House Farm (Yorkshire) long barrow, which is characteristic of rectangular structures, including houses of the Neolithic. The immigrant Neolithic farmers created settlements from c.6000 BC, which were scattered through the countryside with major ceremonial centres about 40km apart.

The very substantial, if marshy, 'land-bridge' with Europe was swamped about 7000/6500 BC as the ice melted and the sea level rose. Hunter-gatherers gave way to farmers, who crossed from Europe and established the first agricultural communities around 4000 BC. Neolithic England then settled as an essentially agricultural economy with internal and external trade across the Channel. Radiocarbon dating to c.4000 BC of the early phase at one of these settler sites, which included a 'mortuary house' below the earthen long barrow at Fussell's Lodge (Wiltshire), makes it one of the oldest dated monuments in England. It now appears likely that the settlers began almost immediately on arrival to create long barrows, substantial burial monuments which also defined landholdings. In common with later invaders and migrants, these people made themselves and their culture highly visible. There are some 300 known long barrows in England. Fussell's Lodge long barrow contained the remains of almost sixty different people, together with pottery and an ox skull, the last placed carefully at the easternmost point. Cremated human remains were later buried in the mound. These monuments were meant to be seen. Typical is the great Belas Knap long barrow in Gloucestershire, sited on the top of a steep Cotswold scarp, where the remains of fifty people were found. Such monuments probably had a variety of purposes for which they needed to be seen in landscapes where, for the archaeologist, remains of habitation have proved elusive. Elsewhere these early people have placed assemblages of artefacts and bones under or within the monuments – antler picks, ox skulls and foot bones, pig remains, pottery, flints and other material. These groups of materials send us a message, but one blurred over the millennia. The great hump-backs of the barrows on skylines or in other prominent places, not to mention their horn-works and the associated ox-remains found within them, may hint at a relationship with some animal, ox or pig, deity. These people clearly valued their dead and thus their past; they also lived with animals in the present. While there are regional variations of types and rites, monuments such as long barrows are found from southern England to northern Scotland showing shared beliefs among different regional groups.

The oldest dated trackway in Europe is preserved in the damp of the Somerset peat. The Neolithic Sweet Track was built, according to dendrochronology (tree-ring dating) from trees cut down in the winter of 3807 BC and the spring of 3806 BC. At 1.8km long, this is a very substantial structure indeed and provides a brilliant insight into the organisational and practical skills of its builders. At the same period the great 'causewayed' camp or enclosure was established at Windmill Hill (Wiltshire), initially in a clearing in the forest. By 3500 BC it extended to 8ha in area and, with a 360m diameter of the outer ditch, it is also one of the largest such monuments known in England. Buried children, scattered adult bones and occupation-refuse identify this as a cultural centre, but its purpose is mysterious. The most widely supported theory is that it was a seasonal gathering point for people living in scattered and isolated farmsteads, for celebration and exchange of goods.

A millennium later the most spectacular monument of the Neolithic Age in England was created at Avebury (Wiltshire). It is a henge monument defined by stone circles and ditches which were established by 2600 BC, at about the traditional date for the introduction of Bronze Age metalworking. Those who created Avebury used beaker pottery and grooved ware. The beaker, as well as being used in funerary practices, was the vessel for that most English of activities, drinking beer (or mead)! References to henge-building, track-construction, drinking and worship remind us that these early people lived as well as died: they have left field systems, exquisite metalworking in bronze and other metals, and evidence of widespread links with the Continent.

Astronomical observations were significant to these early peoples as is shown at the greatest prehistoric monument of all, Stonehenge (Wiltshire), begun about 2950 BC and embellished *c.*2350 BC with bluestones, carried over 300km from Pembrokeshire to Wiltshire and sarsens weighing up to 50 tons each. Like so many grand monuments, both ancient and modern, Stonehenge probably remains unfinished more

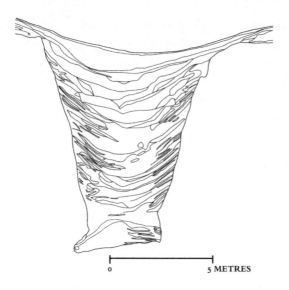

0   5 METRES

Grimes Graves Flint Mines (Norfolk) (3000–1900 BC). This is one of about 450 shafts which were sunk for the excellent flint used to make axes and knives. This shaft, excavated in 1971, is 12m deep and is one of the deepest dug to extract the best flint. Maybe as many as 5 million tools were produced from the site as a whole.

West Kennet (Wiltshire) long barrow, in use c.3800–3300 BC. The largest Neolithic long barrow in England where incomplete remains of some forty people were found. When William Stukeley, a leading antiquarian in the early 1700s, saw it he fancied it was the burial place of 'the archdruid' from nearby Stonehenge. In fact, modern dating has revealed that it predates the great circle by a millennium and the Druids by at least 3,000 years!

because successive generations made additions than because it was conceived as a single-period structure. Recent work, and much heated debate, has led to a re-evaluation of how to display Stonehenge and other monuments which are now rightly seen as elements in cultural landscapes, rather than as isolated collections of stones. This, together with a surge in interest in pre-Christian heritage and religion, has added greatly to the focus on these mysterious monuments. Silbury Hill (Wiltshire) (plate 5), which was developed to its largest extent soon after Avebury and Stonehenge, is reckoned to have taken 1.5 million man-hours to create, further reinforcing the idea of an organised and hierarchical society in late Neolithic England. From the point of view of Britain it is plain that the grandest monuments of the prehistoric period are in southern England, where the climate has always been the most clement.

Whereas it used to be thought that the great civilisations which emerged in the Near East and around the Mediterranean 'diffused' ideas through surrounding areas and eventually to England, recent research and improved dating techniques have established that henges are an indigenous British tradition. Monuments such as Stonehenge were original in concept and were the unique products of those who occupied the landscape around them. Stonehenge enjoys a bewildering range of interpretations of its function. This is not the place to discuss them. However, one thing that everyone can agree on is that it aligned towards the north-east/south-west, as later temples, cathedrals, churches and mosques are also aligned due east. The layout demonstrates that the people who built it wished to acknowledge the rising midsummer sun and the setting midwinter sun, and

Uffington (Oxfordshire, first millennium BC). The Bronze Age White Horse may have been a territorial marker or badge. This eighteenth-century view depicts the outline as having been different from what we see today, showing the value of tracing monuments back in the records. Dragon Hill is adjacent and the horse became associated with the tradition of St George slaying the dragon; another story associated it with Alfred's defeat of the Danes before AD 900.

may have used it for many other lunar and solar observations. All are agreed, on the evidence of scientific dating, that the keepers of Avebury and Stonehenge were not Druids and that it was not the burial place of the British kings who fought the Anglo-Saxons (who came much later), but whoever they were they may have enjoyed 'priestly' status.

Bronze Age peoples who succeeded the creators of Stonehenge in the landscape established their characteristic round barrows in a variety of designs, which were not built after around 1400 BC. The extraordinary White Horse at Uffington (Berkshire), carved in the chalk hillside followed another 500 years later, about 900 BC. With a lack of any scientific dating until recently, a tradition developed in the later Middle Ages that this carving represented not a horse, but the dragon slain by St George, whom the English adopted as their patron saint before AD 1350. While this tale is nonsense, the White Horse reminds us of the growth of interest in and value of the horse in prehistoric societies. Bronze Age people, as their name suggests, were the first to use metal tools. Bronze-working spread westwards, from the Caucasus via the Carpathian mountains into western Europe. Thus those in England were behind other peoples, for example the copper workers of Ireland. It used to be thought that different shaped skulls indicated immigrant populations; the current view is that such differences arise from normal genetic change in a continuous population. But if people were not on the move, ideas certainly were and it seems very likely that there were shared beliefs and a healthy exchange of ideas, as well as regionalisation. Thus while beakers have a wide continental currency, collared urns and food vessels are more localised in England. The development of trade is well attested in the archaeological record: two sunken shiploads dating to 1000–800 BC of Bronze Age artefacts, including axeheads have been found, one off Dover and one off Devon.

Bronze Age monuments were certainly spectacular, but they were comparatively few in number. In the late Bronze Age and during the greater part of the Iron Age (the last millennium BC), new types of monuments such as hill forts appear and novel iron weapons begin to feature. The traditional diffusionist theory suggests that these developments came with yet another series of invaders, collectively called Celts, and were not, therefore, home grown. But it has not proved possible to find an original homeland for these Celts, and extensive and detailed archaeological research has shown that while there were individual tribes who shared artistic and linguistic attributes, and were interlinked by commerce and kinship, they did not constitute a Celtic invasion in the centuries before the Romans came to England. Maiden Castle (Dorset) (plates 2, 3) is the largest and most impressive hill fort, extending to some 45ha, constructed between 500 and 400 BC. This was the centre for the Durotriges, who gave their name to Dorset and who illustrate a local strand in the interweaving of Celtic peoples and material culture which stretched across France and Spain as well as into Ireland, Scotland and Wales. The enormous size of the site with its four concentric rings of banks and ditches illustrates the organisational ability and manpower available to a 'tribe' at the edge of the 'Celtic' world in the pre-Roman period.

Around 1000 BC the climate began to deteriorate and it was around the beginning of the Iron Age, from about 700 BC, that hill forts proliferate. These were often within view of one another. Crickley Hill (Gloucestershire) occupies an impressive hilltop spur, fortified against attack from hill or valley. It developed from about 650 BC and by the 300s BC had a vertical stone wall and rock-cut ditch. Were their builders struggling to secure shares in dwindling resources? Or do the hill forts represent a healthy, wealthy system of exchange between tribes? Many went out of use as major centres about 50 BC, for reasons which are not clear. The most closely studied of these has been Danebury (Hampshire) where evidence of a diversity of structures was found within the grassy banks of this long-deserted site. Houses and above- and below-ground storage structures existed. Its development is broadly contemporary with Crickley Hill, with the major hill fort

Bronze Age (c.2500–700 BC) round house. Growing numbers of circular structures characterise the Bronze Age from multifarious round barrow types, ring cairns and developed stone circles down to the more humble, if complex to build, round houses. The warmer weather of the Bronze Age has allowed survival of numbers of upland field-system landscapes.

works dated to the 400s and 300s BC. Much evidence of occupation later on has been uncovered, perhaps for as many as 300 people, as well as evidence for exchange of goods using 'currency bars'. The presence of defences and trade items, as well as residential and storage structures, provides insight into social stratification in the Iron Age. As in Stone Age and Bronze Age archaeology, the study of environment and landscape has added a new dimension to our understanding. Water supplies and the ephemeral evidence of farms and homes create a picture of a well-peopled landscape with centres of exchange (and defence) at key points. There was evidence of attacks on the main gateway at Danebury, where supplies of unused missiles were discovered. The very existence of so many of these defended structures or forts is evidence of uncertain times as the last millennium BC progressed. There was continuity of use, even if there were also changes of function at Danebury, where an early hoard of bronze tools and weapons of about 600 BC is complemented by series of finds down to about AD 20, by which time Roman commodities were being imported.

On the evidence of the hill forts of Iron Age England violence was not all from within the country, part of it was caused by outsiders. In 55 BC, and again in 54 BC, Julius Caesar appeared in England. It is now doubtful that he intended to capture the island. Though undoubtedly heavily armed, his expeditions are characterised as 'interventions' rather than invasions with the purpose of conquest. He described the wild people he saw, who confronted his troops, standing atop the white cliffs ready to hurl down missiles. The people whom Caesar saw on the sheer cliffs spoke Celtic languages, derived from ubiquitous, ancient Indo-European, which is the basis of virtually all the languages of Europe and India. Thus Caesar, the Roman visitor, had more in common than he, and many subsequent historians, realised with those who defended their island against his forces. These late Iron Age people had fears of attacks from across the sea, as exemplified in their defended promontory lookouts and defences. In a tradition going back to the Neolithic, there is both archaeological and written evidence of cross-Channel economic contacts before Julius Caesar visited. The chalk-white cliffs of the English coast are generally believed to be the derivation of the poetic name 'Albion' (from *albus*, white) for England. Iron Age Britons lived in round houses (contrasting with the rectangular structures of the Romans) on scattered farmsteads some of which were defended, and which often had surrounding field systems and grazing. As in all periods of England's prehistory and history, diversity of altitude, geology and soil led to distinctive regional characteristics.

The ancient peoples of England created varied and sophisticated micro-civilisations of a tribal and chieftain type, which modern scientific dating techniques are helping us to understand. However, their military technology and bravery were no match for Roman armies intent on conquest, and all of Iron Age England was in time to fall victim to the Romans and their south-coast allies. However, when Julius Caesar visited in 55 BC, and again when he marched inland, took captives and extracted tribute in 54 BC, he was not intent on conquest. Even then England had previously witnessed many cultures and had endured previous waves of invaders, migrants and settlers. A century later, in AD 43, a more serious attempt at adding southern England to the Roman Empire began. It is this substantial and active Romanisation of England which separates it so clearly from Ireland (with which trade developed, but which was probably not invaded), and from Scotland and Wales (partially conquered but abandoned). To this day some Irish maintain that the contrast between the free-spirited, outward-going nature of the Irish in contrast to the more regimented character of the English derives from non-Romanisation of their ancient culture. The invasion of Caledonia (Scotland) culminated in a victory over the Picts (Painted People) at Mons Graupius (AD 84), after which the Romans created temporary marching camps perhaps as far north as Elgin. The northern frontier both of Roman Britain and the Roman Empire was established much further south at Hadrian's Wall, built after AD 122 to keep the Picts out, and subsequently at the Antonine Wall across the Scottish Lowlands (AD 143). These northern defences were difficult to sustain: the Antonine Wall was largely abandoned within twenty years of construction. The Romans found Britain north of Hadrian's Wall hostile and, like the Russians in Afghanistan during the late twentieth century, they lost many troops to the northern tribes. A conquest of Caledonia was not a possibility.

Conventionally, Roman occupation began after the invasion of AD 43 under Aulus Plautius on the orders of Emperor Claudius. An abiding image of this invasion comes from the exciting find of a Roman iron ballista bolt during Mortimer Wheeler's 1930s excavations of the Iron Age hill fort, Maiden Castle (Dorset), which was embedded in the spine of the defender it killed, apparently during the invasion of AD 43 as Wheeler, the soldier-archaeologist, interpreted. While this matching of an archaeological find to a historical source may be correct, archaeology has shown beyond doubt that neither the coming to England nor the departure of the Romans was a single historical event. There is plenty of evidence of contacts before AD 43, not least 55 BC and the finds at Danebury. These contacts softened the ground and led to a willingness of the inhabitants of south-east England to submit to the Romans, a view emphasised by the archaeological record. In southern England there was not only prior knowledge of, but acquiescence in, the events surrounding the year AD 43. Further north, though, the Romans made less impact until well after AD 100.

The land which thus passed under Roman control was peopled by descendants of ancient settlers. The Romans used the centres already established by these different groups as their military, urban strongholds, but elsewhere, as between Maiden Castle and Dorchester, they moved centres. The population of England when the Romans arrived was, perhaps, about a million people. Invasion by the Romans was not a simple issue of legions marching in, the local population being wiped out and being replaced by Roman settlers. Roman control depended on the support, or at least the acquiescence, of the natives. Traditionally it has been thought that the Romans invaded through Richborough (Kent) and fought their way westwards. However archaeology has begun to contribute another narrative, that of an invasion through the West Sussex coast, near Chichester, maybe as part of a two-pronged approach. The extraordinary palace complex excavated at Fishbourne (plate 4) in West Sussex – the largest palace west of Rome itself – was probably a reward for a Romanised local lord, Tiberius Claudius Togidubnus. A later inscription dubbed him 'Great King' of Britannia. He may have facilitated the Roman invasion through the south coast, as early Roman supply structures have been found near Chichester, adjacent to Fishbourne. Togidubnus may have contributed to the defeat of the rebellious Boudicca who swept south-west from Essex in AD 60 to meet her fate while crossing the Chilterns.

Roman civilisation – from '*civitas*', a city – differed from societal precursors in England in being based on towns, often developed from forts, and connected by a network of impressively engineered roads. Towns had planned streets, bordered by shops and houses, some laid out round courtyards. Communal facilities at the forum, at temples, theatres and baths were much more highly developed than in prehistoric settlements. Cemeteries lay outside town defences, their

Julius Agricola, a Roman Governor of Britain under the Emperor Domitian
[r.AD 51–96] introducing Roman arts and sciences into England [sic]*, the inhabitants*
of which are astonished and soon become fond of the Arts and manners of their cruel
invaders'. From Edward Barnard's History of England *c.1791 quoted by Martin*
Henig. Since Barnard the wheel has turned almost full circle: today Henig argues that
Roman Britain was largely the creation of the Britons themselves.

location dictated by all-pervading Imperial law. Roman
engineers transformed valley bottom sites, in contrast to prehistoric Britons whose major defended sites were often on
hilltops. At Chichester, Colchester and Winchester, for example, rivers were diverted to facilitate the development of
low-lying sites for walled towns.

Soon after the conquest of Britannia the wealthy Romano-
British élite created a comfortable villa culture in the

countryside of lowland England. The development of this culture is the strongest indication of England being part of the wider culture, the bigger system, engendered by Rome. Residents were confident of protection by the greatest army they had ever seen, whose camps and outposts have been excavated the length and breadth of the country. Evidence of mosaic floors and hypocaust heating systems, together with embossed red Samian ware from Gaul, glass, metalwork and coins abound on such sites. However, the vast majority of the conquered peoples lived much as before in round-timber, and mud huts, a design found especially in Britain over the last two millennia BC. The grains for their bread and the animals they raised similarly continued unchanged, although the Romans did introduce some new fauna and flora to England, probably including the vine.

In common with their prehistoric predecessors the Romans worshipped a variety of gods. There were four main strands: official Roman gods, Celtic deities, oriental religions such as Mithraism, and Christianity. Some intermingling of these strands took place. Thus at Bath (in Somerset) the Celtic Sulis and the Roman goddess Minerva became conflated (plate 6). A famous representation of this deity found there shows female Minerva with an unmistakable bushy moustache, precisely the facial adornment Caesar had noted among the natives he had fought. It was Roman policy to accommodate local deities of conquered peoples, just as Christianity in Saxon times accommodated local saints.

Constantine, whose father died at York in AD 306 and who was proclaimed emperor there, converted to Christianity in AD 312. Christianity subsequently became the official religion of the Romans. Pacifist Christianity gave way to the military Church parades. Christians whose predecessors had been martyred for refusing to fight now found the army a principal locus of the newly favoured religion. Christianity became an institution. The link between the Church and the military survives today in war memorials sited in and around churches and the flags blessed and hung in churches. The earliest '*chi-rho*' (plate 47) (Christian) monogram found in England was at Hinton St Mary (Dorset) and dates from *c.*AD 350, while wall paintings of Christians at prayer from Lullingstone (Kent) and a Christian church at Colchester (Essex) also date from this period of Roman Christianity. Ecclesiastical organisation based on towns was established after AD 350 and may have been designed to combat a resurgence in paganism. The contrast between town and country under the Romans is highlighted here, for 'pagan' means country dweller. There are a number of finds of later Roman silver from England adorned with Christian symbols suggesting a breakdown of order, as the hidden hoards were never recovered by their owners.

By one recent estimate people were distributed under the Romans in a ratio of 1:4 between town and country, with perhaps 2 million people living in the countryside and half a million in towns at the height of Roman power. Estimates of population are difficult to make for the Roman period and rely on guesswork derived from perceived density of settlement, for example in towns where there were generously spaced houses, and on the rise and fall of numbers of burials in cemeteries at different dates. With the vast majority of the Romanised British living in the countryside it is not surprising to find strong evidence of Roman rural management. The system of roads enabled rapid movement of troops and therefore an ability to smother uprisings rapidly. Thus the rural villa culture flourished.

Recent archaeological work has moved outwards from the villas to piece together the landscapes in which they were set. Work on field systems through examination of aerial photographs and their transcription onto maps has begun to reveal the patchwork of Roman fields, while study of earthworks in woodland areas amplifies the picture where woodland cover has protected them from the damage inflicted by modern deep ploughing. This has reduced many 'lynchets' or hillside agricultural platforms to mere scatters of debris. Study of the size of Roman fields across England has shown that varying status among Roman agricultural landlords can be deduced from the size of fields they exploited – the larger the fields, the higher the status. The study of Roman field banks in woodland has contributed to the view that a substantially larger area than previously thought was under cultivation and, in turn, that there was much less 'ancient' or 'primary' woodland from the era of the last Ice Age in the Roman period, and thus even less today.

Although the term 'Roman' is generally used for some 400 years after AD 43, the number of Italians in the military forces was never very great. Both tomb stones and grave goods tell us how people from within and without the Roman empire came to England under the aegis of the imperial government and army. The south coast came under attack from as early as *c.*AD 200 by Saxons from north Germany. This led to the creation of a series of forts along the shore to defend the coast and to provide harbours for the Roman fleet or *Classis Britannica*, which while based in France had the task of defending Britannia, as well as a transport function, up to the

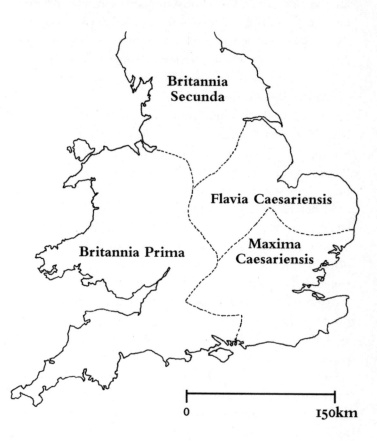

Roman provinces of southern Britain c.AD 250. Classical writers suggest that the inhabitants called their land Albion in pre-Roman times, while the Roman name Britannia was a corruption of the 'Pretani'. After early administration as a single unit, Britannia, from time to time torn by civil strife, was divided into a number of provinces, a fragmentation which looked backwards to Iron Age tribal divisions and forward to Saxon kingdoms.

AD 300s. The coast was clearly in need of further defences from the era of the Saxon Shore forts of the AD 200s. The 'Painted House' at Dover (Kent), where excavations have revealed some of the most extensive Roman wall paintings in England, was a high-status building cut through by the erection of the shore fort there.

Attacks on Roman government did not come only from beyond the sea. Allectus, a local official, usurped power; he became a local 'emperor' in the AD 290s. At that stage central Roman power was sufficient to crush such an upstart. A century later things were different as archaeology shows. Evidence reveals how an opulent town-house culture flourished at urban centres until *c.*AD 350. Thereafter richly appointed houses went out of use and, although urban populations grew, people lived in relative poverty, squatting in the ruins of the great mansions and in more flimsy dwellings. Road surfaces, gravelled and swept to a clean orange finish for three centuries, become patched and uneven. Finally, burials in the formerly ordered cemeteries became haphazard and petered out shortly after AD 400, signalling the end of Roman military authority here. Latin as the language of Romano-British society as far down as urban artisans and soldiers, died out in the two centuries that followed. Perhaps this was due to a disastrous decline in population in England? On the Continent, by contrast, a form of Latin took root among the invading tribes. In England the language which held sway until about 1100 was the Old English of the Anglo-Saxon invaders, with Celtic languages at the fringes of England and beyond.

Thus to the question 'Who lived in Roman Britannia?' the answer must be: descendants of the country's disparate Iron

Roman tombstone from South Shields (County Durham). Inscriptions such as this, to the Catuvellaunian Regina, wife of the Palmyrene Barates, remind us of the racial mix in Roman Britain – Tacitus, for example, had commented (c.AD 100) that the southern British resembled the Gauls and noted the redhaired Caledonians. Inscriptions also invite discussion of the extent to which Latin and/or native languages were used by the population at large.

Age tribes welded together by Roman civilisation and culture. Careful archaeological study of Roman villas has shown much continuity from their Iron Age predecessors back into deep prehistory, and in the same way there was to be much continuity in the post-Roman period.

2

Arthur and Avalon

English and Normans AD 400–1327

Britain, an island in the ocean, formerly called Albion, is situated between the north and the west, facing, though at a considerable distance from the coasts of Germany, France and Spain... This island at present... contains five languages and four nations, English, Britons, Irish, Picts and... Latin which has become a common medium through the study of the Scriptures...

Bede, *Ecclesiastical History*, c.AD 731

The shadowy King Arthur defended western Britannia against invading Anglo-Saxons which action c.AD 500 provided the final act in the passing of Roman Britannia. Some believe he was a gentleman Roman Briton, Ambrosius Aurelianus; others that he was of humble birth but chosen as leader because of his military skills. Archaeology and place-name studies have associated Arthur with locations from Scotland to Cornwall. In one of his twelve battles Arthur is said to have 'borne the image of the Cross of Christ on his shoulders'. The site of his final battle, Mons Badonicus, in which

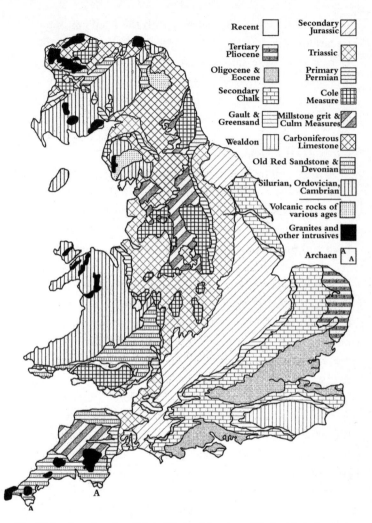

Legend:

Recent

Tertiary Pliocene

Oligocene & Eocene

Secondary Chalk

Gault & Greensand

Wealdon

Secondary Jurassic

Triassic

Primary Permian

Cole Measure

Millstone grit & Culm Measures

Carboniferous Limestone

Old Red Sandstone & Devonian

Silurian, Ordovician, Cambrian

Volcanic rocks of various ages

Granites and other intrusives

Archaen

Simplified geology of southern Britain. The banded geology of England is the key to vegetation and settlement. Settlement in Anglo-Saxon England, for example, was concentrated in the southern and eastern areas of the country, where there was also a concentration of forest, familiar to the German immigrants. Geological divisions encouraged diversity from region to region.

he personally killed 940 people (with the Lord's assistance) is uncertain. It is not even clear whether Arthur and Mordred were on the same side or were opponents. However, he was a clearly a Christian fighting pagans. Elements of the story were worked up in detail 600 years later, as is explained later (p.60). Arthur has been brought out of history on a number of occasions at the behest of monarchs and nations, for example under the Tudors after 1485.

Arthur's enemies were the pagan Angles, Saxons and Jutes, whom he opposed from his bases – most likely in the south-west of England. These German invaders from north-west Europe came into the south-east and east of the country. Like prehistoric peoples and the Romans, contacts were well established with northern Germany before any systematic occupation began in the late AD 400s. At Hod Hill in Dorset, evidence shows Anglo-Saxons in southern Britannia prior to the invasion period. Anglo-Saxon settlement petered out before it got deep into the West Country. Britons did not cease to exist, but adapted, for although Anglo-Saxons never overwhelmed the natives numerically, their language – English – began to predominate. The archaeology of 'Arthur's England' has focused on cemeteries, dealing with the issue of whether weapons and other grave goods with continental associations belonged to invaders (or invitees) or to defenders.

One of the problems for this period is the lack of settlement-evidence: cemeteries abound, but few settlements have been discovered, a ratio of forty cemeteries to one settlement in the archaeological record. However, we do have excavated Anglo-Saxon post-built wooden halls and character-istic subsidiary structures called sunken-floor buildings

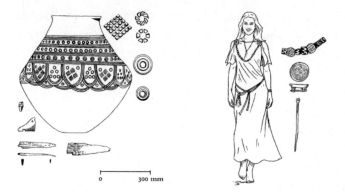

Left: *Early Anglo-Saxon cremation urn from Sancton (East Yorkshire c.AD 500–700). Some inhabitants of Anglo-Saxon England especially in the south practised inhumation, enabling analysis of size and clothing etc., but in eastern and northern areas cremation was the preferred method. Decoration of urns such as this may provide evidence about the individual whose remains were found within it, if we could interpret the incisions.*

Right: *An Anglo-Saxon woman. We know much more about the early Anglo-Saxons (400s to 600s) from cemeteries than from settlements. Some cemeteries contain taller men with weapons, maybe Anglo-Saxons, and smaller men without. However, women do not show the same characteristic groupings by size, but are distinguished by goods according to age cycle. This one shows the trappings of biological maturity.*

(*Gruben-häuser*), built over rectangular pits – for storage or for working looms with weights. Despite their names and currency in northern Europe, they are particularly associated with England, examples being found in the east of the country and on the Isle of Wight. Both types of building are found dating from the AD 400s to the early AD 700s and reconstructions can be seen at West Stow (Suffolk) (plate 48). Flimsy wooden structures are hard to capture in the archaeological record so it is especially fortunate that West Stow had been covered by sand dunes after its abandonment. The paucity of Anglo-Saxon buildings may be partly explained by the obvious fact that many Anglo-Saxons, a rural people, used the farmsteads which had been occupied by the Romano-British before them. The Anglo-Saxons were not natural villagers.

Historians, especially those writing in the late nineteenth century found these German invaders very much to their taste in searching for the English roots of British world domination. The unification of Germany in 1871, the close family links with the Germans of Queen Victoria, soon to be the queen-empress, focused attention on England's far off Anglo-Saxon Germanic roots. Germany was all the rage – it is hard to remember that today! John Richard Green, Honorary Fellow of Jesus College, Oxford (a College paradoxically with strong Welsh links) in his *Short History of the English People* (1874), a bestseller until the First World War, opened his 900-page text: 'For the fatherland of the English race we must look away from England itself'. Warming to his task he included a section about the AD 400s and AD 500s called 'Extermination of the Britons' and came to the point with the statement, 'What strikes us at once in the new England is, that it was the only purely German nation which rose upon the wreck of Rome'. Geographers weighed in, the great Professor Freeman (father-in-law of the journalist and archaeologist, Arthur Evans) at Trinity, wrote in 1882, 'No part of European history is to me more attractive than the early history of the German kingdom'... continuing a few pages later under the heading 'Europe: an Aryan continent':

Whether we look at Europe now, or whether we look at it at the earliest times of which we have any glimmerings, it is preeminently an Aryan continent. Everything non-Aryan is at once marked as exceptional.

He continues to tell us that these 'exceptional' groups included Celts in the north and west, and 'Fins' and Basques elsewhere; the English were quite definitely in the magic circle. Archaeology has not been able to identify Aryans any more than the elusive Celts, and today it is believed that if the Aryans had anything in common it was Sanskrit and a suggested Indian homeland! Green and Freeman concerned themselves with racial origins of the English, Green further identified personal liberty as the fundamental trait of the incoming English. The seal was set on these ruminations by Professor Maitland, Downing Professor of the Laws of England, Cambridge. In his 1887 lectures Maitland traced the origins of English law to King Ethelbert of Kent *c.*AD 600 as the point at which English law drew away from Roman law in this island. The fundamentals of Ethelbert's law were its Christianity and, notably, it was 'the earliest laws ever written in any Teutonic tongue'. Personal liberty within a Christian legal framework, therefore established the origins of English individualism, what Maitland called her 'individualistic path'.

Back in Germany Wagner was completing his operatic excursions into the heroic origins of his country: the 'Ring cycle' was performed in its entirety at Bayreuth for the first time in 1876, providing an overwhelmingly romantic view of the distant past in an age when opera was replacing church-going as entertainment. Thus people began to think that if English descendants of German invader-migrants could rule the world, what might a united Germany achieve? With hindsight we know where that led in the twentieth century – to more extermination and bids for racial purity.

Green's thesis became received wisdom. Another Oxford don S.R. Gardiner wrote in the 1890s that the invading

English (as he chose to call the Anglo-Saxons) found little time for the natives:

> The conquerors looked on the Britons with the utmost contempt, naming them Welsh, a name which no Briton thought of giving to himself. It is an English word which signifies one who talks gibberish.

He compared 'English' attitudes to the barbarian gibberish of conquered peoples with the disdain the Latin-speaking Romans felt for languages of those they had vanquished. Gardiner concluded on linguistic grounds (the survival of the British word 'mattock', for example) that all the natives in the south were slaughtered, the only survivors being 'many women and many agricultural labourers [who] were spared by the conquerors'. This cleared the way for German purity, Saxon rule eventually being extended from the powerhouse of Wessex to benighted western and northern England.

So much for the wisdom of scholarship, such pro-German notions became highly unfashionable after 1914 and remained so for the rest of the twentieth century. What of the evidence? If there was a single event which marked the end of Roman Britain it may not have been the often stated refusal of Honorius to send further support to these shores *c.*AD 410. A more likely candidate is the Great Death or plague of Justinian, as contemporaries called it, of the first half of the sixth century, reported variously in AD 534 (when it 'fell off the edge of the world' beyond Ireland) and AD 547. This plague may have been the determining factor in the collapse of urban life in Britannia. It was at this period, for example, that the great baths complex at Wroxeter

(Shropshire) (plate 49) which had struggled on, increasingly ruinous, during the AD 400s, was levelled. Christianity, introduced in the early AD 300s, died out in much of the south, engulfed by paganism although the candle of Christian veneration continued to burn in the north and west.

The ruined towns were accorded names which often ended in '*-ceaster*' (–chester). Chester, Dorchester, Gloucester, Silchester and Winchester, among others, were places recognised by the Saxons to have been Roman centres. These ruined urban centres contained much in the way of gigantic remains, of administrative and military structures such as town walls, of collapsed columns (for example that seen today re-erected by York Minster) and much else. The ruins protruded from a thick layer of 'dark earth' composed of rotted wooden structures and horticultural remains deposited by early migrants from rural backgrounds who had colonised these abandoned towns. Not surprisingly legends abounded that the great Roman structures had been created by a nation of giants!

The widespread Great Death may well have been the cause of the reduction in the European population and thus of migrant settling and raiding after the age of Arthur *c*.AD 500. Within a century more peaceful newcomers were seen in southern and eastern England. A revival of Christianity opened with the conversion of the Kentish royal family during the mission of St Augustine in AD 596–597. The most spectacular find ever in English archaeology dates from soon after AD 600: the Sutton Hoo (Suffolk) ship burial. As a ship this find chimes well with English enthusiasm for their maritime past, which heightened public interest. It was found in the summer of 1939 when the storm clouds of war were

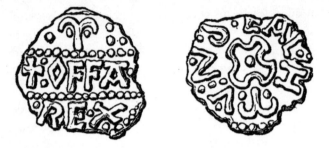

Coin of Offa (r. 757–96). The great king of Mercia ruled a large area of central England. He had ambitions to marry his daughter to a son of Charlemagne. He ran an exceptionally well-organised administration which not only reformed the coinage, but also produced the labour force which created the great Offa's Dyke, separating his kingdom from the Welsh and running from the Dee estuary to the Severn estuary.

gathering across the Channel. The ship contained the cremated remains of a man, perhaps a king of East Anglia. Among the jewels and symbols of power, were spoons inscribed *Paulos* and *Saulo*s, suggesting that this cremated king – if such he was – had embraced Christianity. Some believe, but it cannot be proved, that he was Raedwald, king of the East Angles, who had been baptised in Kent, but who had kept his religious options open by sustaining both Christian and pagan altars in his residence. The range of the origins of the Sutton Hoo artefacts reminds us again of England's extensive trade links: the hanging bowls were British but the exquisite helmet was of Swedish manufacture; silverware, including the spoons were made in Byzantium (Istanbul), while the Frankish kingdom was represented not only by a magnificent sword but also by thirty-seven gold coins each minted in a different place in Francia.

Within a generation of the conversion of the Kentish royal family the missionary Paulinus was preaching in Northumbria,

By c.AD 600 southern Britain had fragmented into a number of kingdoms. The most powerful were East Anglia, Essex, Kent, Mercia, Northumbria, Sussex and Wessex. This was the period of the reintroduction of Christianity after AD 597. Christian (and pagan) symbols were found in the royal ship burial of this date at Sutton Hoo, burial place of the Wuffingas kings of East Anglia.

where he converted its ruler Edwin and founded the see of York in AD 627. Birinus was a missionary in Wessex after AD 635. An extraordinary palace site from this period at Yeavering (Northumberland) was possibly founded by King Edwin after AD 600, significantly on a former British site to strengthen links with the past, and was extended to include a large wooden fort, over a dozen halls, a possible church and an unique 'grandstand' structure. The date and the existence of the grandstand have led to the suggestion that it was here that Paulinus preached in AD 627.

Europe fragmented when the grip of the Roman army disappeared. In England competing kingdoms emerged – East, South and West Saxons, Jutes in Kent and elsewhere, with Mercia, Bernicia (Durham and Northumberland) and Deira (Yorkshire) in the Midlands and north. One of the key-stones of this new order was Christianity. After AD 597 Christianity took root in Kent and spread northwards and westwards in England, providing a key foundation stone for English development as the pagan Saxons, with their exotic grave goods, were converted to Christianity. Grave goods thus gradually disappeared by about AD 700, but a new English urban culture developed at the same time, producing another revival of Roman civilisation alongside Christianity. Economic growth was based around coastal emporia and international trade. These 'Middle-Saxon' ports were wealthy and largely undefended. Their '-*wic*' place-name endings, Aldwych (London), Ipswich, Hamwic (Southampton) are characteristic and the wealth they generated was associated with the return of coinage at this time. Among those who appear on these new coins was King Offa, who ruled Mercia from AD 757–796. He banished the Welsh behind the great

The Alfred Jewel is the most famous relic of the age of Alfred, inscribed 'Alfred ordered me to be made'. That king's driving forward of education and scholarship is epitomised in material terms by the survival of this jewelled end of a pointer, probably for a reader following a religious text. Alfred is said to have commented that literacy had so declined that not a single scholar south of the Thames could read or translate a word of Latin. The Jewel was presented to the Ashmolean Museum as long ago as 1718.

Coin of Alfred (d.899), the best-known pre-Conquest king. He is credited with much including the establishment of a written administration, a refined coinage and with the historic defeat of the Danes at Edington (878), which prevented a Danish conquest of England. It is also said that he created a navy against the Danes and revived in learning. He captured London in 886, beginning the process of the conquest of England by the house of Wessex.

Cnut (r. 1016–35) and Emma making a presentation to New Minster, Winchester. New Minster had been founded after AD 900 by Alfred's son Edward the Elder as a public church and as a burial centre for Saxon kings. Alfred was laid to rest there, but even so not all his successors were. It was King Cnut who declared Winchester his capital and from there ruled his extensive kingdom in Britain and Scandinavia. Emma (d. 1052) was the mother of Edward the Confessor by a previous marriage.

westerly dyke which bears his name, and extended Mercia into Essex and Kent. So powerful was he that a tradition – now disputed – emerged that he actually called himself 'King of the English' (*Rex Anglorum*). But Offa overstretched his power-base and failed to see the threats beyond his kingdom.

The Anglo-Saxon England of Offa and his successors was not poor as their Norman successors later trumpeted. It was the wealthy and undefended nature of Anglo-Saxon settlements which encouraged the depredations of the Scandinavian Vikings from the late AD 700s. Raids are documented on Lindisfarne (Northumberland) in AD 793, where the monastery was destroyed, and on Portland (Dorset) in AD 789. Eventually the Vikings consolidated their hold on England from the north, capturing York in AD 867, and establishing settlements with their distinctive '-by' and '-thorpe' place-name endings. The *Anglo-Saxon Chronicle*, for AD 876, records that their leader 'shared out the lands of the Northumbrians and they proceeded to plough and support themselves'. A group of distinctive 'hog back' Viking tombs is associated with this northern culture, apparently modelled on the form of their houses. These unusual artefacts were developed in England and were not copied from Scandinavian prototypes, where stone sculpture was not known.

In response to Viking attacks, the defences of southern England were consolidated. This prompted the establishment of communal 'burhs' or forts in the era of King Alfred (d.AD 899) who, following an uncertain start, achieved military successes against the raiding Vikings and captured London in AD 886. Alfred has some claim to be the greatest of English kings. If Alfred's biographer Asser and the chroniclers are to be believed, he can be distinguished from other English kings by outstanding qualities of military leadership and with the establishment, temporarily, of a navy – an achievement especially prized by his later English biographers. By all accounts he was also an able administrator. It is likely, though uncertain, whether Alfred himself could write, he could definitely read. If writing was one of his accomplishments, it was another 450 years before another English king could write – Edward III in 1330. When Alfred died his son Edward the Elder established a mausoleum for their dynasty for which the great New Minster was built in Winchester. Alfred is known to have visited Winchester only once, well on in his reign, to send some Vikings to be hanged. In death he established a hold over the city which despite the subsequent loss of his bones, he has retained ever since.

Alfred contributed to the rise of Wessex over its neighbouring kingdoms in the late Anglo-Saxon period. The defended burhs were an embryonic urban network. The need for taxation to fight the Danish Vikings (or to pay them to keep away) may have been a driving force in the organisation of proto-village life on a new footing from the AD 800s onwards. This income contributed to the dominance of Wessex. In time this dominance was further emphasised by the choice of Winchester, with its longstanding links to the royal household of Wessex, by the powerful international ruler Cnut (Canute) (1016–35). Cnut's Scandinavian connections were continued under the Norman-educated Edward the Confessor (plate 57) and the invader William the Conqueror (1066–87).

Demographically, England experienced growth in the period AD 800–1300, contrasting with the crises of the Great Death in the AD 500s and the Black Death (plate 62) in the

William the Conqueror's administration was excellent. His great seal, seen here, was the authenticating agent of government in a era when kings could not write. The compilation of Domesday Book in 1086 is the enduring legacy of the Conqueror's ability as an administrator.

Extracts from a calendar produced in England before the Norman Conquest. Typical scenes of agricultural life in the Middle Ages are seen: shepherding (May) and haymaking (July). The short clothes of the Saxons are apparent, but otherwise such scenes continued to appear in calendars for the next half-millennium, reassuring landowners of the clockwork round of peasant agricultural activity which produced their wealth.

1300s. Such growth was a pan-European phenomenon. Among other things, this prompted the Viking settlements throughout the north Atlantic region.

The Norman Conquest of 1066 was an outer ripple of this movement. The battle of Hastings is a traditional watershed in English history. The invading Normans, led by their duke, William the Bastard (who after the battle became William the Conqueror), vanquished the Anglo-Saxons under Harold Godwineson, who died with an arrow in his eye. The Norman Conquest certainly led to changes at the top of the hierarchy, in the way the country was policed (castles), in landholding patterns, and in the monastic orders recruiting and developing in England. But there was also much continuity: the majority of the population carried on as before in their agricultural activities. The intention of Domesday Book of 1086 was to see who had owned what when William came to the throne and to test the extent, if any, of usurpation of his land and of royal authority in the previous twenty years. Domesday reveals significant regional variations: how far ahead, for example in provision of mills, East Anglia was economically compared to southern and western England. It shows as clearly as any document drawn up before or since how governable England is, with its girdle of sea and its territory shading off into the mountains of Scotland and Wales. When the Conqueror died in 1087 the Viking diaspora was a spent force. New theatres of war were opening up, most notably in the Holy Land as the crusading movement began to harness the warlike leaders of the west and to direct their energies eastwards towards the infidel.

Before crusading fervour reached England, the Conqueror's sons fought amongst themselves after his death. The warlike Rufus, William II, seemed to his father the most appropriate person to rule rebellious England rather than docile Normandy. Contemporary writers contrasted in their views of Rufus (1087–1100) and his brother Henry (1100–35), who was to rule as Henry I. To monastic chroniclers Rufus and his knightly, chivalric court were scandalous and shameful: but the generosity of Rufus to his friends and his considerable skill as a soldier made him popular with many of the knightly class. He was a generous patron of building, his crowning achievement being the unsurpassed Westminster Hall, the cavernous interior of which is still used on major occasions, such as for the lying in state of monarchs. Henry 'Beauclerk', who could read (unlike his father), appealed more obviously to monkish sensibilities, emphasising the significance of intellectual qualities to the religious orders of the 1100s.

Both Rufus and Henry I were hunting in the New Forest on 2 August 1100 when Rufus was killed by an arrow. Henry moved quickly to secure the treasury and in 1106 defeated another brother, Robert, who challenged his power at Tinchebrai (Normandy). Henry saw himself as a born commander rather than as an active warrior like Rufus. He dealt decisively with perceived wrongdoers: blinding, flaying and castration were the punishments he meted out to those he thought responsible for irregularities in minting money. Such rigour against maladministrators provides an insight into Henry's achievement as a monarch and into the developing Norman governmental system. The island boundaries of England to the south and east – the most populous regions – facilitated the establishment of a clearly defined area in which a written administration could flourish. It seems likely that the Exchequer (an accounting tool named after the chequer or chess board) came into existence early in Henry's reign, providing a reckoner of monies expected and received. Through the common pain of increased taxation and through feudalism, laws, language and parliament, the nation was readily drawn together within highland and sea boundaries.

The notion of 'new men' raised from lowly status to serve monarchs on whom they relied completely is often associated with the fifteenth-century Yorkists and Tudors, but is clearly seen in the reign of Henry I. An excellent example is Roger, bishop of Salisbury. An obscure Norman clerk, Roger came to the notice of the king and who became valued, it was said, because he could say Mass in record time! He was raised, eventually, to be first minister of the Crown. Henry I realised that sound administration was the key to political success, the wealth of Saxon England having been one of its chief attractions to the Norman invaders. In addition, the wars which Henry was forced to wage in Normandy were a considerable drain on his resources. He was significantly poorer than Rufus had been, but this was compensated by efficient management.

Rufus was attacked by monastic chroniclers for alleged homosexuality. The chroniclers were, however, much kinder to Henry whose knowledge of Latin endeared him to churchmen, although his private life was scandalous by the standards of any age. His tally of some two dozen children, of whom only two were legitimate, may have provided in time, a flow of loyal supporters in church and state, but his only legitimate son, William, died in the White Ship disaster of 1119. A lack of reaction to this immorality among contemporaries may have been inspired by Henry's violence against perceived wrongdoers, or may be a sign of the times. In the 1600s, Charles II (plate 28) likewise fathered over twenty bastards, but had the misfortune to be the contemporary of puritanical, Protestant detractors.

Norman kings, like their Anglo-Saxon predecessors, worked closely with the Church and the Normans actively supported the reforming popes of the late eleventh century. New religious orders were introduced to England to augment the Benedictine houses, the sole monastic order available to Saxon England. The first of these newcomers were members of the Cluniac reform movement, from Burgundy. This order was followed, among others, by Augustinian canons, whose priories spread rapidly in the early 1100s and were populated by groups of priests who lived together under a common rule.

Augustinian houses were the most numerous religious houses in England by the end of the monastic period. Within a generation, in 1129, the first Cistercian house was founded in England, at Waverley in Surrey, to be followed by Rievaulx (plate 52) and even later by Fountains (plate 53), Tintern and many others in the wild north and west.

Henry I married Matilda, daughter of Malcolm III of Scotland who had made feudal submission to the Conqueror at Abernethy in 1072. David I (1124–53), son of Malcolm III, had been prominent at the court of Henry I before he became king of Scotland, where he introduced many changes which had been promoted by the Normans in England: he fostered the introduction of new religious orders and introduced the first Scottish coinage. Above all he introduced Norman castles and the concomitant military machine. Thus it was that the Norman conquest of England filtered northward and provided subsequent royal houses in Scotland, for the Bruces (*Brus*) and the Balliols (*Bailleul*) bore names derived from places in northern France.

Henry I died in 1135 leaving a disputed inheritance. His daughter Matilda, had married Geoffrey, count of Anjou, in 1128. Her father's death made Matilda and her husband heirs to the throne of England, but Geoffrey never set foot in England. Far from uniting the kingdoms of England and Anjou, Henry's death led to twenty years of destructive civil war both in both kingdoms.

The throne was occupied from 1135 by Stephen, son of the Conqueror's daughter Adela, who had married Stephen of Blois. His reign is known as the 'Anarchy', a time of intermittent but fierce warfare accompanied by the consolidation of baronial power through the construction of personal castle fortresses. The question of the succession was resolved only a year before Stephen's death when he disinherited his son Eustace, in favour of Henry Plantagenet, the young, active and ruthless son of Matilda and Geoffrey. Henry II (plate 54) ruled from 1154–89. He brought the anarchy to an end and built on the administrative system of the Exchequer (finance) and Chancery (writing) offices that Henry I had established. From early in his reign the records of the Exchequer run virtually without a break until after 1800.

It was during the 'anarchy' that Geoffrey of Monmouth fleshed out the story of King Arthur from the uncertain bones of the sixth-century evidence. He added the knights who have subsequently remained associated with the Arthurian setting at Avalon. These stories proved popular and were further developed in the reign of Henry II by the addition of the notion of the Round Table. Arthur emerged and gained currency to support the incoming Angevin dynasty not only as an exemplar of kingship, but also as a heroic leader in a time of civil war, a parallel between the 1130s and 1140s and the age of Arthur *c*.AD 500.

The 1100s were a time of continuing demographic and economic growth, the expanding trade network, in particular, furnishing the funds which flowed into the centralised Exchequer. New towns were founded, while throughout Europe areas of forest were claimed for habitation and assarting (from the French '*essarter*' – to grub up a tree) was the order of the day. The new-found wealth, reflected in architecture, also manifested itself in the creation of expensive and labour-intensive aristocratic and ecclesiastical forests, deer parks and in flights of fishponds, the larders and deep-freeze equivalents at the élite's scattered residences. The Normans are credited with bringing new species of animals and birds into England. Fallow deer appeared in the forests and deer parks so beloved of the new ruling class. The rabbit, managed in warrens, had been working its way northwards across Europe from the Mediterranean since the AD 800s and is a well-known example. Before 1200 the pheasant, originally from China, had made its way into England as a farmed creature.

Great monastic buildings were created by the new and old religious orders alike. In remote places, such as those favoured by the Cistercians, land was cheap and their system of employing lay brothers who worked both from monastic sites and from remote granges, ensured that, for the moment, they were wealthy and expanding. Archaeology has illuminated the diverse range of activities at monastic sites alongside religious worship. Such ancillary work included masonry carving and tiling (both floor and roof), iron smelting, milling using water wheels. Income to support these activities came from the great flocks of sheep producing wool which was stored at monastic granges, producing wool. As the Middle Ages progressed a vigorous futures market developed as Italian entrepreneurs rode from monastic house to monastic house buying up the future wool supplies and thus enabling the financial planning which resulted in the magnificent buildings.

During the 1100s the temporary wooden castles of the Conqueror's time, some possibly brought prefabricated with the invasion force, were rebuilt in stone and became more comfortable. Town mansions and undefended palaces appear in town and country alike – reminiscent of the best Roman properties. Archaeology has shed a light on this period: material remains of stone houses and the cultures of the

Following Henry II's success in limiting ecclesiastical power through the Constitutions of Clarendon (1164), Archbishop Becket fled abroad. This is probably the earliest representation of the martyrdom of Becket in his cathedral at Canterbury in 1170. He has remained a controversial figure: hugely popular after his rapid canonisation in 1173, he became a target for Protestant reformers of the sixteenth and seventeenth centuries.

townspeople who occupied them from before 1100 feature in urban archaeology, while at the other end of the scale the flimsy wooden houses of the poor have also come to light. The wooden precursors of stone castles (as at Abinger in Surrey) and the humble wooden structures which preceded the great stone monasteries have been revealed by archaeology (at Fountains Abbey, Glastonbury Abbey and Norton Priory). The material culture of daily urban life and industry have been illuminated by digging (for example at London, Northampton, and Winchester). Local and imported pottery, functional and decorative ironwork, tools, gold, silver, copper and lead have all been found. The greatest range of metal material has come from water fronts where timbers can be precisely dated to the 1100s and where layers of artefacts dumped as infill provide core samples to which random finds can be matched (as at London, and in the canals at Salisbury).

The Church became increasingly powerful and new doctrines brought more wealth. The notion of purgatory began in the 1100s. Thenceforward people strove to shorten their stay in that misty no-man's-land between their earthly and heavenly lives. The stay could be lessened by giving to the Church. Gifts of land to new, stricter, religious orders increased and advowsons (the right to appoint clergy to parishes) were often handed by lay persons to the Church, often to orders such as Augustinian canons who could provide ordained clergy to celebrate the sacraments.

Those at the head of the English Church were often wealthy, aristocratic and cosmopolitan ecclesiastics. The greatest of the twelfth-century churchmen was Henry of Blois, brother of King Stephen. Bishop Henry had trained at Cluny in Burgundy. He was appointed both abbot of Glastonbury and bishop of Winchester, a diocese whose lands – many the gifts of Saxon kings – encompassed Taunton in the west and Southwark in the east. Furthermore, Henry was a major patron of the arts: a key figure in the twelfth-century renaissance of architecture, manuscript illumination, sculpture and metalwork. He brought back *spolia* (which included classical sculpture) from Rome to adorn his palaces. The great Winchester Bible, which he sponsored, was enormous in concept and execution, although the decorative illuminations were never completed. It required the skins of 250 calves to make the pages; the scribe who copied out the text is estimated to have spent twenty-five years on that task, while teams of illuminators set about the task of colouring the intricately drawn capital letters of the books and chapters using a wide range of pigments, including exceptionally valuable crushed lapis lazuli from far off Afghanistan and less precious sheets of gold leaf.

With such conspicuous wealth among the clergy, the potential for conflict between Church and State grew and came to a head with the crisis involving Archbishop Thomas Becket. As his grandfather had done with Roger of Salisbury, so Henry II elevated Becket as a new man. But circumstances were different this time. By appointing an archbishop from his own following, Henry II expected to have a compliant Church. With the Constitutions of Clarendon (1164) Henry sought to limit papal power in England. An antiquarian plaque attached to the romantic ruins of Henry's Clarendon palace deep in the Wiltshire forest claims that this legislation, which arose from the 'spirit awakened with these walls' struck the first spark of a slow-burning fuse that led to the English Reformation nearly 400 years later. Standing in the ruins of the great hall there, and reading chroniclers' accounts of knights passing to and from separate chambers where Henry II and Archbishop Becket each sat with their supporters, it is not difficult to imagine that fiery confrontation in which the strong-minded king was resisted by an archbishop determined to sustain his Church.

The outcome of the row in 1164 was the murder of Becket in 1170, apparently by royal command, in his cathedral at Canterbury. Not surprisingly the monks of that house believed the lightning-strike which set their church on fire in 1172 was an act of God in judgement on Henry II rather than on their 'turbulent priest', Becket. From the ashes of this political and religious disaster an architectural phoenix arose. The monks employed the Frenchman William of Sens to oversee the rebuilding of their burnt choir in the new gothic style, the first project in that style on such a scale in England. Rib vaults,

Salisbury (Wiltshire) Cathedral was completed as part of the development of the city of New Sarum between 1220 and 1258. It epitomises the Early English style in which England drew away from continental models and Englishness became the fashion. Sculpture from the nearby palace at Clarendon is in a similar style, and Henry III (1216–72) named his eldest son Edward, harking back to pre-Conquest Saxon times when Edward the Confessor reigned.

pointed windows, buttresses and slender columns of Purbeck marble provide the skeleton of this remarkable scheme, with stained glass and novel tiled floors to flesh it out. As for William of Sens, he fell from the scaffolding and damaged his back. He was the last overseas master of works on such a scheme. Thereafter the gothic in England developed under English masons into the national style dubbed 'Early English'.

The shrine of Becket, first in the crypt but soon elevated to the east end of Canterbury Cathedral became an internationally significant site. His bloody death became legendary, a contemporary chronicler describing how the murderous knights sliced off the top of his cranium and then stamped on his neck spreading his blood and brains across the floor.

This holy blood sanctified the well in the cathedral whence water was drawn to fill *ampullae* (small containers) which were sold to the thousands of pilgrims who flocked to Canterbury. These small lead pilgrim tokens depicting elements of Becket's life and death have been found from Scandinavia to Spain and all over the British Isles. An especially large group was recovered from the river at Canterbury itself, suggesting that pilgrims may have cast them into the stream as they left the city, to bless their journey home. Two centuries later, in the 1380s, Geoffrey Chaucer (plate 61) was to immortalise this pilgrim route in his *Canterbury Tales*, testifying to the continuing importance and popularity of the shrine. For the moment pilgrimage struck the imagination in popular religious belief. Henry II himself was among the first to pay his respects on his own journey establishing the route for others from his disembarkation point at Southampton along the south downs to Harbledown on the outskirts of Canterbury, where traditionally the name suggests, pilgrims hobbled the last stretch of their long walk to the great cathedral church.

Publicly and within his family, the later years of Henry II's reign were less happy. Despite the crowd of sons borne by his wife Eleanor of Aquitaine (plate 56), who had been disposed of as a queen by Louis VII of France because they had no sons, Henry II suffered anxieties about the succession. He had his eldest son, also called Henry, crowned king during his lifetime but his wife and sons frequently rebelled against him. Young Henry eventually died during a rebellion against his father. Henry II's lands, which stretched from the Scottish border to the Pyrenees, were tiring to perambulate and complex to rule, even for a man of his extraordinary energy and vitality. At the time of his death in 1189 he was once again locked in combat with his sons.

Despite the unhappiness of Henry II's later years, he reinforced the administrative systems of England to such good effect that his successor Richard I (1189–99) (plate 55) could be absent from the realm for almost all of his reign without administrative mishap. John (1199–1216) enjoyed his father Henry II's physical fitness and interest in administration. He was highly active and never in the same place for more than a month during his seventeen-and-a-half-year reign. This mobility and engagement in the detail of governing through local courts – otherwise seen as interference – made him unpopular with chroniclers and civil servants: the latter would no doubt have preferred to settle down at Westminster rather than trail behind a monarch ceaselessly roaming the realm, stopping in places where no king had been seen for generations. This active government is one of the reasons contemporaries wrote disparagingly about him, causing him to be been seen as a 'bad' king. By no means all the places called 'King John's house' were visited by him, but their ubiquity is itself revealing.

John's reign witnessed conflicts: with the Pope, which led to England being placed under a papal interdict; with his first wife, which led to divorce; and with his magnates and churchmen, which led to the *Magna Carta* (Great Charter) in 1215. This was certainly a landmark in feudal relationships between monarch and the greater families, whose resentment was provoked – *inter alia* – by the king taking residences from bishops and by taking wives of barons to bed without their husbands' consent. One searches the charter in vain for principles which applied to ordinary people. In any case, within

Rex henric. Alienora.

Henry III (r. 1216-72), came to the throne on the death of his father, King John aged only nine. From an early age Henry showed an interest in architecture and building, and fine structures such as the Great Hall of Winchester Castle were built during his minority. In 1236 he married the twelve-year-old Princess Eleanor. They had a long and companionable marriage enjoying creating buildings and gardens together through good times and bad. Their reign saw the strengthening of the notion of Englishness.

De reditu Regis in Angliam.
a Wafeoina
Rex
Regina.

Henry III was less successful in foreign policy than in his pursuit of the arts. Here he returns home in 1243, defeated after an unsuccessful campaign in France against his great brother-in-law St Louis (Louis IX). Matthew Paris the chronicler who decorated his chronicle with this and many other drawings was one of many who supported baronial opponents of Henry, using this opportunity to highlight the king's discomfort.

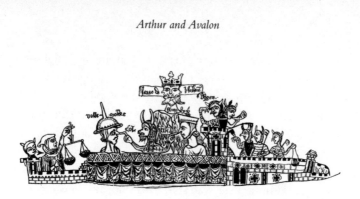

The rise of the concept Englishness in the twelfth century had a downside. Jews, who led a separate religious existence, and who engaged in moneylending, forbidden to Christians, were obvious outsiders. In 1290 Edward I expelled them, partly on the advice of his magnate advisers who owed large amounts of money! Here we see the multi-faced, wheeler-dealer Isaac of Norwich, crowned in mockery in a record of 1233.

a year John was dead and, for the moment at least, the Great Charter's precepts died with him.

Once more the administration triumphed. Despite the presence of a French army in southern England in support of the baronial faction, John's son, Henry III (1216–72), a child of nine at his father's death, inherited the throne without disorder. This king became the champion of the new gothic style in architecture during his long reign. His lavish spending was possible because the 1200s produced even more wealth for landowners than the 1100s. Henry III's projects included the beginnings of the rebuilding of Westminster Abbey. He was present at the laying of foundations of Salisbury Cathedral, begun in 1220, while a foundation stone at Netley Abbey in Hampshire also records his presence there. Salisbury Cathedral, the finest monument in the Early English style, was built on a virgin site and was, amazingly, completed within two generations.

The whole question of who was English and who was 'alien' came to the fore at this time. Within the limited horizons of

most medieval people, 'foreigners' came from the neighbouring community and 'aliens' from abroad. Among the difficulties of the thirteenth century was that the nobility of England,
descended from Norman invaders of 1066, were becoming
more insular and thus more anglicised. The loss of French lands
by John certainly contributed to this for, unlike his father Henry
II, John did not for long have lands that were centred on Anjou
in France, although he was able to sustain his lordship over
areas of south-west France and Ireland. Paradoxically by the
early 1200s, as the population became more wedded to their
'Englishness', they had almost stopped using Old English
names, such as Alfred and Edgar, and adopted French names.

Henry III married Eleanor of Provence, one of whose sisters was married to Louis IX of France and whose other
sisters were married to the younger brothers of Louis and
Henry respectively. These unions brought the royal families of
England and France close together. Henry imported various
relations of Eleanor's, such as Peter of Savoy who created the
Savoy Palace (site of the Savoy Hotel) in the Strand. The
English magnates, those who considered themselves the king's
'natural councillors', began to resent such incomers and this
was one of the causes of the Barons' Wars in the middle of
the century. There were other causes too: Henry III had failed
to pay a dowry to Simon de Montfort when that baron married the king's sister.

The close links between Henry III and Louis IX, and the
difficulties with the barons had a noticeable long-term effect
on English relations with France and, as a by-product, encouraged the development of parliament. Henry III was not a
warrior and really had no success in winning back the lands
lost in France by his father. At the Treaty of Paris in 1259 a

deal was offered – Henry would acknowledge the loss of his father's territories in northern France by abandoning the titles 'Duke of Normandy and Count of Anjou' and Louis, in return, would guarantee English rights in southern areas, Aquitaine and Gascony, acquired by Henry II's marriage to Eleanor of Aquitaine. Henry III, in difficulties with Simon de Montfort, was willing to give the necessary undertakings and Louis agreed for his part, if necessary, to support Henry with force against the barons. These events were highly significant less than a century later when Edward III became a claimant to the French throne.

Henry's lavish expenditure was frowned upon by the barons, who attempted to cut off his supplies of money. With the benefits of non-baronial financial support and the promises of French aid, Henry defeated the barons and Simon de Montfort was killed at the battle of Evesham in 1265. Henry died in 1272. It is noteworthy, on considering a growth of the idea of nationhood in the 1200s, that Henry III acted almost as though the Normans had not existed when choosing names for his children, Edward, named after Edward the Confessor, and Edmund. At the end of his life, having provided a splendid new shrine for his hero Edward the Confessor (d. 1066), Henry III had his own remains interred in the Confessor's former coffin, a remarkable tribute to England's patron saint at that time.

Edward I (1272–1307) was away crusading for the first two years of his reign, leaving the realm once more in the hands of civil servants. He was crowned on his return in 1274. Thereafter he set about building up the laws of England through a series of statutes which attempted, among other things, to restrict the amount of land donated to the 'dead hand' (*mortmain*) of the Church, an institution which never died, and thus taken out of feudal circulation in the land market. In the 1280s he turned his attention to Wales and conquered the previously independent princedom. He created the remarkable series of castles which dominate north Wales at Conwy, Harlech, Beaumaris and elsewhere. The walls of Caernarfon bear decorative banding, a scheme employed at Constantinople, which crusaders including Edward's master of works, had seen.

When Edward had subdued the Welsh, he turned to Scotland. Here that most popular of medieval motifs, the wheel of fortune, came into play, for the king of Scotland, Alexander III, rode over a cliff in 1286 and was killed leaving a disputed succession. Edward, who was a substantial figure in European politics, had already been called upon to adjudicate in a succession dispute in Sicily. In Scotland he adjudicated correctly, on the basis of the evidence, in favour of John Balliol, who became its king in 1292. But Edward insisted on being designated overlord of Scotland, which was unsurprising in view of the recent request for him to choose their king. In attempting to exercise power in Scotland, Edward provoked the Scots into rebellion and Balliol was removed from the throne after the English victory at Dunbar in 1296. The next thirty years or so are known in Scottish history as the 'wars of independence', led early on by William Wallace, then by Robert Bruce (r. 1306–29) who emerged as king of Scotland after murderous machinations. He was the victor over Edward II at Bannockburn in 1314 and lived to gain recognition of the principle of Scottish independence, backed by French diplomacy, in the Treaty of Northampton in 1328, which was known in England as the *Turpis pax* (shameful peace). Of at least equal significance was the agreement by the Pope that the kings of Scotland should be anointed, which set the seal on an independent monarchy north of the border by making the coronation rite equivalent to that in England. This freed Scottish monarchs, for the moment at least, from feudal subjection to England.

Edward I's plans to subjugate Scotland failed. Even the wealth of high medieval England was insufficient to bring Scotland under the English control. On his death in 1307, the throne passed to the youngest of his fifteen children, Edward of Caernarfon, who became Edward II.

Around 1300 it can be argued that there was a turning point in the history of England. The outward-looking positive spirit of the crusades had long been waning: the fourth crusade of 1204 had resulted not in the capture of Muslim Alexandria but of Christian Constantinople. In 1216 a papal edict required that everyone should go to church at least three times a year, which suggests that attendance was much less regular than is generally supposed. By 1300 the papacy no longer gave the lead it had in the past, soon afterwards it chose to leave Rome for Avignon, just beyond the border of France and was considered, at least by the English, to be effectively a French institution.

European population growth, steady for half a millennium, slowed down. In 1315, the year following Bannockburn, the great European famine broke out. People were trampled to death in bread queues in London and elsewhere, and a series of disastrous harvest failures followed. The effects were particularly pronounced in the numerous towns where provisions for food storage against such an eventuality had never been established. The famine affected the whole of the British Isles. In Ireland its effects were exacerbated by a campaign led by Edward Bruce, brother of the

Scottish king, which aimed to force the Irish into a Celtic alliance against England.

A period of war between England and Scotland ensued and, from the 1290s, increasing tension and skirmishing with France sought to unsettle the English monarchy by supporting Scotland. The English used their residual lands in Gascony as a base from which to harass the Capetian kings of France. The house of Capet had ruled France without problems of male succession since AD 987, but finally ran out of male heirs in 1328. Among the claimants was Isabella, sister of the last Capetian king, who had been instrumental in the deposition of her husband Edward II in 1327. Isabella now ruled England with her partner Roger Mortimer, on behalf of her son Edward III.

With the English and French monarchies in turmoil, with the papacy comparatively subdued and ineffectual, and with a decline in economic growth which inhibited the already weak resolve of the English to fight, Robert the Bruce took his opportunity to strengthen the basis of the Scottish monarchy. But the wheel of fortune turned against him too and he died in 1329, leaving a son of five threatened by the Balliol faction, whom Robert had excluded from power when he took the throne in 1306. The political barometer was set at 'Change' in 1330 and those who wished for change indeed got just that and, as we shall see, experienced it in abundance.

3

Enter St George

Black Death to Henry VIII, 1327–1547

In 1348, about the feast of St Peter ad Vincula the first pestilence arrived in England... it lasted in the south country around Bristol throughout August and all winter... in 1349 the pestilence began in other regions of England and lasted for a whole year, with the result that there were scarcely sufficient living to bury the dead.

(*Anonimalle Chronicle*, 1348–49)

The lives of the Black Prince and Henry VIII, who died in 1547, bracket this period. They had much in common: both were stylish princes who followed fashion; both admired French culture, yet battled against French power; both had stormy private lives which involved mistresses, bastards and previously married wives, though Henry had six wives to the Black Prince's one. Both men died prematurely leaving under-age heirs to the throne – Richard II (plate 65) and Edward VI, neither of whom left direct heirs. If life in the royal family was much the same in the mid-1300s and 1500s, much changed beyond the palaces. Dynasties came and went;

Edward the Black Prince (d.1376) in his armour from a wall painting in the royal chapel at Westminster Palace discovered and recorded in 1800, but destroyed in the fire of 1834. A good warrior at Crécy and general at Poitiers and Najera, the Prince was less effective as a ruler of English Gascony in south-west France. His premature death in 1376 led to the coronation of his son, the ten-year-old Richard II.

the longest war in English history was fought – and lost; the necessity for war funds transformed parliament; and Christian worship was altered significantly with the beginnings of the Reformation.

Edward II was only forty-three when he was horribly murdered in 1327, it is said with the thrust of a red-hot poker in punishment for his alleged homosexuality. His grandson, Edward the Black Prince, eldest son of Edward III, was born in 1330. With an heir in place, Edward III acted quickly to terminate Isabella and Mortimer's usurpation by force. Mortimer was executed and Isabella banished to Norfolk.

The price of internal stability is often foreign wars. Edward III gathered a group of young nobles and promoted career soldiers, who became a war party at the English court. This support was formalised first by the foundation of the Order of the Round Table in 1344 and substantiated by the establishment of the Order of the Garter in 1348. Only a king as

Edward III (d.1377) is among the greatest of English monarchs. His fifty-year reign began in turmoil with the murder of his father, Edward II, resulting from a plot by his mother. Edward drew a group of effective young nobles around him, and triumphed in the war against France. Towards the end of his life, however, he was less successful and increasingly unpopular, especially after the death of his wife Philippa in 1369.

powerful as Edward III could have founded an enduring order of chivalry based on an article of women's underclothing!

It is likely that the foundation of the Order of the Garter was accompanied by the adoption of St George the martyr as patron saint of England. Perhaps this patron saint of soldiers was more appropriate for a jolly gathering of begartered young men (as the first knights were) than the previous patron saint, the holy Edward the Confessor. George was also an appropriate choice as England was engaged in wars on two fronts: against Scotland and France. Whatever George achieved in his lifetime was long forgotten even by the AD 500s, when it was recorded that his deeds 'were known to God alone'. George, then, was something of a blank sheet on which to write. It was in this late medieval period that he evolved into a rescuer of the maidens and slayer of dragons – quite in keeping with his chivalric, soldierly attributes. Following the battle of Agincourt in 1415 his feast day was elevated to the highest rank and thenceforward he appeared in modern armour with his red cross on a white background. The formalising and limiting of the spread of coats of arms, occurred at this time with the appointment first of an officer by Henry V and later with foundation the College of Arms under Richard III (plate 13). These actions secured George his place in the new hierarchy. His cult grew and the White Horse at Uffington was reinterpreted as 'the' dragon George had slain. This brought the Bronze Age monument well within the Christian period!

Confident on his throne, Edward III challenged the rulers on his borders. First Scotland, where Robert the Bruce's untimely death followed by regency provided an opportunity to settle scores – especially for the descendants of John Balliol, adjudged king of Scotland by Edward I but disinherited by the Bruce faction. Edward Balliol, supported by the English, invaded Scotland in the early 1330s.

Second, Edward claimed the throne of France through his mother, Isabella, the late Charles IV's sister. As Philip VI of Valois was not minded to give France away, war followed – the Hundred Years War (1337–1453). French raids on England in the late 1330s excited fears of a full-scale invasion but this did not occur because the French fleet was largely destroyed at the sea battle off Sluys in 1340 (plate 8). This English victory was a defining moment as fighting took place thereafter on French soil.

English and French exchanged verbal and other abuse: 'England, shit of men' was the opening salvo of the Frenchman in an imaginary contemporary dispute with an Englishman. He continues, 'We drink the liquor of the vine; the lees are sold to England'. The Englishman retorts that the

Frenchman speaks in a womanly way, has a mincing gait and 'surrenders other parts to be used like a woman's'! As for Philip VI, the king of France, he was condemned as 'bleareyed', to which the French retaliated by spreading rumours that Edward III was a rapist and the Scots (whose king, David II, was dubbed 'the shitter' (*cacator*), allegedly having defecated on the altar during his baptism, weighed in with claims that Edward had murdered his brother in Perth in 1336. National stereotypes go back a long way, the undiscerning English, the sexually charged French, and the violent and depraved Scots.

For the English 1346 represented a pinnacle of success with the defeat of the Scots at Neville's Cross (Durham) and victory over the French at Crécy, followed by the capture of Calais in 1347. Edward consolidated his dynasty on the European stage by contracting a marriage between his daughter Joan and King Pedro of Castile. Joan set off with the baggage train which included chapel furnishings, kitchen utensils and herbs for use along the route, and a chair on which to sit while her hair was washed. But Joan never arrived. She died suddenly at Bordeaux in 1347 of a plague now known as the Black Death. This virulent disease caused the greatest catastrophe in European history and spread to England in the summer of 1348.

The Black Death was a mixture of bubonic (swellings in the armpit and groin etc. at the nodal points of the lymphatic system), pneumonic (spread to lungs by coughing, sneezing, kissing etc. without the agency of rats and fleas) and septicaemic (blood poisoning) plague. For a century and more it has been accepted that in the main the plague was bubonic, spread by rats and their fleas. Recently there have been challenges to this theory: some claim it was anthrax, others finger

The lasting damage done by plague was as much in the continuing return of the disease every few years between its first arrival in 1348 and its disappearance in 1670. This detail from a broadsheet on mortality in Oxford in 1577 reminds us that plague became increasingly an urban phenomenon, and in the last quarter of the sixteenth century was joined by famine once again.

different diseases, while some argue cogently and copiously that it was not bubonic plague at all, but cannot produce an alternative explanation. Archaeology has cast new light on the Black Death with identification of rising populations of rats and rat predators – cats and dogs – in the century or so before-hand. A scientist in France claims to have found the plague bacillus in the soft-tissue of teeth belonging to individuals in a plague cemetery. This claim is disputed on this side of the Channel, all adding to the controversy about the worst catas-trophe in history. Contemporary accounts which describe symptoms and the varied times that different manifestations of the disease took to kill people leave little room for doubt that the epidemic was plague. However, scholars still hotly debate every aspect of the plague, its nature, causes, long and short term effects and spread. The effects were immediate and dra-matic. Fifty per cent of the entire population died, with clergy being particularly hard hit, leading people to question God's attitude to his clergy and, in time, the fundamentals of church doctrine. All levels of society were affected and suffered deaths, including the archbishop of Canterbury, abbots, merchants and peasants in countless thousands. In three years the population of Europe was reduced from 80 million to 30 million people. Before the Black Death the population of the British Isles was probably six to eight million people. By 1450 it had fallen as low as two or even one million. Life would never be the same again. Perhaps the worst thing about the plague was that it recurred every ten years or so for the next 300 years, becoming endemic in some parts of the country. The disease continued to affect England regularly until, as suddenly as it had come it disappeared, soon after the Great Plague of London of 1665.

There are examples of English communities that were immediately wiped out by the plague in 1348–51, for example Quob in Hampshire and Tusmore in Oxfordshire. It was the long-term effects of successive outbreaks of plague that contributed to change in many spheres of life, from agriculture, architecture and military affairs to politics, religion and the role of women. Population fell so low that there were shortages of people in all occupations from soldiery to shepherds. It can be argued that this disaster caused a true break in the development of England. After the low point around 1450, new generations grew up in the Tudor period, they had different ideas and ideals. If the Black Death was the prehistory of enclosure, it was equally the prehistory of the Reformation. That these changes were more startling and far-reaching in England than elsewhere in Europe was because the population fell so low in England that the pool of expertise and labour was almost entirely drained.

In agriculture, peasant tilling of open fields and hill farming was reduced as large areas of land were enclosed for grazing by

Peasant tilling of fields was the backbone of the English economy for much of the Middle Ages. There was little technological advance in the equipment – though the harrow was a medieval invention. After the Black Death peasants could, and did, demand higher wages: some marginal settlements were abandoned as farmers retreated to the better lands.

sheep: this changed the face of the English countryside, with humps and bumps replacing former settlements and farms. Twentieth-century archaeologists and historians founded a special group to study deserted medieval villages, which focused on those communities which failed. The excavation of the deserted village of Wharram Percy (plate 63) in Yorkshire ran for over thirty years and proved to be a revelation about the ebb and flow of settlement there throughout the Middle Ages: at the height of the economic boom of the 1200s, there were probably as many as 300 people occupying houses and gardens at Wharram where there were two mills and an active parish church. About 200 years later there was only a parson and a shepherd: blocked arcades along the north and south sides of the church show where aisles, added to accommodate the high numbers of the pre-plague village, had first fallen into disrepair and were then demolished. Some churches, like Wharram, were left isolated and adrift in the green fields as communities disappeared. Enclosure of grazing and arable land previously held in common by peasants and the conversion of such lands to private sheep pasture, which required fewer workers, was a major and divisive economic issue from *c.*1350 to 1500. Similarly, in architecture, the labour-intensive Decorated style with its expensive 'seaweed' encrusted stonework gave way to the plain, more cheaply produced, window mouldings of the Perpendicular, often referred to as the 'English style' of architecture. The innovative William Ramsay, the royal master mason and contemporary leading exponents of the Decorated style, died in the Black Death and the style more or less died with them. Indeed all the plastic arts were affected in England: manuscript illumination, stained glass manufacture, sculpture, tomb-brasses and wall painting suffered. Work was halted at Lichfield where the masons over from York died and at Exeter where statue niches were left unfilled for a generation.

In military affairs post-plague English success continued for a while. At Poitiers in 1356, the Black Prince won an astonishing victory over John II of France, who was captured. Whether because of the reduced human resources as a result of the plague or because it was beyond their capability, the English were unable to capitalise on their windfall victories by imposing their rule on France. Edward III might have cut off King John's head and declared himself king of France, but triumphant, chivalric, English pragmatism triumphed. After his victory the Black Prince chivalrously waited at table on John, who was brought to England and accommodated at the Savoy Palace in the Strand. Edward III sought a substantial ransom and territorial concessions.

England was safe for the moment. The enormous ransom for King John enabled Edward to indulge in extravagant building projects such as the modernised and transformed Windsor Castle, while at Westminster Palace the completion of St Stephen's Chapel (plate 19), begun by King Stephen over 200 years before, was achieved.

The ransom also gave a sense of security. Before 1356 the king had bankrupted the state, its Italian bankers and financiers from the city of London – hence, no doubt his pragmatism in victory. So confident was he of his new-found wealth that in 1363 he agreed to a demand that taxation should not in the future be levied without the consent of parliament. This transformed the role of parliament, whose powers thereafter steadily grew until it could clip a king's wings by refusing aid or ultimately sweep a king aside. Taxation thenceforward became inevitable as parliamentary agreement to taxes was on behalf of the people it represented. But financial worries were coming. In 1364 John II died, still in captivity, and the funds dried up. His successor recaptured the lands ceded to England by the treaty of Calais (1360). By 1369, Calais apart, all the territorial gains resulting from Crécy and Poitiers, and the ransom which had accrued from the capture of the French king were gone. The Black Prince died in 1376, so when Edward died in 1377, the throne passed to his grandson, the ten-year-old Richard of Bordeaux.

The failing war with France required considerable new money to revive English fortunes. The regency council imposed a poll or head tax for 1377. This seemed logical: it took account of the loss of population in the plagues by changing the basis of taxation from the community, which paid a lump sum, to individuals. Thus it taxed the survivors. But it was poorly organised and in addition did not

A selection of the Canterbury pilgrims from an early edition of the Canterbury Tales, *which appeared in 1387. The organisation of the pilgrims as they set off down to Canterbury by rank and 'degre' by Chaucer may have been designed to reassure the courtly audience of the social status quo. Social order had been disrupted by the Great Revolt of 1381, when some of the rebels had marched up from Canterbury, terrified the king and cut off the archbishop's head.*

distinguish wealthy from poor in its rates. Implementation involved the obtaining of detailed knowledge of individual households. The cocktail of unfair taxation, inquisition into personal affairs and continuing lack of success in the French war led to the Great or Peasants' Revolt in 1381, when the new wealthy peasants and some of their immediate masters turned on the royal government, beginning with the savaging of the tax collectors in Essex and Kent.

Despite the oft-quoted text 'when Adam delved and Eve span, who was then the gentleman?', there is little evidence that the Great Revolt was primarily proletarian. It was an alliance of people from different social groups who were disaffected for various reasons – with the government, with the war, with the Church and other institutions, and with neighbours. A second conflict arose between the king and a group of nobles which included members of his own family. Richard's beloved wife, Anne of Bohemia, died in 1394. Thereafter his reign declined into tyranny. When Richard dispossessed his cousin Henry Bolingbroke of his rightful inheritance in 1399 (plate 7), Henry rebelled and deposed Richard, who was murdered in Pontefract Castle (1400).

Henry IV (Bolingbroke) (plate 66), an usurper, was always anxious on his throne. He was a warrior and many had hopes of a renewal of war against France. But Henry was too preoccupied with affairs at home to pursue overseas wars. At the battle of Shrewsbury in 1403 he quelled an uprising by the Percys, who had helped him to the throne but with whom he had fallen out over the ransoms of Scots prisoners. The Welsh led by Owain Glyn Dwr also rebelled, while the Scots under Robert III threatened too as well. Although Glyn Dwr was defeated and James I, Robert's heir, fell into English hands in 1406 en route to his new kingdom, the pressure became too much. Henry IV suffered from mental prostration for the remainder of his reign. When he died in 1413 there had already been a number of attempts to depose him, most notably by his son, who became Henry V.

Similar motives to those which had led Edward III into war with France also inspired Henry: dynastic uncertainty following the deposition of Richard II; a desire to unite dissident nobles and factions at home with a foreign war which might offer lands and spoils otherwise beyond royal resources; a claim

*Among subsequent opponents of Henry IV was Henry Percy and his son 'Hotspur',
disaffected by the new king's apparent failure to honour commitments over ransoms due
to them. The Percies had been key supporters in Henry IV's snatching of the throne.
Hotspur met his end at the battle of Shrewsbury, illustrated here, on 21 July 1403 at the
hands of the royal army.*

to the throne of France. After initial plots against him had been
overcome, Henry V focused on the French war. At first the
policy was successful, especially at the battle of Agincourt in
1415. As at Crécy and Poitiers, an expeditionary force, trying to
avoid confrontation with numerically superior French forces,
was brought to battle under able generalship, in this case of
Henry V himself. Like Crécy and Poitiers, Agincourt owed
much to archers and projected the warrior-king of England to
the centre-stage in European politics. Henry created a small

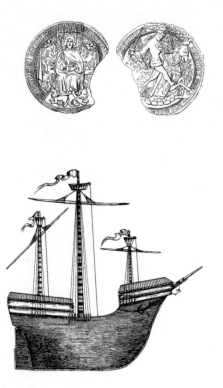

The Seal of Owain Glyn Dwr who led rebellions in Wales and the Marches from 1400 for almost ten years and declared himself Prince of Wales as shown here. There were widespread grievances at all levels of society in the West, and the reign of the new, uncertain, king of England from 1399 opened the door to revolt.

Henry V's great ship, Grace Dieu, *planned in 1414 and completed in 1416. At 1,400 tons and over 200ft long it was larger than other ships of the time: a recent analysis suggests that the mast was over 200ft high! Victory at Agincourt in 1415 changed the political geography of the Channel as the English occupied and administered much of France, which made the ship less essential to national security. Struck by lightning in 1439, she sank at Hamble and her remains may still be seen at low tides.*

but impressive navy (plate 8), building the giant *Grace Dieu*, the biggest ship to be constructed in England before the reign of Charles II and even bulkier than *Victory*. Emperor Sigismund, disillusioned with the sad court of the aged and insane Charles VI of France, was impressed with England where great festivities followed the victory of 1415 (plate 9). Henry and Sigismund took joint action, encouraging councils of the Church to try to resolve certain of Europe's problems, notably in the matter of the papacy which was weak and divided.

The untimely death of Henry V from dysentery at the age of thirty-three brought the glory days of the Hundred Years War to an end. Like a sinking ship, English enterprises in France gradually settled lower in the water from Henry V's death in 1422 to final defeat in 1453. Various factors contributed to the English failure: the continuing inexorable decline in population; lack of funds in the royal treasury in England; the unwillingness of the French to accept the baby Henry VI of England as ruler of both England and France as proposed in 1420 under the Treaty of Troyes; divisions within the royal family into war and peace parties and failure of alliances, especially that with powerful Burgundy after 1435. Apart from the population issue, perhaps the most significant reason for the loss of the war was the failure of the English to invest in updating their military strategy and tactics. The establishment of a standing army and investment in cannon by the French effectively meant the end of English pretensions in France (plate 10). During the resurgence of French military power at the time of Joan of Arc in 1429, it was prescient that the earl of Salisbury was killed by cannon fire, while in the final battle of the war when Gascony was overrun in 1453, Sir Thomas Kyriel was blasted from his horse by cannonade, while increasingly ineffective archers struggled against guns far beyond their resources to silence.

With military success the French monarchy was more positive about its future and this, coupled with the virtual extinction of English territory in France, undermined the necessity for the 'auld alliance' between Scotland and France. In 1424 James I of Scotland emerged from eighteen years' incarceration in England with a wife who was a cousin of the English king (plate 22). By the time he was released the 'auld

The baby Henry VI, born on St Nicholas day (6 December) 1421 to Henry V and Katherine Valois. The French agreed at Troyes in 1420 that a son of their princess and Henry V should be king of both France and England. Henry's birth was, therefore, a triumph for the English. But Henry V's premature death from dysentery when the prince was under a year old made his son's position as dual monarch difficult to sustain.

alliance' was at a low ebb. Scots forces, serving in support of the French, had been destroyed by the English at Verneuil. Thereafter Scots ceased to play an active role in the conflict, to the relief of the English and also, according to contemporary accounts, that of the French. Although wars between England and Scotland were to recur, the fifteenth century was largely a time of peace between the two nations.

The Scottish monarchy was not without problems at this time, for James I was murdered in 1437, James II (plate 31) was blown up by one of his own cannons in 1460 and James III was killed fighting rebels in 1488. Despite all these difficulties there was consolidation north of the border, where politics were, briefly in the fifteenth century, less violent than in

England and where there was a burgeoning of scholarship with the foundation of several universities beginning with St Andrews in 1410. This gave Scotland, numerically and late in the day, more seats of higher learning than England's Oxford and Cambridge founded two centuries earlier.

Unsuccessful war exacerbates internal dissension and the failure of the war in France in 1453 focused attention on difficulties at home. Trouble was compounded when, in early August 1453 and probably on receipt of the news of the fateful battle of Castillon two weeks earlier, the gentle and saintly Henry VI suffered a mental breakdown which left him more or less incapacitated for life. With the depressive Henry IV as one grandfather and the chronically mentally ill Charles VI of France as the other, genes were not on his side.

Civil war in England followed failure in France and offered an outlet for numerous frustrations. The conflict was between descendants of the two sons of Edward III: John of Gaunt, duke of Lancaster (1340–99) and Edmund Duke of York (1342–1402), from whose titles the warring factions took their names. A pit excavated near the battlefield of Towton (1461), an especially bloody encounter, revealed the extreme violence of head wounds and other injuries sustained by combatants, some of whom appeared to be veterans of previous battles which had already left them scarred.

The war lasted for thirty years and witnessed the deposition of Henry VI and, temporarily, of Edward IV, the murder in the Tower of Edward's sons, Edward V and Richard Duke of York, and the final battle at Bosworth in which Richard III (plate 13) lost his crown to Henry Tudor. Henry VII's 'claim' to the throne was through Catherine of Valois, the widowed queen of Henry V, who married Owen Tudor, a junior court official – in fact no claim at all! Their sons, uterine brothers of Henry VI, were brought up at court. The elder, Edmund Tudor, earl of Richmond, married Margaret Beaufort, a great-great-granddaughter of Edward III. The Beauforts were illegitimate offspring of John of Gaunt and Katherine Swinford, nanny to his legitimate children, and were barred by statute from inheriting the throne. Margaret and Edmund's son, Henry VII, united the families of York and Lancaster by marrying Elizabeth, sister to the late kings Edward IV and Richard III (plate 13). The Tudors, genealogically speaking, brought the succession to a low ebb and introduced another phase of that most English characteristic, being ruled by foreign dynasties, in this case Welsh.

The fifteenth century was a time of low ebb not only for the monarchy but also, in the civil wars, for the nobility. There was, as we have seen, significantly reduced population which affected England's ambitions abroad. There was a desperate financial shortfall in the treasury and there was a perceived breakdown in law and order, betokened by the building of defensive gatehouses even at monasteries and the widespread establishment of moated sites in the countryside. Weakened by plague, villages were deserted, especially in upland areas such as the Lincolnshire wolds. Monasticism faltered as new recruits failed to materialise. Religious leadership was lacking. Papal fortunes reached their lowest ebb when the popes in Rome were challenged by French-backed popes in Avignon and even, briefly, in Pisa. Thus the papacy was under threat from increasingly nationalist governments in western Europe. Secular leaders such as Henry V and the Emperor Sigismund took the lead in religious matters. Henry V, for example, dissolved priories which owed allegiance to mother houses in

John Wycliffe (d.1384) was an early nonconformist voice against the papacy, seen in England as a French institution while based at Avignon; England and France being at war. Wycliffe was supported, although for different motives, at court in his complaints about the Church. Eventually, towards the end of his life, he became so strident in attacks on Church doctrine, landholding and much else that he lost support. After his death his remains were exhumed, burned and cast into a river to deny him a pilgrim following.

France. In the late 1300s England had developed its own home-grown heresy, Lollardy (based on another word for incomprehensible babbling), with John Wycliffe taking a lead. This called for vernacular (English) language for services, and received some support at court. Wycliffe himself was eventually banished to rural Lutterworth in Leicestershire. His brand of internal reform of the Church had a wider currency, being 'exported' to Bohemia where, under the leadership of John Hus it stirred up war. As for Wycliffe, he died peacefully. Only later were his remains dug up and cast into a river so that there should be no shrine to this reforming zealot.

There was much in the fifteenth century that suggested decline. But the 150 years after 1350 saw an unparalleled rise in the fortunes of women: 'a golden age of women and a golden age of bacilli'. Women stormed the bastion of male-dominated burgess groups in towns, secured apprenticeships in crafts and ran their own businesses, not only in traditional areas but also in more unlikely ones, such as the foundation of guilds and activities such as bellfounding. Female mystics such at the Kings Lynn woman, Margery Kempe, (suspected of Lollardy) and the women who come into focus in the letters by the Cely and Paston families give a clear view of the generally happy conditions of life for those who survived the plague, for those who were left benefited enormously from the lands and possessions of those who had disappeared. In general shortage of labour, then as later, brought women into the workforce: rising population in the sixteenth century forced them, willingly or not, back into the kitchen.

As demographic decline provided more space but a less skilled workforce, there were significant developments in architecture. The focus on private space, already visible before 1350, becomes more apparent afterwards. Monastic accommodation became increasingly private, from separate and grand houses for abbots and priors to cubicles for monks in divided-up dormitories. Stylistically the Perpendicular, with its regimented mullioned and transomed windows, was not as glorious as the Decorated but was at least uniquely English in its simplicity and grace, and impressive to behold. Late Perpendicular, otherwise Tudor, architecture became ornate once more, as can be seen at King's College, Cambridge, founded by Henry VI and completed by Henry VII.

Like Henry IV, Henry VII was also uncertain on his throne: he stayed near London, the centre of power. Following the distribution of spoils to family and supporters in 1485, royal palaces were reduced to a handful in and around the capital. The early Tudors, Henry VII and Henry VIII, concentrated their rule and their residencies in the south-east and were unwilling to travel their kingdom as much as their predecessors had done.

Henry VII re-established the equilibrium of the English monarchy and its finances. He was a meticulous man in every respect. A striking example of this is found in his papers relating to his search for a wife after his queen, Elizabeth, died. Ambassadors were dispatched to examine possible young princess-brides. The king sent detailed instructions, to which ambassadors responded with written replies. In the case of the young queen of Naples (who was not selected), the questions enquired about the shape of her nose, the length of her neck, the size of her breasts (and nipples) and whether she had hair about her upper lip or not! The ambassadors were hard pressed to answer such explicit questions and the contortions of their replies – especially on those parts of the body they could not see – are good reading. The whole episode reminds us of the problems encountered in such matchmaking before travel was easy and throw into perspective Henry VIII's difficulties with the portrait and actuality of Anne of Cleves. The only portrait of Henry VII we have, shows him as a thin-lipped, hollow-cheeked man in middle age, was made to show his face to prospective wives – it does not reveal the 'few black teeth' referred to by Polydore Vergil.

The premature death in 1502 of Prince Arthur, the heir to the throne, propelled Prince Henry into the unexpected role of prospective king of England. On his father's death in 1509 this accomplished young man duly inherited the throne. Like Henry V, Henry VIII was also son of a usurper. At first he was happy to be guided by his ministers. Thomas Wolsey, ambitious to be Pope, came to hold a number of wealthy positions in the English Church, including archbishop of York and

Henry VII (d.1509) was a parsimonious and well-organised monarch who clung tenaciously to the crown. After the death of his queen, Elizabeth, in 1503, Henry searched far and wide for a replacement, sending out ambassadors to seek every detail of the young women he considered eligible. Portraits of the king were circulated – none showing his black teeth, as observed by a contemporary.

bishop of Winchester. It was Wolsey who, within a year of Henry's accession introduced the latest Italian building schemes to England in his creation of his palace at Hampton Court. Although his palace was taken over by Henry VIII when Wolsey fell from power, recent research has shown that the plans and structures established following 1510 brought Italian Renaissance styles to England over a century before Inigo Jones's (plate 18) creations of the seventeenth century, traditionally believed the first in England in the new style.

This Henry was able, scholarly (for a monarch) and enquiring, if tyrannical. He was also competitive and imitative. At the Field of the Cloth of Gold in 1520 where he met Francis I of France, he strove to impress that modish bearded monarch by the splendour of his pavilions, dress and chivalric skills. Having confronted the king of France in this way, Henry

Cardinal Wolsey (d. 1530) was the son of an Ipswich butcher who rose within the Church and state through his sheer ability to be an international figure. He commanded wealth perhaps second only to his master, Henry VIII. Wolsey eventually overstepped the mark, and was on his way to London to face the royal wrath when he died.

contrived a meeting with his contemporary ruler, the Emperor Charles V. In 1522 Charles visited England and was shown King Arthur's round table hanging on the wall of the great hall at Winchester Castle. This icon brought together a number of themes: it suggested (quite misleadingly) that the Tudor dynasty was antique in showing a bearded Henry as King Arthur (Henry's beard was modelled on Francis I's) presiding over a table of chivalric courtiers with a Tudor Rose as the central motif. Importantly, from Henry's point of view, the castle was a centre of power in the 'ancient capital', where his elder brother had been born and baptised thus adding to the Tudor myth. Archaeology has considerably deepened our understanding of this apparently straightforward artefact. While it was painted in *c.*1520, the table itself, which now hangs on the wall of Winchester Castle hall, dates from much

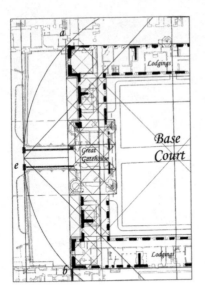

Recent research by Jonathan Foyle, illustrated here, has shown that in creating his palace at Hampton Court Wolsey employed the latest principles of architecture imported from Italy. This remarkable discovery shows that Renaissance architecture was established in England over a century before Inigo Jones, who has traditionally been considered the initiator of Renaissance architecture in England.

earlier – but not from the time of King Arthur. It is likely on the best evidence we have to date either to the period of the foundation of the Orders of the Round Table and Garter in the 1340s, or more likely to the late thirteenth century, when Edward I held an impressive tournament at Winchester.

By far the most dramatic piece of Tudor archaeology is the *Mary Rose*, raised in November 1982 from the seabed off Portsmouth, where she had lain since capsizing on 19 July 1545, under the gaze of the king himself. The raising of the wreck gripped the nation, as did the treasure trove of finds from the contents of the barber-surgeon's cabin to the long-bows of the soldiers on board, not to mention weapons of all other sorts, clothing and even some remains of the men themselves. The *Mary Rose*, in her wet-storage time capsule still has much to tell us as the painstaking research and renovation

Henry VIII by Hans Holbein, who joined the court in 1536, just at the time when Henry was disposing of Anne Boleyn. Henry bears a challenging and fearsome look in contrast to his previous youthful, narrow-faced appearance, although he was only in his mid-forties. By this time the king had changed his mind over Catholicism, had broken with Rome and was beginning the process of dissolving the monasteries.

proceeds. Yet again archaeology has revealed a wealth of evidence, which could never have been discovered from documentary sources.

Henry VIII's propaganda at first was against those who criticised the papacy. Henry joined Charles V in opposing the reformist programme expounded by Martin Luther and was rewarded with the papal title *Fidei Defensor* (defender of the faith), which still appears as *FD* on coins today. In view of Henry's subsequent designation as head of the Church in England it is often wrongly believed that his title was a Protestant origin, a popular misconception condoned if not promoted through the coinage.

To the insecure Tudor dynasty the necessity to produce an heir was paramount (plate 14). It may be that Henry VIII's determination to secure the future of his line moulded almost all the events in the latter half of his reign: his disposal of Wolsey; the removal and subsequent execution of Lord Chancellor Thomas More (plate 67) in 1532; his establishment as head of the Church in England (1534); the marriage to and execution of Anne Boleyn (1533–36); the marriage to Jane Seymour (plate 68) and the birth of Prince Edward in 1537.

Henry VIII is remembered for the beginnings of the Reformation. Financial disputes with the papacy were a primary cause of the train of events. His pliant chief minister Thomas Cromwell and Archbishop Thomas Cranmer paved the way for the break with Rome by sanctioning Henry's divorce from Catherine of Aragon against papal opposition. Henry's elevation to be head of the Church in England and the Dissolution of the Monasteries between 1536 and 1540 saw this first phase of the reformation accomplished. Ever insecure, Henry allowed most of the monastic lands to be redistributed amongst his supporters, who became known as 'augmentations families' from the euphemistically entitled Court of Augmentations which gathered in the possessions of the dissolved monasteries.

Glimpses of England in the latter years of Henry VIII's reign were recorded by John Leland in his *Itinerary*. Leland, who was sent out by the king to survey monastic libraries in a frenzied search for Arthurian texts, recorded much before and during the dissolution: how some of the sites lay vacant and ruinous, while others were rapidly turned into private houses. Leland's mental health gave way in 1547. The notes of this early exponent of archaeological fieldwork, which have survived, are greatly valued today as snapshots of his turbulent experiences.

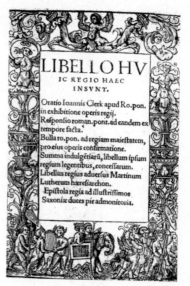

Title page of Assertio septem Sacramentorum adversus Martin Lutherum *(1521). Almost certainly composed by Henry VIII in opposition to the renegade monks' pamphlets, it earned the king the title of* 'Fidei defensor', *which is to this day on coins of the realm. An eyewitness reported that Thomas Wolsey, Henry's polemic in his hand, presided over the public burning of Luther's works in St Paul's churchyard in May 1521 before a crowd of 30,000.*

Anne Boleyn by Holbein. Portraiture, and biography, in the early Tudor period were skills often practised by foreigners in England, where such skills were not to be found. Anne Boleyn, who in turn delighted and infuriated Henry, was probably still under thirty when she was executed in 1536 not long after this portrait was made.

Thomas More's Utopia *was published in 1516. In view of its heavy satire on existing institutions, and More's ambassadorial duties on the continent at the time, it is not surprising that it was published abroad, and in Latin. It was part of a European debate. However, it contained plenty of criticism of the England he knew – especially the exponential growth in sheep farming which was devouring the countryside. His masters should have taken note that this public servant was a threat as well as a boon.*

Archaeologically the dissolution is revealed most obviously in the landscape of 'bare ruin'd choirs' and the roofless skeletons of the once vibrant monastic centres of English intellectual life. Among the debris found by archaeologists are the clasps from medieval books burnt by the reformers, the dividers used for ruling out the pages of music and other manuscripts, and in Yorkshire lead ingots marked with the royal crest, the former lead roofs melted down to become royal property, but buried during over-enthusiastic demolition. These ruins and artefacts demonstrate as clearly as any text the wreckage caused by the reformers.

By 1547 the population of England had begun to rise once more. Some towns, notably London, were beginning to expand rapidly. London began the process of transformation from a middle-ranking European city of some 50,000 people in 1450 to the largest in Europe by 1700. The basis of the Tudor Poor law was established as towns responded to an increasing tide of mobile poor, many of whom had been pushed off the land by enclosure, so roundly denounced by Thomas More in his *Utopia* (1516), in which he argued that the countryside, formerly the domain of people was being occupied and devoured by multitudes of sheep, of which there were at least as many as there were people in the countryside. Pain for the poor and benefits for gentry were to be significant characteristics of the next century of English history.

4

Gloriana and Shakespeare
Antiquaries, Puritans and Civil War, 1547–1650

I know I have the body of a weak and feeble woman, but I have the heart and stomach of a king, and of a king of England too; and think foul scorn that Parma or Spain, or any prince of Europe, should dare to invade the borders of my realm.

Elizabeth I, *Speech to troops*, 1588

Between 1547 and 1650 England witnessed the advance of Protestant reforms, and enjoyed the brilliant reign of Elizabeth, Shakespeare's works and the unification of the thrones of England and Scotland. It is a strong contender to be hailed as the most triumphant century in English history. The period opened with the death of the Catholic king Henry VIII and closed with the shutting down of the theatres, Civil War and the end, for the time being, of the monarchy.

There was a sharp rise in consciousness about England's past at this time of disruptive change and foreign Catholic threat. Early in the field was John Leland, the king's antiquary, who died in 1552 without publishing his notes. William Camden (d.1623), whose *Britannia* ranged widely from Hadrian's Wall to Stonehenge and was first published in 1586, took up the mantle with the aim of 'restoring antiquity' to his country. *Albion's England* by William Warner traced the history of England from Noah to the Norman Conquest and was published in the same year. The notion of England's history beginning with Noah may seem odd to modern eyes. However, to the Elizabethan and Jacobean antiquaries who walked the high Cotswold and Chiltern hills and found marine fossils there, it was plain that these uplands were once drowned by the Great Flood. The antiquaries were at sea in their divinations of dates in prehistory; and some contemporaries found them rather a joke as shown in the 1641 play *The Antiquary* where it was observed that a collector might sit:

> *All day in contemplation of a statue*
> *With ne'er a nose*

However, the antiquary himself sums up the archaeological viewpoint with blinding clarity when he says, 'Antiquities... are the registers, the chronicles of the age they were made in, and speak the truth of history better than a hundred of your printed commentaries'. If it was impossible to date antiquities, scholars felt they should be able to date documents more readily, especially the Bible. The hilltop fossils reinforced notions of the historicity of the Bible, whose texts Protestants closely scrutinised. Thus James Ussher (d.1656) a Protestant prelate, poring over his books in Ireland, established to his own satisfaction that the world had been created in 4004 BC,

John Knox (d.1572) was by turns a Catholic priest, galley slave and chaplain to Edward VI. He worked in Calvinist Geneva during Mary's reign and returned to Scotland in 1558, publishing his blast against female rulers – the 'Monstrous Regiment of Women' at that time. A bearded prophet (as opposed to a tonsured priest or monk), he took a leading role in the Scottish Calvinist reformation after 1560, when papal authority was abolished and the material culture of Catholicism vigorously destroyed.

at 9 o'clock on a Monday morning, a date which was long accepted as a fact, his dates were even printed in the margins of some eighteenth-century bibles.

But these calculations were the background to the glories of Elizabethan and early Stuart culture. Key elements of Englishness today date from this period: the Church of England with its oft-quoted prayer book and Authorised Version of the Bible; the plays of Shakespeare and his contemporaries; addiction to tobacco brought to England in the early 1600s, despite a counterblast from James I; and the classical 'ideal' architecture of Inigo Jones. But there was a dark side: the burnings in the name of religion, the fear of foreign invasion and the eventual descent once more into Civil War in 1642.

Coronation procession of Edward VI in 1547. He was only ten at his accession, and his mother's brother, Edward Seymour became Protector. Edward showed some of his father's hardness of heart when he acquiesced in his uncle's execution in 1549. His mentors pursued the Reformation with vigour in the young king's name.

Henry VIII had broken with Rome and dissolved the monasteries. This forceful monarch who made himself head of the Church in England but who died a Catholic, may be seen as England's last medieval king. Some would say that whereas the arrival of the Tudors on the throne of England was the end of the Middle Ages for historians, the Dissolution of the Monasteries and the Henrician reformation provide an 'archaeological' end to the Middle Ages. But even within our island such dates may be challenged: John Knox did not preach 'pull down their nests that the craws may build na' more' until 1559, which resulted in the summary end of monastic Catholicism in Scotland at the hands of local mobs.

In England the minority of the little Edward VI, only nine at Henry's death, provided an opportunity for his masters to pursue Church reform at a parochial level in a much more vigorous campaign than his father had done. This was accomplished in the young king's name by his maternal uncle the duke of Somerset. Key elements of this reform were the abolition of the chantries (where masses were said for the souls of the dead), the destruction of shrines including that of Becket at Canterbury and the introduction of the Protestant prayer book (plate 15), a text of worship in English. The prayer book is largely a direct translation of the Latin it replaced. Endorsed by parliament in 1549, the prayer book was edited into a more Protestant text in 1552 and the Catholic Mass was abolished.

The Reformation was not an immediate success. It took about a century to work through society. Many gentry and MPs continued their allegiance to the old religion well into the 1600s, and some beyond, simply ignoring legislation against Catholics. Outlying areas of the British Isles, including much of Ireland and small communities, such as South Uist off the west coast of Scotland, never experienced reformation. Pre-Reformation parish finance was geared to celibate clergy and the emoluments were limited. This influenced the quality of married clergy who came forward as the incomes were so small. Their poverty-stricken and often large families could be more of a burden than a benefit in a parish. Few 'reformed' clergy were as ignorant as the Herefordshire parson who, when asked by a visiting bishop in 1549 to distinguish between Jesus and Judas (who betrayed him), was unable to do so. The bishop's following question, which required the hapless man to recite the Lord's Prayer, received an equally dumb response.

The duke of Northumberland ousted Somerset and had him beheaded in 1552 on behalf of Edward VI.

A fragment of a drawing of the shrine of Becket at Canterbury, seen here on the eve of its destruction, it had been a magnet for pilgrims from all over Europe for over 350 years. Note the bones and what appears to be the sliced through cranium on the chest in the foreground. A Venetian wrote in 1500 that it was 'all covered with plates of purest gold... scarcely seen because it is covered with precious stones... sculpted gems... and cameos, surpassed by a ruby'. It was swept away in 1538 for the benefit of the royal coffers.

Execution of Archbishop Cranmer, burned at the stake in 1556. Thomas Cranmer had been archbishop of Canterbury before the Reformation under Henry VIII: subsequently he was the first Protestant archbishop. His gift for sonorous expression is found in the Edwardian prayer books. Returning Catholicism under Mary was a problem for Cranmer. After vacillating, he was burnt as a heretic at Oxford.

Northumberland succeeded in having his daughter-in-law, Lady Jane Grey, named heir to the throne by the ailing boy-king who died in 1553. Support for Grey was insufficient: she was executed and the rightful heir, Mary, succeeded. The problems during Edward's reign and the succession crisis highlight the continuing weakness of the monarchy and the power of the nobility.

Mary resolved to return England to Catholicism. Her marriage in 1554 to Philip, heir to the throne of Spain, reinforced the old religion. The Catholic marriage was soon followed by the burning of leading Protestants: Bishops Latimer and Ridley in 1555 and Archbishop Cranmer in 1556. Much could not be restored, for example the monastic houses had largely been demolished or converted to other uses and their communities scattered. Mary did, however, re-establish a Benedictine monastery at Westminster and small religious houses elsewhere. In the parishes, churchwardens' accounts graphically show how church furnishings were restored, altars re-erected, statuary replaced, bells re-hung and the old service books returned.

The succession remained a problem for the childless Mary. Pathetic documents drawn up in preparation for the announcement of the birth of an heir survive among the public records, with blanks to be filled in once the birth had occurred and the sex of the heir was known. But there were only false pregnancies and on Mary's death in 1558, her sister Elizabeth came to the throne.

For Elizabeth (plate 20), the first and most pressing issue was religion. A settlement was made: the queen became Supreme Governor of the Church in England replacing the Pope. A less severely Protestant version of the 1552 prayer book was introduced which allowed considerable religious latitude. Religious conflict came to rest with the establishment of Protestantism, but this did not mean unanimity. The matter was hotly debated: radical Puritans wished to rid the country of vacillating 'popish massmongers, men for all seasons'. Puritans sought to return to what they perceived as ancient apostolic Christianity, with congregations choosing their ministers: Presbyterianism. The religious establishment feared the rooting out of the whole ecclesiastical polity. However there was sufficient doctrine and a scriptural basis in common, together with a shared anxiety about Catholicism, to keep Puritans and Anglicans from physical conflict. Elizabeth gave a lead and must be credited for bringing decades of ferocious religious struggle under control.

In contrast to her predecessors, Elizabeth called parliament comparatively infrequently: there were only ten parliaments

English troops on the march in Ireland. Elizabeth's reign was characterised by the comparative poverty of the public purse. The war in Ireland swallowed up more English resources of men and money than all Elizabeth's other military commitments.

This woodcut from The Groundeworke of Conny-Catching *(1592) appeared in a grim decade of famine and plague. It warns of two types of sturdy beggar the 'upright man' posing as a gentleman fallen on hard times, and the 'counterfeit crank' whose ubiquitous bar of soap could make him foam at the mouth. The surge in poverty, after the Dissolution of the Monasteries resulted in the workhouse, a Utopian ideal in 1516, being introduced without a murmur in the parliament of 1576.*

in her reign of forty-five years (plates 16, 17). Parliament was called to address particular problems. Her intentions and parliament's were not always coterminous, so the sessions were often short. An account of major issues which parliament addressed provides a check list of the major considerations of the reign: the religious settlement (1559, 1563); the Treason Act (1571); the Poor Law (1572, 1576, 1598, 1601) – in 1576 the parliament took the opportunity tentatively to petition the queen to marry, a matter not mentioned since a major row in 1566; to cut off Mary Queen of Scots's (plate 69) head (1587); and to finance the war in Ireland (1601). The 1601 parliament is a good example of a parliament called for one purpose which diverted its attention to others, including attacks on monopolies and a codification of the Poor Law, which remained on the statute book until 1834.

The basis of the Tudor Poor Law was simplistic and badly flawed. It assumed that everyone had come from an identifiable parish and that, when the location of that parish was known, individuals could be sent back there and the problem solved. The weakness of this assumption was that every vagrant presumably left their parish for a reason and, in a time of high rural population and enclosure, work for all was not available in their native parish. A second fundamental of this Poor Law was that it divided the poor into those who deserved relief and sturdy beggars who could, but would not, work. Workhouses which were considered Utopian early in the century, were established by statute in 1576, without a voice in parliament against the proposal and proved another enduring feature of provision for the poor and the unemployed.

These statutory changes are reflected both in the landscape and in surviving monuments. Churches bear the scars of demolished altars and screens, defaced shrines and wall paintings. Artefacts which replaced them are seen today: boards with paintings of the Ten Commandments and royal coats of arms as monarchs took over from the papacy as leaders of the Church. A Protestant 'temple-style' of architecture slowly evolved, bringing a revival of the rounded Romanesque arch (plate 60) in contrast to the gothic style of recent centuries. In towns and the countryside the distinctive close-studded timber framing of the 'Tudor' style of architecture emerged as farmers gained long leases of land, which encouraged them to rebuild or build anew. This represented growing security as the peasants of medieval England re-emerged with their consolidated wealth and holdings as the yeomen of England. Their fenced and hedged farms contrasted sharply with the open fields of medieval England and the shared wasteland and wood pasture. By driving villagers out, the enclosing of the landscape contributed to the perceived necessity for the Poor Law to manage these migrants dubbed 'sturdy beggars' by parliament.

Queen Elizabeth's government was increasingly afflicted by faction, especially in the 1590s when the earl of Essex and William Cecil, Lord Burghley, battled for power at court. Eventually Essex was executed for plotting against the queen. Nonetheless, power remained very much with the aristocracy who had the resources to involve themselves in politics and who could help to fund the ambitions of an increasingly impoverished Crown.

Queen Elizabeth realised that many wealthy families in England had derived fortunes from the dispersal of monastic lands, but by her reign only a tiny amount of monastic land remained in royal hands. In default of monasteries to provide hospitality and because her grandfather had disposed of the scattered rural palaces enjoyed by medieval monarchs, summer progresses beyond the area around the Thames valley and London where Henry VIII had assembled some sixty palaces, involved queen and court travelling between country houses belonging to other people. Entertaining Elizabeth became a heavy burden which some sought to avoid by leaving their houses when the queen was known to be coming. Elizabeth requisitioned such houses and stayed there despite the owners' absence. Others, who were more ambitious to share political power and to shine at court, and who possessed sufficient resources, built magnificent houses with an eye to providing accommodation for the monarch and her court. Longleat and Theobalds are examples of such 'prodigy' houses.

Architecturally, however, even the greatest Elizabethan and early Stuart houses such as Hardwick Hall (1590s) and Hatfield House (after 1607) were not a match for their

Elizabeth I and her huntsman from Turberville's Noble Art of Venerie *(1575). Hunting was always a major royal pastime and Elizabeth enjoyed it heartily. On her visit to Clarendon (Wiltshire) in 1574, the hunting book records that almost 350 deer were killed in one day!*

The Elvetham Entertainment, 1591. By 1590 rewards, wars and other expenditure had removed all the profits which had accrued from the Dissolution of the Monasteries. Elizabeth relied on her nobles to provide entertainment and, often to their great displeasure, would descend on them with her court.

continental counterparts. The finest English architectural creations of the age were those of Inigo Jones who travelled to Italy to sketch classical architecture first-hand, thus setting a new general standard in the early seventeenth century at the Queen's House, Greenwich (1616–35) and at the Banqueting Hall, Whitehall (1619–22), picking up where Wolsey had begun in 1510 at Hampton Court. These distinguished buildings stand out from other 'Renaissance' structures in England, which derived from classical models filtered through Northern Europe, and were built by patrons and artisans who had only a partial understanding of the classical forms and decorative schemes they were trying to recreate.

But if the English were no match for the continental powers in architecture, they continued to triumph when confronted in war. The defeat of the Spanish Armada in 1588, by a small and heroic English fleet against numerical and technological odds, gave heart to a nation beleaguered by powerful and Catholic neighbours. Like the battles at Crécy, Poitiers and Agincourt, this was another triumph of David over Goliath. The Armada set sail from Spain as a crusading fleet blessed by the Pope. Its defeat by the English and further destruction by storms which drove the ships round the north of Britain, reducing the fleet from 136 to eighty ships, effectively ended hopes of a Catholic revival in England. Maritime archaeology has recently revealed that the ships of the Armada were loaded with siege weapons to facilitate the work of the invasion force they carried towards England. There was more than religious tension between England and Spain. Economic interests in an expanding world brought conflict. In Henry VIII's reign privateers who raided Spanish treasure ships returning from the colonies in Central and South America were welcomed at

Sir Francis Drake (d.1596) was the greatest Elizabethan sailor, who circumnavigated the globe, 'singed the king of Spain's beard' at Cadiz in 1587, and famously found time to win his game of bowls, at Plymouth in his native Devon, and 'to thrash the Spaniards too' at the time of the Armada in 1588, which, of course, he did.

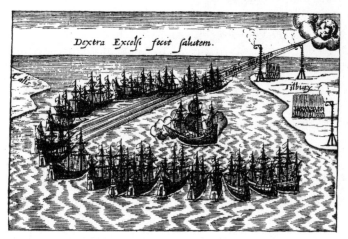

The Spanish Armada off Tilbury, 1588. From George Carleton's A Thankfull Remembrance of God's Mercy in the Deliverance of the Church and state in the reigns of Elizabeth and James I. *England was saved by courageous sailors and the blast of the south-west wind which blew the Armada steadily north until many ships were wrecked on the coasts of Scotland, and eventually Ireland. Archaeology has shown the Armada ships were carrying cargoes of invasion machinery for capturing towns in England.*

Sir Walter Raleigh (ex.1618) was a handsome adventurer who dazzled the Elizabethan court with his plans and projects, and flattered the queen with his proposed colony to be called 'Virginia'. That he brought the blessing of potatoes and curse of smoking to England epitomise his Jekyll and Hyde life. Mostly popular with Elizabeth, though having bitter enemies, he aroused the hostility of James I who eventually had him executed, probably justifiably, for his involvement in Spanish interests. His legacy includes his History of the World *(1614); after death he was more popular than in his lifetime.*

Court by the king. English ventures in the New World lacked the religious zeal of the Catholics and, equally importantly, were invariably undercapitalised, as in Brazil *c.*1540 and in Virginia during Elizabeth's reign where Sir Walter Raleigh tried unsuccessfully to found a colony in the late 1580s.

Nor were all Elizabethan sailors as competent or faithful as might be wished. A memorable example is Thomas Hood who, in spurning the new-fangled compasses and quadrants with the quip 'I give not a fart for all their cosmography', set sail for China. Unsurprisingly, he never arrived but ended up on the River Plate in Argentina where one of his boats was wrecked and its occupants captured by natives who enslaved the fittest and ate the rest. Sir Walter Raleigh was long believed to have been executed for puncturing the inflated ego of James I. Recent work has shown, however, that Raleigh received substantial payments from none other than the Spaniards themselves!

The centre of gravity of European commerce was shifting from the Mediterranean, whose merchants had dominated European trade for centuries, to the Atlantic coast of Europe. Here cities such as Antwerp flourished, with a population of 100,000 by 1560, attracting merchant communities from all over Europe including England and Scotland. But, like England, continental Europe was riven by religious dissention which, while it threatened England, also produced some useful side effects.

The economy of England was bolstered by this shift in trade to the Atlantic and by influxes of religious refugees from Catholic Europe. These were often young and energetic people with skills new to England, especially in the 'new draperies' such as serge-making, which flourished in harness with traditional broadcloth manufacture. The arrival of such new skills, distinct from native work, was supported by workers in sufficient numbers to provide for a market anxious for new products and was a great success.

'Alien' skills had long been in demand in England in banking (hence Lombard Street taking its name from its medieval Italian bankers), insurance and the development of credit facilities. Foreigners continued to be in demand under the Tudors and Stuarts. Hans Holbein, well known for his portrait of Henry VIII, came from Augsburg. Similarly, Anthony van Dyck from Antwerp came to the court of James I and set the style for court portrait painting under Charles I and thereafter. Alongside these exceptional imported talents, which made their way into the England as the country reinvented itself as the leading Protestant power in Europe, was found quality 'alien' artisan work in, for example, glazing (all known glaziers in sixteenth-century Southampton were 'alien'

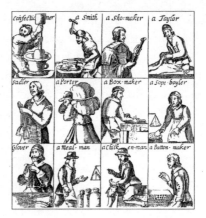

Tradesmen of the Tudor period. As population rose once more in the sixteenth century, following a century and a half of decline and stagnation after the Black Death, England's skills base began to be re-established: good for men, but not so good for women, who found less work outside the home.

immigrants) and in metalwork, exemplified by fine Tudor imported tomb-brasses, some of which have survived reformist zeal. It is plain that in the two centuries following the Black Death of 1348 the skills base in England remained very low in many areas and that the country benefited substantially from the diffusion of innovation in artisan and artistic skills.

Demographically, Elizabeth's reign saw the population rise to, perhaps, 5 million by 1600 in the British Isles as a whole. This led to pressures on the land and also the towns. Plague continued to afflict the country but was an increasingly urban phenomenon returning to many towns every ten to fifteen years or so, culling up to 25 per cent of the population and sometimes more. The effects of plague are readily seen in parish registers instituted by Thomas Cromwell in 1538. Queen

The Gunpowder plotters of 1605 were Catholic terrorists who insinuated kegs of gunpowder into the undercroft of the parliament building at Westminster. Their plan was foiled by an informer, and the plotters paid a heavy price in torture and death after trial. Some have seen them as Catholic martyrs, others as anti-Scottish protesters against the accession of James VI of Scotland as James I of England.

Elizabeth's reign ended as it had begun with a violent epidemic. She died at the palace of Richmond on the Thames and her ring, a token of succession, was dropped from an upper window to a waiting horseman, who galloped off to tell James VI of Scotland that he was to become James I of England. The Welsh Tudor dynasty gave way to the Scots Stuarts.

Unification of the thrones of England and Scotland was thus painlessly achieved. Paradoxically, at the time when the monarchy became monolithic, divisions in Britain were growing. Religion was the chief cause of division. Fears of King James's liberal attitudes to religion and of his Presbyterian background were amongst the causes of the celebrated Gunpowder Plot of November 1605, in which the plotters, led by Robert Catesby aimed to blow up parliament. The plot was betrayed and Guy Fawkes, a former soldier in the Spanish army in the Netherlands, was discovered with the gunpowder beneath the Houses of Parliament. He was tried by the Lord Chief Justice, Sir Thomas Fleming, and was hung, drawn and quartered. It was long suspected that the story of Guy Fawkes was a propaganda coup against the Catholics. However, recent research has shown that gunpowder was taken from the palace of Westminster into the arsenal at the Tower of London (plate 51) immediately following the discovery of the plot.

Respect for scripture is a fundamental core of Protestantism and perhaps the most enduring achievement of James's reign in England was the publication in 1611 of the Authorised Version of the Bible. This scholarly work drew on the best elements of previous translations, both Catholic and Protestant, and was produced by a team of several dozen scholars. The Authorised Version was part of a broader vision, that of making England, clearly the most powerful and populous Protestant country in Europe, a leader among Protestant states. James I's vision was shared by many leading English Protestant intellectuals. When Sir Thomas Bodley re-established the university library at Oxford in 1602 he appointed Thomas James, a red-hot Protestant from New College, as 'Librarie Keeper'. Bodley himself had been in exile at Geneva (during the later years of John Calvin's theocracy in the city) in Mary's reign on account of his religion and between them patron and librarian began to build an international Protestant library. James was especially interested in studying the early Church Fathers, whose works he believed had been deliberately falsified by Roman Catholic theologians. The Protestant nature of the library was further emphasised by a portrait frieze of 200 scholars round the top of the walls in the Upper Reading

Room, emphasising recent Protestant scholarship, and claiming many ancients, posthumously, in the cause at the same time. A joint catalogue was produced from Oxford including those texts in the Cambridge University Library. After James retired from the library in 1620 he collated texts, building on his 1611 *A treatise of the Corruption of Scripture by... the Church of Rome for the maintenance of Popery and Irreligion.* By the time he died in 1629 James's equally zealous Protestant nephew Richard, who wrote 760 pages on the 'decanonisation' of Becket, was in charge of the other great Protestant library, that of Sir Robert Cotton, now the basis of the British Library. It was plain which way the English Protestant scholars and their patrons were tending. But the death of James I and the accession of Charles I brought a change of religious atmosphere away from this kind of Protestantism.

The language of the Authorised Version is mirrored in the works of William Shakespeare, whose final and experimental plays, which included *The Tempest* with all its allusions to the New World, were written *c.*1611, at the same time as the Authorised Version. Shakespeare is universally acclaimed as the finest writer of the English language and his plays, have stood the test of time, like no others. His contribution, not only to the culture of his own age but to succeeding generations and now worldwide, is a major reason why late Tudor and early Stuart England is seen as a literary golden age. Shakespeare's brilliance is apparent in the astonishing breadth of subject matter with which he engaged. For all its Renaissance vernacular, however, English literature was slow to grace the shelves of the Bodleian Library; only three out of 5,000 titles in 1605 (Chaucer, Lydgate and Puttenham) were in English, as Bodley considered such titles a waste of shelf-space as 'riffe-raffe' books. Thus it would be unwise to imagine that there was a national agenda in the arts, literature and theology as subsequent ideological and theological divisions, and the closure of the theatres in 1642 were to highlight.

The introduction of printing by William Caxton (plates 11, 12) before 1500 made literature more readily available. Court culture began to permeate a broader audience. This was achieved partly through noble patronage of the theatre. Plays were brought to a wider audience through theatres such as the Globe, although poetry remained in the grip of courtier-poets such as Spenser, who eulogised Queen Elizabeth or 'Gloriana' as he calls her, in his *Faerie Queene*. So-called 'Renaissance individualism' encouraged authors to identify themselves, while the Reformation led to a growth in secular drama. Individualism and reform contributed to

The ducking stool. Belief in witchcraft survived from the medieval period and enjoyed something of a revival in the early seventeenth century. Shakespeare's later plays, such as Cymbeline *(with its English story) and* The Tempest *incorporate elements of magic in the romance and recognise this trend. Witchcraft declined with the rise of newspapers a century later.*

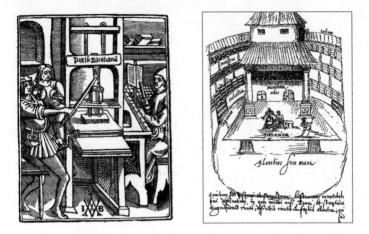

Left: *A printing press from a 1498 book by Iodocus Badius Ascensianus. The printing press revolutionised the circulation of pictorial and written material following its introduction to England in the 1470s.*

Right: *The Swan Theatre, Southwark, London, is important today because this surviving view of its interior c.1595, soon after it was built, is our sole reliable record of an Elizabethan open air auditorium. It was demolished c.1637. Southwark, across the river from the city of London, was notorious in the early modern periods for low-life entertainment, including brothels and theatres.*

the end of the anonymous urban guild drama of late medieval England, replaced by larger than life dramatists whose careers can be traced, for better or for worse, beginning perhaps with Nicholas Udall, poet at the coronation of Anne Boleyn and writer of the play *Ralph Roister Doister c.*1550, hailed as the first English comedy. Udall was sacked as head of Eton College for making off with funds (which he denied) and for interfering with the boys (which he did not deny). The involvement of Marlowe in spying, and Shakespeare's purchase of a large house in Stratford and his interest in the Globe Theatre are details which flesh out these men's lives

The Globe Theatre (Visscher, 1606). The Globe was built in 1599, Shakespeare being one of the four shareholders and here many of his greatest plays were performed including: Twelfth Night, Julius Caesar, Othello and King Lear. The theatre burnt to the ground 'in two hours' during a performance of Henry VIII in 1613, when a stage cannon's wadding set fire to the thatched roof. It was rebuilt in the 1990s and once more provides plays in a Shakespearean atmosphere.

The Redcross knight (clearly St George) from Book 1 of Edmund Spenser's chivalric allegory The Faerie Queene, which first appeared in 1590. This edition appeared in 1598. The work emphasised the cult of Elizabeth I, variously seen as Gloriana and Belphoebe 'a most virtuous and beautiful lady'. It is a work deeply imbued with Protestant bias against the falsehoods of Rome – very popular after the failure of the Catholic Spanish Armada in 1588.

and help us to understand their place in society. There was certainly a broader spectrum of occupations and professions supporting the work of the *literati* by 1600 compared to Civil Service poets such as Chaucer, a comptroller of customs' dues, and Hoccleve, a bored public servant in the 1300s and 1400s.

If the production of the Authorised Version of the Bible in 1611 represents a high point of scholarly achievement in the reign of James I, thereafter there was downward slide notably in government achievement. This was partly precipitated by the death in 1612 of Robert Cecil, who had negotiated James's succession and acted as treasurer until his death. Thereafter James relied on men whose contemporaries deemed unsatisfactory as chief advisers: Robert Carr, earl of Somerset, and George Villiers, duke of Buckingham, both of whom had been rapidly elevated to the peerage by the king. King James doted on these men and was accused of allowing homosexual infatuation to cloud his judgement. The king had a tendency to be autocratic and made much of the doctrine of the divine right of kings, according to which a king is accountable only to God. Despite his Presbyterianism, he pursued a Spanish marriage for his son Charles. In the end Charles married the French Catholic princess, Henrietta Maria.

Charles inherited James I's attachment to the doctrine of divine right, as well as his father's favourite, Buckingham. The latter was assassinated, in the course of an unsuccessful attempt to relieve beleaguered Protestant Huguenots at La Rochelle in 1627. The murder was a relief to many, though Buckingham was deeply mourned by Charles. The imprisonment in the Tower by the king of a group of intellectuals including the bibliophile Sir Robert Cotton following the murder of Buckingham shows on the one hand a growth in the breadth

Above: *Entry of Prince Charles, the future Charles I, into Madrid in 1623. James I's reversal of Elizabethan anti-Spanish policy did little for his popularity in England and Scotland. The hoped for marriage to the Spanish Infanta would have secured a union with the great Catholic power, but it failed. However, after he became king, Charles married Henrietta Maria, a Catholic French princess, and thus alienated the puritan English.*

Below: *Contrasting responses to Charles's rejection in his Spanish marriage venture of 1623. James I comforts his son, while the Londoners celebrate with bonfires and toss their hats in the air.*

of opposition to the king, and on the other determination of Charles I to suppress any opposition. The king's autocratic adherence to divine right, inevitably brought conflict with parliament in the face of the necessity to raise funds to govern and pursue foreign policy. At first parliaments were frequent, in 1625, 1626 and 1628–29, but, from Charles's point of view, unsatisfactory. He was, in a sense, a victim of the long-term development of parliamentary power over finance stretching back at least to 1363. In the 1620s the parliament was dominated by Puritan members, who took particular exception to Charles's Arminian (high church) outlook and who were suspicious of his Catholic wife. He resolved to do without parliament and this he did from 1629 to 1640.

During this eleven-year period he relied on two ministers, the earl of Strafford and Archbishop Laud. Strafford implemented the king's personal rule and was rewarded for so doing by being given effective control of Ireland. His unpopularity stemmed from his 'thorough' policy, which centred upon the strengthening of royal power. His colleague and overseer of the church was Archbishop Laud. Laud attempted to impose uniformity on both Catholics and Puritans, the counterpart on the king's behalf to Strafford's secular policy. His attempt to force Episcopal administration and the Anglican prayer book on the Scots, who had covenanted against bishops in 1637, led to the Bishops' Wars of 1639–40. War was beyond the scope of Charles's finances and he was forced to summon what became known as the Short Parliament, which was highly critical of royal policy and, as a result, lasted only from April to May 1640.

A Scots victory forced the recall of parliament in November. This brought the Long Parliament into existence, which in effect sat for twenty years. The parliament attempted to impose

A (1201)
PERFECT
DIVRNALL
OF THE
PASSAGES
IN
PARLIAMENT.

From the second of *Ianuary* to the ninth of *Ianuary*.

Collected by the same hand that formerly drew up the Copy for William Cooke in
Furnivals Inne. And now Printed by I. Okes and F. Leach and are to be
sold by Francis Coles in the Old Baily.

Munday the 2. of Ianuary. 1642. /3

Journal of the Long Parliament for January 1643. Civil war had already broken out at this point. The parliament, summoned in 1640 to raise funds for furthering the king's war against the Scots on whom he had attempted to impose an English religious settlement with bishops. It sat, with purges and intermissions, until the Restoration in 1660.

A Doctor Vsher, Lord Prima-
le of Ireland.
B the Sheriffes of London.
C the Earle of Strafford
D his kindred and Friends.

Execution of Thomas Wentworth, earl of Strafford on Tower Hill in London, May 1641. Strafford, an ally of Charles I, had shown himself an efficient and 'thorough' (Strafford's own word) administrator and gave sound advice to the king in the 1530s. His advice to bring troops from Ireland, which might have saved the king in the early 1640s was ignored. Strafford was sacrificed by the king early in the dispute with parliament.

reforms on the king and impeached his two leading ministers for maladministration – there was particular fear relating to Catholic massacres of Protestants in Strafford's Ireland (plate 23), which fuelled anxieties about what might happen in England should the conservative religious outlook of King Charles become even more dominant. Strafford was executed and although Laud escaped initially, saved by the House of Lords, he was eventually executed in 1645 at the intervention of the Commons (plate 24). An attempt by Charles to arrest five members of parliament by force in 1642 caused the parliament to assume control of the militia. The closure of the theatres and the end of outstandingly creative architectural achievements by Inigo Jones were further indications in 1642 of the dark days ahead.

After failing to arrest the five members in parliament, Charles left London (plate 32). In the Civil War, as so often before, regional considerations were key issues, though not the only ones. The king headed north, seeking supporters from the more Royalist and conservative north and west. He raised his standard at Nottingham in August 1642. The Civil War had begun. At first, mounted Royalist Cavaliers had the better of parliament's Roundhead foot soldiers. In time, both sides developed cavalry and infantry regiments. Parliament enjoyed two decisive advantages: London and the navy. Charles found it increasingly difficult to secure a base or to import foreign soldiers or weapons.

The battle of Edgehill in October 1642 ended in a bloody stalemate. The Royalists then advanced on London but were halted by the city's trained bands. Parliamentary forces then thrust into Charles's northern territory and won victories at Marston Moor in 1644, which secured York and at Naseby

Mounted dragoons (1644). Cavalry played a key role in the decisive battle of the Civil War, Marston Moor (Yorkshire)in 1644, a parliamentary victory which delivered royalists the north of England.

A contemporary woodcut of soldiers of the New Model Army: a targeteer (left) and an officer of infantry (right) which was formed by Sir Thomas Fairfax in 1645, and contributed to the parliament's victory at Naseby in that year. It amalgamated militia from different areas of England, notably from East Anglia where Oliver Cromwell was commander. Cromwell became commander-in-chief of the New Model Army in 1650.

(Northamptonshire) in 1645 which secured the Midlands. The Scots first favoured the Stuart king. Marston Moor persuaded them otherwise and when they captured Charles in 1646 they sold him to parliament. Terms were offered which Charles rejected and he escaped from captivity. He had little option, despite past experience, but to throw himself on the mercy of his compatriot Scots. A Scottish invasion of England followed. Oliver Cromwell marched north again and crushed the Scottish Royalist forces at Preston in 1648. Charles was re-arrested.

Defiant to the last the king refused terms and after a trial whose outcome was a foregone conclusion, was sentenced to

Left: *Trial of Charles I in Westminster Hall, 20 January 1649. The king refused to plead demanding to know the authority by which he was called to the court.*

Right: *Charles I in regal splendour from a patent document. The king was exceptionally short – only 4 feet 10 inches, which meant, wherever possible, that he choose to be depicted either on his own, or on horseback.*

execution. The historian Macaulay, writing in the 1820s during the reign of the profligate George IV, summed up Charles I thus: 'selfish, cruel and deceitful… a bad man, in spite of all his temperance at the table and all his regularity at chapel'. The diminutive figure of the king – he was under 5 feet tall – was brought to execution on a high scaffold outside the Banqueting Hall in Whitehall on 30 January 1649. Macaulay attributed Charles's apparent popularity with posterity to 'his Vandyke dress, his handsome face and his peaked beard' (plate 25). Divine right and the aura of kingship could not save him. The monarchy, for the present, was at an end.

5

An Englishman, Scots and a Dutchman

Interregnum, Restoration and Glorious Revolution 1650-1702

God put an end in one month (for it was the first of May that the king's letter was delivered to the parliament, and his majesty was at Whitehall on the twenty-ninth of the same month) to a rebellion that had raged near twenty years, and had been carried on with all the horrid circumstances of parricide, murder and devastation, that fire and the sword in the hands of the most wicked men in the world, could be ministers of...

Clarendon, *History of the Rebellion*, on 1660

After the execution of Charles I in January 1649, England became a republic whose leader emerged as Oliver Cromwell, parliament's most effective general and probably the most English person ever to rule England.

Cromwell had to address the central problem of the government of the country. As those members who were more sympathetic to the king had been excluded from parliament in 1648, the resultant 'Rump' had little claim to be a constitutional body. At the other end of the spectrum 'levellers' –

Oliver Cromwell (1599–1658). 'God's Englishman' – lawyer, parliamentarian and general and one of the few truly English people ever to rule England. He was as Lord Protector, backed by the army from 1653–58. This Dutch engraving, with severed heads (see that of Charles I, bottom right) recalls his route to power. In common with other usurpers, such as Henry IV, Cromwell had to rule pragmatically, for example, making alliance with Puritan Scots and Catholic French.

radicals who proposed all adult male heads of households should have a vote – were scattered in 1649. Cromwell, President of the Council of State, used his all-conquering army to dismiss the 'Rump' in 1653 (plate 27), when, in an act symbolic of the dominance of the army in politics, he entered the Commons with soldiers in attendance.

Detractors of the parliament which followed called it 'Barebones' after a member, Nicholas 'Praise God' Barebone – a London leatherseller. It was, however, composed largely of gentry whose religious outlook was independent of the Church of England, as Anglican worship had been abolished. This parliament did useful work on social matters, but it did not provide an answer to the all-important question: 'Who should govern?' In December 1653 the army ejected a hard-core of radical members and produced 'An Instrument of Government', which made Cromwell Lord Protector for life, and proposed elections. The parliament which resulted was, however, critical of Cromwell's decision to allow freedom of conscience (except for Catholics) and so he dismissed it.

Charles II riding out of Worcester after the crushing defeat of his supporters and their Scots allies, 3 September 1651. This was the end of his campaign to win back his father's throne and he fled abroad. The bushy trees in the background remind us of the legend that the twenty-one-year-old king was obliged to hide in an oak tree to avoid capture after the battle.

Cromwell fought a trade war with the Dutch 1651–54, following his Navigation Act of 1651. This Dutch satire of 1652 shows him dreaming of the crown, 'Impotent ambition shown to the life in the present government of England'. Cromwell is beleagured by fanatical, puritanical levellers, while a queue of suppliants stretches down to idle ships in London docks.

Alongside his campaigns in Ireland and Scotland, Cromwell engaged in European wars, first against the Protestant Dutch, who were commercial and imperial rivals, and subsequently against Catholic Spain. Another parliament was called to fund the war. This parliament offered Cromwell the title of king, rightly convinced that making him king was the best way of reducing his dependence on the army. He was probably flattered by the idea and certainly did not reject it utterly but hesitated, no doubt because an emphatic message came from sections of the army that he should not accept the title. Cromwell dismissed parliament and resorted to the army to help him collect taxes. Before a resolution to the question of kingship was achieved, Cromwell died in 1658. By the end of his life Oliver Cromwell was far from the puritanical general of the 1640s and early 1650s. He relished the power which his role as Lord Protector brought and enjoyed masques and long weekends at Hampton Court. Surprisingly, in view of the usual gloomy view of Puritanism, opera, that most Italian of art forms, was welcomed in England during Cromwell's Protectorate. This is the more surprising in view of the response to opera in the eighteenth century (addressed later), but it can be seen that opera did not take root in England of the late 1600s.

The death of Cromwell brought the succession question to a head. In the event his son Richard was the Lord Protector's successor. All the usual problems of lack of continuity of policy associated with the passage of power from one ruler to the next were transformed in this case, because Oliver Cromwell's position had been unique and unprecedented. Richard Cromwell lacked the support of the army which had sustained the Protectorate. Richard was not an accomplished general and he soon abandoned his 'reign'. Within two years

English and Scottish troops embrace during a truce in the Civil War. The English invaded Scotland under Charles I in the late 1630s; the Scots fought on the parliamentary side for much of the Civil War, but after the execution of the king in 1649, supported Charles II and were defeated at Preston and at Dunbar by Cromwell as well as at Worcester. Scottish troops garrisoned various parts of England, including the Isle of Wight where a contemporary recorded that their 'begetting of bastards' was almost the undoing of the whole island.

of Oliver Cromwell's death, the monarchy was back and Charles II was king.

What had the Civil Wars and the Interregnum achieved? Obviously the king had been defeated and executed. Although many kings had previously lost their thrones, they had never before been tried and publicly executed on the orders of commoners. This was revolutionary. The monarchy could never be the same again. England was effectively ruled by a quasi-military dictator, supported by a standing army. Like the trial and execution of the king, this was highly experimental. It is noteworthy that neither of these experiments has been repeated in our history. Additionally, Scotland and Ireland were forced into a closer relationship with England than ever before.

Religion remained the catalyst for much conflict in the early modern period. Now the pendulum swung towards the

Puritans. Cromwell's troops, who sang psalms as they marched into battle led by puritan gentry, show how deeply Protestantism had penetrated society. The Church of England with its bishops and prayer book was abolished by Cromwell. This was a religious revolution of the kind sought by Elizabethan Puritans in the 1570s. During the Civil War some churches were ransacked and some cathedrals were used as stables: the work of the Reformation was extended. With the Church of England in flight from the religious radical Fifth Monarchy Men, Independents, Presbyterians, Quakers, naked Ranters and others, Catholicism vanished underground.

Socially and economically the period from 1642 to 1660 has caused much debate. Key questions which have been asked include the following: 'Who supported king and parliament?', 'What was the role of the gentry?', 'What was the nature of the change in landholding brought about by the Dissolution of the Monasteries, the so-called prehistory of the Civil War?', 'Who were the neutrals and why were there so many of them?', 'In what ways did "popular" politics and religion come to prominence?' and 'What were the effects on women?'

Much of country had split allegiances, though there is some merit in the traditional idea that the Royalists' power base was chiefly in the north and west (among those who had least experience of the monarchs themselves) and that of parliament in the south and east. However, many MPs who at first were critical of Charles's rule but whose estates lay in Royalist regions, joined the king. Divisions for and against the king were not simple either regionally, in terms of class or rural against urban. Some aristocrats, for example the earl of Essex, were parliamentarian, some towns Royalist, although London was for parliament. Ordinary people had little involvement in the war, except the soldiers, but there is evidence that they used the opportunity to settle old scores. Groups like the Dorset clubmen took matters in their own hands, beating men of both persuasions, in a good old English dislike of extremism whatever it was. To what extent the mobility of the army throughout the country and prizes of lands in Ireland, opened new horizons to ordinary people is still debated.

The question of the role of the gentry has generated most debate, for that was the body of MPs who had opposed Charles I. It is clear they were a key element, but how many were 'rising', economically buoyed up by landed wealth derived from former monastic estates or 'declining', weighed down by increasing taxation, remains at issue. By ignoring parliament in the 1630s Charles I incensed MPs and thus the gentry as a group. The extent of Puritanism amongst the gentry is another significant issue: Cromwell himself was a parliamentary Puritan. Puritanism, with its concentration on personal religion and reading of religious texts in English, went hand-in-hand with education. MPs certainly became more educated in sixteenth and seventeenth centuries; this undoubtedly led to their questioning the status quo. Puritans 'prostrated themselves before God while setting their foot on the king's neck'.

Charles II, who was expediently invited back from exile in May 1660, had plenty of time during Cromwell's rule to plan a return to power. He had no standing army to enforce his rule; economically his realm was bankrupt. But he did exercise political skill, especially in his early years. He promised to pardon his enemies, except regicides, to allow freedom of worship and agreed to let parliament sort out vexed problems relating to a land settlement. It is apparent that some lands had already been returned to Royalists before 1660. Edward Hyde, earl of Clarendon, Charles II's chancellor, father-in-law to the duke of York (later, James II, whose scandalous pre-marital affair with Anne Hyde almost led to her execution), wrote his substantial work *The History of the Rebellion and Civil Wars in England*, published by his sons after his death as an act of filial piety. He claimed God for the Royalists and concluded his great work which has been seen as a Tory apologia:

> God put an end in one month [May 1660] to a rebellion that had raged near twenty years, and had been carried on with all the horrid circumstances of patricide, murder, and devastation that fire and the sword, in the hands of the most wicked men in world, could be ministers of; almost to the desolation of two kingdoms and, the exceeding defacing and deforming of the third.

Thomas Hobbes (d. 1679) was another eyewitness who, although he remained a Royalist during the Civil War, reconciled himself to the Commonwealth (plate 26). By contrast with Hyde, he saw that the Civil War and Protectorate had been momentous in our history and not merely a nightmarish interlude: 'If in time, as in place' wrote Hobbes, 'there were degrees of high and low, I verily believe that the highest of time would be that which passed between 1640 and 1660'. Hobbes's philosophy was not, however, at all times so positive as it was he who gloomily (reflecting his Englishness?) noted in his *Leviathan* the potential of disorder: 'No arts; no letters; no society; and which is worst of all, continual fear and danger of violent death; and the life of man, solitary, poor, nasty, brutish and short.'

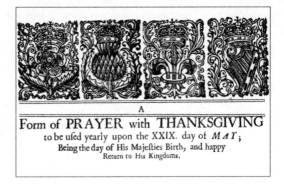

A

Form of PRAYER with THANKSGIVING
to be uſed yearly upon the XXIX. day of *M A Y*;
Being the day of His Majeſties Birth, and happy
Return to His Kingdoms.

Heading to the form of thanksgiving for Charles II's restoration, from the Book of
Common Prayer. *Religion was at the centre of much bitter debate and fighting in
the seventeenth century. Charles I with his Catholic wife, support for bishops and
opposition to Calvinism and Presbyterianism; Cromwell's toleration of most religious
leanings apart from Catholicism and episcopalianism; Charles II presided over
toleration, his ministers such as Clarendon steering a middle course based around the*
Prayer Book, *opposing extremes of Catholicism and Protestantism.*

After the initial euphoria, Charles II repudiated most of his
Restoration promises. However, the Church of England was
re-established, bishops were reinstated and, in 1662, use of the
prayer book became once more a requirement for clergy.
However, in 1672, Charles did away with the anti-Catholic
legislation in return for large cash payments from Louis XIV
of France for English support against the Protestant Dutch.
However, the following year parliament introduced the Test
Act, which required office holders in civil or military positions to adhere to the rites of the Church of England and to
reject the Catholic doctrine of the Mass.

The disbanding of the standing army, which had proved
ruinous to national finances, gave parliament a free hand in
government. But there was no consensus. Indeed opposing
parliamentary parties developed, defined by terms of abuse:

the anti-Royalists 'Whigs' opposed Royalist 'Tories' – the birth of confrontational politics as we know it today. In a notably English fashion these political parties were not named after English groups at all: Tories were dispossessed Irish 'bog-trotters' who murdered English settlers; Whigs, Scottish Presbyterian exclusionists against James II. Contemporary pictures and archaeological surveys of the remaining archi-tecture of Parliament House, reveal its shape and form up to this date. It was formerly St Stephen's Chapel, its church architecture of opposing stalls encouraging parliamentary confrontation. When, during the Reformation, the canons were ejected from the royal chapel, parliament moved in occupying the canons' stalls. There was no room for cross-benchers in such a chamber. When this chapel/parliament house was burned down in 1834, the replacement Commons was equipped with facing seats, thus sustaining politics pur-sued from government and opposition benches. It seems never to have occurred to the architects why the previous building was the shape it was or to think about function and purpose: they merely, unquestioningly, replicated the past 'mother of parliaments' as series of opposing benches.

As politics changed, so scientific discoveries were harbin-gers of a new, more secular outlook. Discoveries and impetus for science included: the circulation of the blood, published by William Harvey in 1628; the foundation of The Royal Society (1662); and Newton's observations on gravity, while on enforced home leave from Cambridge during the Great Plague of 1665. In the arts, painting was restricted by the eschewing of religious subjects. Lely, born of Dutch parents, painted for both Charles I and Cromwell before producing his best work after the Restoration. He continued the limited portrait

This woodcut, originally of 1625 but much reprinted, neatly gathers up the elements of a plague epidemic, such as the Great Plague of 1665: its urban nature, the triumph of death, the blotches of the buboes on the victims in the foreground, fleeing citizens and the miasma cloud settled over London with lightning striking randomly across the city.

tradition of van Dyck. Christopher Wren's St Paul's was a significant example in the new architectural style, English Baroque. However, his original design was to adapt Old St Paul's (plate 21) – the Great Fire (plate 30) which destroyed that great, gothic medieval church with its shrine to the obscure Anglo-Saxon St Erkenwald, provided him with a unique opportunity to go further. A chance for a great rebuilding in the city of London also accrued – but such plans were largely frustrated by characteristic English compromise: the churches and the new St Paul's were built but only part of Wren's planned city of boulevards and mansions was constructed. Like so much about Charles's reign, the creation of St Paul's Cathedral is a cause of debate. Was Wren's great domed structure an appropriate Protestant cathedral for the capital of England, to match St Peter's at Rome, or was it a Catholic church in European style, which signalled the king's increasing inclination towards the Old Religion? Or was its classical style a reference to the secular inspiration of ancient Rome? The English could make what they wished of it.

Royalists who had lived abroad during the Interregnum came back to England full of new continental ideas. Among these was the grand house, of which Edward Hyde's Clarendon House in Piccadilly, built in 1664–67 on land donated by the king was a fine example. It was praised by John Evelyn, who came minded to be critical, but was obliged to declare it the greatest house, or even palace, in England. Roger Pratt the architect was the best exponent of the new architectural form in which the shape of the house was regular, by contrast to the sprawling 'organic growth' of medieval and early modern grand houses and palaces. The key feature of the new style had no English term, only *piano nobile* – the raised ground floor approached up steps. Servants and

Many thought the only sure response to plague, such as the Great Plague of London of 1665, was to run away from it, but this remedy not an option for the poor. However, as this seventeenth-century woodcut shows, travellers could take death with them aboard their coaches. We know, but they did not, that it was carried by fleas or spread by coughing.

services were crammed into semi-basements. Functional areas, kitchen, public rooms and sleeping accommodation, were no longer visible as separate buildings, but were encapsulated within the symmetrical block of the house contributing to notions of hierarchy and privacy which were emphasised by the horizontal divisions of the buildings. Many of these ground-breaking houses have been lost over time, and perhaps the most perfect example of Pratt's work, Coleshill (Berkshire), was demolished after a fire in 1952.

Those who had served the monarchy were rewarded with royal lands, salvaged at the Restoration. The ruin of the former royal palace at Clarendon (Wiltshire), its park and estate stripped of ancient oaks for naval vessels and the deer long slaughtered, went to George Monck (plate 29), duke of Albemarle. Monck, a younger son of a West Country squire, was a larger than life character. His capacity for drinking was legendary as was his capacity for work. He had been committed to the Tower, but emerged (to marry his laundress) and had led heroically in Cromwell's defeat of the Scots at Dunbar. He was instrumental in restoring the monarchy, while Edward Hyde acted as chancellor. What these great men shared was a hatred of extremism, whether Catholic, Puritan or Quaker. For them the Church of England was the right religion and it might be said of their initial achievement that they achieved what Henry VIII had begun, the Protestant Reformation. But neither lasted long under the new regime. The portly Clarendon, who had originally frightened Charles II so much that the restored king was too nervous to speak in council, was dismissed in 1667 and went into exile until his death in 1674. Among many reasons for his dismissal was his anxiety about the king's religious tendency towards

Catholicism. Monck died in 1670, having turned from managing the Restoration to managing London during the Great Plague of 1665. He was given a grand funeral recorded in a fold-out series of prints which show a great procession with Albemarle on his bier.

Economically England recovered comparatively quickly after the Civil War, although demographically there was a steady decline from a high point at well over 5 million in England in 1651 to under 5 million in the 1690s. Imperial and trade competitors such as the Dutch were engaged in wars, so dockyard towns grew as the navy was upgraded. Chatham and Deptford with populations of *c.*5,000 in 1700 became leading dockyard towns, while Falmouth, Plymouth and Portsmouth also developed rapidly. London in particular grew and flourished, becoming the largest city in Europe, with a population of 575,000 by 1700. This dwarfed all other cities in the realm, providing a market for grain and meat and encouraging farming, but stunting growth in towns throughout southern England.

Charles II had many mistresses and numerous bastards but failed to leave a legitimate male heir to succeed him. The licentious morals of the Court, as depicted in portraits of bare-breasted women, was an almost unimaginable contrast to the Puritan ethics of Oliver Cromwell's regime. How much of a contrast there was within the lower orders before and after the Restoration is not so clear cut. Radical Ranters during the Commonwealth certainly sought the abolition of traditional sexual morality. After the Restoration immorality was not confined to court: the diarist Samuel Pepys tells us of his affairs with married women which, in contrast to Charles II's behaviour, at least promised legitimate status for any offspring!

The battle of Sedgemoor (1685). The protestant duke of Monmouth, an illegitimate son of Charles II led a rebellion from the West Country against the accession of the Catholic James II. The ill-armed peasant supporters of the duke were defeated, and James used the law through Judge Jefferies to exact retribution in the 'Bloody Assize' which sentenced 320 to death, 800 to transportation and hundreds more to prison.

Some feared that Charles was gradually preparing for his kingdom to be returned to Catholicism. His panegyricist, poet laureate and court playwright, John Dryden, was amongst many who openly professed Catholicism by the end of the reign. In 1679, six years before Charles died, an Exclusion Bill was introduced into parliament which aimed to prevent the king's Catholic brother James from inheriting the throne. As time passed and there was no heir for Charles, James gathered more power to himself and his accession became apparently inevitable. An attempt by the Rye House plotters to murder Charles and James on their way back from the races at Newmarket in 1683 was unsuccessful. Despite Charles's failure to call a parliament in the closing years of his reign, public sympathy for the monarchy increased and when Charles died in 1685, James's succession was widely welcomed.

A precipitate rebellion in 1685 by the duke of Monmouth, a Protestant but illegitimate son of Charles II, failed, despite the bravery of his West Country supporters who were crushed at Sedgemoor. Judge Jeffreys, acting on King James's orders, led a fierce reaction, effectively discouraging any claims to the throne by Charles II's numerous illegitimate offspring. James, like his late brother, felt sufficiently secure to rule without parliament as, indeed, Cromwell had done. James promoted Catholics in the central government and, more alarmingly, in the army. He dismissed city governments in the regions and put in his own people to ensure the return of Catholics to parliament. After the death of his Protestant first wife, Anne Hyde, James married a Catholic, Mary of Modena, who bore him a son James, who later became known as the 'Old Pretender'. James II already had two Protestant daughters, both of whom were destined to be queens of England: Mary, married to the Protestant William of Orange, and Anne.

James's tyranny and his Catholicism, coupled with the power of Louis XIV of France, who was engaged in a war with the Protestant Dutch, focused the minds of both Whigs and Tories. Parliament asked William and Mary to occupy the throne. James, his navy becalmed in London and deserted by his chief general John Churchill, fled into exile and William and Mary were crowned joint monarchs.

The offer of the English throne was most welcome to William of Orange who was fighting the Catholic Louis of

The coronation of William and Mary (1689), seen here in a contemporary ballad, marked the triumph of Protestant monarchy following the 'Glorious Revolution' of 1688, which deposed James II. Mary was a daughter of James II by his first wife, Anne Hyde, whose Protestant father had administered the realm and the restoration of Charles II.

France. England promised troops, a navy and financial resources. For its own part, there was much to recommend the arrangement to the English parliament: Stuart succession in the form of James II's Protestant daughter Mary would be achieved and parliament could strengthen its base by circumscribing the foreign King William. This they did by the Bill of Rights in 1689 which, among other things, forbade monarchs to suspend parliaments and insisted on parliamentary consent to taxation. There was to be no standing army in peace time. The Catholic struggle for the throne of England came to an end for the moment with the battles of the Boyne (1 July 1690) (plate 33) and Aughrim (12 July 1691). In these extraordinary encounters the Catholic James's army fought the Protestant William's army; James supported by the French,

William supported by the Pope! Protestant victory ensured continuing Protestant English rule in Ireland. Today the Protestant 'Unionists' march on 12 July to celebrate these Protestant victories, to which the Pope contributed; such are the complexities of Irish politics.

Queen Mary died in 1694. Her obsequies were accompanied by Henry Purcell's famous funeral music, the doleful beat thumped out on kettledrums borne on the backs of foot soldiers. Within months Purcell, England's greatest composer, was dead and the music was used again at his own funeral. Parliament, meanwhile, continued to strengthen its position by passing the Triennial Act of 1694 which demanded elections every three years. When William died in 1701, the Act of Settlement was passed which required a Protestant succession and went further in forbidding anyone 'born outside the kingdoms' to be an MP or hold military or civil positions under the Crown.

The Act of Settlement also dealt with the succession in the longer term. If Anne were to die childless, the succession would pass to the family of Sophia of Hanover, granddaughter of James I. This proposed resolution of the succession extended the long tradition of having monarchs whose roots lay outside England. This dated back to pre-Conquest Danish kings and beyond, and this continued, broadly speaking, down to the present. Particularly with the unification of the British Isles, it was politic to have a monarch who was not from the dominant English. However, briefly between 1653 and 1658, Britain was ruled by an Englishman – 'God's Englishman' – Oliver Cromwell. On his death the nation rejected English rule and returned to the rule of the Scots' Stuart royal house.

The Civil War strengthened parliament and weakened the monarchy irretrievably. The army became prominent and its leaders received rich rewards. Kings could be summoned, as was Charles II; driven out, as was James II; circumscribed in their religious outlook, as Anne and her successors were; or earmarked for the future by parliament, as were the Hanoverians. Thenceforward, the country was in the hands of parliament, which levied taxes and whose members, divided into opposing parties, struggled for power.

6

English Landscapes and Foreign Acquisitions
The First British Empire, 1702–1760

Rule Britannia!
Britannia rule the waves

James Thomson, *c.*1740

Between the accession of Queen Anne in 1702 and the death of George II in 1760, Britain established itself as a major power on the world stage by addressing problems within the British Isles, and by extending lands and trading links abroad. Within the British Isles the settlement of Ireland, begun under the Tudors, was brought to a high point of Protestant landowner-ship. In Scotland the Act of Union was agreed in 1707 and rebellious tendencies snuffed out at Culloden in 1746 when the Young Pretender's forces, charging downhill with broad swords and round shields, were destroyed by the duke of Cumberland's musketeers. It has been argued that this defeat ended any Scottish rights to independence. Meanwhile foreign trade and colonies grew in Africa, the Americas and by 1760, in India.

Despite the advances in parliamentary power which followed the Civil War, the monarchy retained some, if diminished, authority under Anne (1702–14), who could nonetheless choose her own prime minister, her generals and her admirals. This being the case, credit for John Churchill, duke of Marlborough's, victories over Louis XIV and his allies must reflect upon her.

Marlborough, after playing a key role in the crisis of 1688 when he changed sides to oppose James II, fell from favour in the 1690s because of his supposed Jacobite tendencies. Under Queen Anne he returned to favour and his victories over France, which began at Blenheim in 1704 and culminated in the slaughter at Malplaquet in 1709, thwarted French ambition to dominate Europe for almost a century. The parish and the medieval buildings at Woodstock were given to Marlborough by a grateful parliament in 1705 and grants were made to build Blenheim Palace, where Winston Churchill was born in 1874. Marlborough's spirited wife, Sarah, oversaw the demolition of the medieval palace to make way for the new building. It was designed by Sir John Vanbrugh, but he was sacked before it was completed. Initially it had a formal garden, but later Capability Brown did away with the 'military garden', establishing gardens and a lake, below Vanbrugh's great bridge, engulfed the medieval landscape in a triumph of the modern over the antique. In 1711 Sarah Churchill's wilfulness led to

Queen Anne (1665–1714), like Mary, was a daughter of James II and Anne Hyde. As this coin from the end of the reign indicates, Anne was pleased to see her 'Augustan' reign compared to the palmy era of Augustus Caesar. It was the age of Addison and Pope, Swift and Dryden. This calm intellectual brilliance was in sharp contrast to her life as a parent: she bore seventeen children, only one of whom lived long beyond birth, but died as a child.

John Churchill (1650–1722) 1st Duke of Marlborough and scourge of the French in the War of Spanish Succession (1701–13) in which he won a string of victories in the Low Countries and northern France. He was rewarded with the Woodstock estate, renamed Blenheim after his famous victory. A hundred years on in the era of Napoleonic War the French produced this cartoon recalling the long-dead English general's enduring reputation.

the dismissal of Marlborough by Queen Anne who was angry at the hectoring way in which Sarah treated her. However, Marlborough's continental war had been won by then.

Among the changes which were occurring during Queen Anne's reign was a developing interest in landscape gardens to accompany the new great houses which had come into fashion during her grandfather's time following the Restoration. In the year of her death Stephen Switzer defined the new, Baroque gardens as 'extensive or forest gardening'. The emergence of the landscape garden in the 1700s has been hailed as a English contribution to world civilisation. In the Georgian period these gardens began to appear under the auspices of Charles Bridgeman (d.1738), Stephen Switzer (1682–1745),

William Kent (1674–1748), Henry Flitcroft (1697–1769) and their younger disciple Lancelot 'Capability' Brown (1715–83). Lakes, curvilinear paths and 'natural' plantings amidst grand landscapes are a characteristic of this English work.

From such grand beginnings these Whiggish landscapes, commensurate with their one-party domination of England at the period, provide a fruitful area of study for garden and landscape archaeologists, who are now recovering their origins and plantings using such techniques as pollen analysis and topographic survey to rediscover these great, English achievements. Although the achievement was English, the inspiration was varied and included much that was continental, especially classical and Italian. Like Handel's English oratorios, this garden work represented the taking of 'foreign' ideas and successfully anglicising them into a language with which the English could feel comfortable. English weather was never going to show the pines of Rome's clear-cut shadows as the hot sun of Italy did: but the ensemble of deciduous plantings together with conifers at Stourhead, for example, makes at least as brilliant a contrast on a sunny autumn day.

The best of these varied garden landscapes include Stowe (1716–51, Bridgeman, Kent, and from 1740, Brown), Paston Manor (1718, Switzer), Chiswick (1725, Kent see later) and Stourhead (1741–69, Flitcroft). Close study is revealing how landscapes reflect authority, power and politics. It is not the kings in the eighteenth century, but generals and politicians who establish their credentials by the landscapes they created. Whigs created landscapes with their houses protected from animals by the ha-ha, thus apparently floating in an undulating open parkland landscape as at Stowe or Castle Howard. These unimpeded vistas accorded with their unimpeded power. Tories on the other hand, out of power and belea-guered, created enclosed landscapes with enclosed areas, often on a smaller scale (they had no access to the public purse) and in touch with their localities building adjacent to those gentry from whom they sought support.

At that same time as these landscape garden wonders were unfolding in the English countryside, horizons were extending abroad beyond Europe, another aspect reflected in the confident, open, created country landscapes. The Treaty of Utrecht of 1713 was an important milestone, bringing the acquisition of territory which included Gibraltar and at the same time the empowering of British slave traders to sail direct to Iberian South America. By 1729 it could be claimed by a merchant that the great rise in national wealth was derived from sugar and tobacco tended on plantations by that most profitable of commodities, negro slaves.

So, once more in our history, successful foreign wars helped to heal divisions at home, this time between England and Scotland. After 1700 relations between the two nations had deteriorated: the Scottish parliament refused to agree to the Act of Settlement (1701). They threatened to restore the Stuarts and the English feared a return of the Franco-Scots 'auld alliance'. However, religious differences between Catholic Highlanders and Protestant Lowlanders, as well as between Episcopalians and Presbyterians, were among many divisions in Scotland. The Highland/Lowland division within Scotland was nothing new, for in language, culture and family names there were sharp distinctions. These divisions were too wide for unanimity north of the border in support of a Catholic Stuart monarchy. Anxieties in both England and Scotland, led to the Act of Union under terms of which forty-five Scots MPs with sixteen Lords were to be returned to Westminster. Scotland accepted the Act of Settlement and free trade between the two countries was assured.

Marlborough's victories abroad no doubt contributed to the union of England and Scotland. The Scots wanted a part of those successes. Profit was an ever more reasonable proposition after union. Some Scots felt that the failure of the Darien Scheme at the Panama isthmus at the turn of the century had resulted from lack of British support against the Spaniards. Queen Anne's reign thus witnessed a settlement with Scotland which existed until the establishment of the Scottish parliament in 1999. Support for the rule of the male Stuart line was in evidence in England as well as Scotland. In England there was Tory support for James Edward, the Old Pretender. Up to 1708, though less thereafter, Anne was careful to choose both Whigs and Tories as her ministers. However, during the last two years of her reign, negotiations began with James Edward Stuart over his possible succession. He was unwilling to give up his Catholicism so Harley and Bolingbroke gave up their plan. Thus the Elector of Hanover, great-great-grandson of James VI and I became king as George I. George was confronted by a xenophobic Tory smear campaign against him, which can be summed up in restrained language as follows: he was an alien who spoke little English and who used German advisers. He was further accused of using his two Turkish servants 'for abominable purposes'. This latter claim is interesting in that William III, Dutch and homosexual, had proved acceptable to an earlier generation. The difference presumably was that whereas George was German, William was Dutch.

Such wild claims were the resort of desperate men: Tory support for the Jacobite uprising of 1715 was a last throw of the dice. The fragmented 1715 rebellion in Scotland did not secure French aid for the Old Pretender. The 1715 revolt was fatally divided. It was a ragged alliance of Episcopalian Scots (the backbone of Jacobite sentiment), the implacably Catholic Old Pretender, English Catholics and xenophobic Tories, these last with no wish for a French alliance. The rebellion fizzled out. The Tories were discredited. James Edward went abroad and died at Rome in 1766.

Fear of a return of a Catholic Stuart king was among the reasons why both George I (1714–27) and George II (1727–60) relied heavily on the Whigs to govern the country. Robert Walpole was the key minister in this period acting as prime minister from 1721 to 1742 with the support of the kings. Walpole's success is attributable to his unwillingness to innovate and to his executive efficiency. He was not in favour of foreign wars – although war did break out in the latter years of his ministry and lasted from 1739–48. Trade was encouraged through stability of the one-party system at home: the Whigs lowered customs duties both on goods leaving and entering the country, and they lowered taxes in general. This pleased landowners, whose land-tax bills were less, and the international traders whose fortunes grew apace. The population at large was excluded from decision-making: in 1715, for example, less than 5 per cent of men voted.

After some fluctuations between 1700 and 1750, population freed of plague had grown by 1760 to 6 million, up a million on 1700 and perhaps double the number in 1550. People gravitated towards the towns: by 1750 a quarter of England's population lived in towns, double the proportion in 1550. Leisure facilities flourished. Early in the century, thousands flocked to Bath (plate 34) where Beau Nash was master of ceremonies from the time of Queen Anne to the beginning of George III's reign. Mercantile towns such as Liverpool took off, growing between 1705 and 1770 from 8,000 to 35,000.

However, none matched London which continued as the largest city in Europe in growing from its 575,000 inhabitants of 1700. One in eight of the English population lived there by 1750. London affected the economic development of town and country alike, especially in south-eastern areas. The dominance of London contributed significantly to the development of national consciousness and more significantly to a national market. Covent Garden became a market for the nation's fruit and vegetables. The cloud of smoke over the capital from coal fires rewarded the labours of gangs in the mines of north-east England, whose owners created great houses and gardens on the proceeds. An integrated national coal market began.

Cock-fighting by Hogarth (1759). This gambling sport was long established when it was recorded here. Some effort was made to find alternatives at this time: cricket was a fledgling betting sport which was intended to divert resources from cock-fighting.

1 'Cheddar Man' lived some 9,000 years ago in the Middle Stone or Mesolithic Age, early in the post-glacial period. Here we see a local resident today, who has been linked by DNA to his ancient ancestor. The use of DNA samples in archaeology has contributed to the beginnings of studies in distribution and mobility (or lack of it!) in ancient populations.

2, 3 Maiden Castle (Dorset). A Neolithic site of c.3800 BC, it was developed to its greatest extent in the Iron Age c.500 BC to make it the largest and most impressive hill fort in Britain. Maiden Castle went out of use soon after the Roman invasion, by about AD 100. Here Mortimer Wheeler's 1930s excavations are in progress. Mortimer Wheeler's excavations uncovered this apparently native spine (below) pierced by a Roman ballista bolt. For the soldier-archaeologist this epitomised the triumph of the Roman army over the southern British. But was the victim a fleeing Celt or – from the careful burial – a victim of 'friendly fire'?

4 *Fishbourne (Sussex) – Roman palace garden. Fishbourne was perhaps the largest Roman palace near the Alps and was possibly the first point of contact in the invasion of AD 43. Excavation showed the layout of the gardens, which have been reconstructed as seen here.*

5 *Silbury Hill (Wiltshire) is a giant structure of mysterious purpose. There are no apparent burials there. Built in its present form c.2200 BC it contains some 350,000 cubic metres of chalk, created by an estimated 1.5 million man-hours.*

6 *Bath (Somerset), Celtic goddess from a Roman building at Aquae Sulis. The Romans were willing to embrace local deities to placate conquered peoples – the Celtic goddess Sulis equated to the Romans' Minerva. Here we see a mask of Neptune conflated with the goddess Minerva's Medusa bearded and moustached mask from a grand temple.*

7 Jean Froissart was one of a number of people from the Low Countries who came to England following Edward III's marriage to Philippa of Hainault. Froissart recorded the valorous deeds of the knightly classes in the early phases of the Hundred Years War. Here we see the court of Richard II in the late 1390s. The king is banishing Bolingbroke (later, Henry IV) and Norfolk. Froissart was a brilliant writer, despite numerous inaccuracies, though his perspective changes according to his French or English patron of the day!

8 Sea power was always important for England, but it was expensive. French sacking of English ports in the fourteenth century was stemmed by the great English victory at Sluys (1340), but French resurgence led to further raids later in the century and the establishment of a serious navy by Henry V. However, Henry VI could not afford to sustain such a navy and the English became increasingly worried about invasions, especially after their final defeat at Gascony (1453).

9 Henry V and Richard Beauchamp, earl of Warwick. Beauchamp was a hero: a knight errant who visited the Holy Sepulchre and eastern Europe, served Henry V in his successful wars and acted as mentor to the boy-king Henry VI in the 1420s. The Holy Roman Emperor, Henry V's ally Sigismund, called Beauchamp 'the father of courtesy'. Beauchamp died in 1439. His superb chantry chapel and tomb are seen at St Mary's Warwick – the complex work almost all undertaken by foreign craftsmen as none of sufficient quality, in Beauchamp's opinion, were to be found in England even a century after the Black Death.

10 *Although the English were initially successful under Henry VI, with the dukes of Bedford and Gloucester and the earl of Warwick playing their parts, it was difficult to sustain their effort. Although they had some cannon, as seen here, it was the French use of the 'private' cannon of the Bureau brothers, which relentlessly reduced English-held castles in northern France. England, depopulated and cash-strapped had neither the resources of men nor money to hold out and were expelled in 1453 – except for Calais, which continued to be a national financial black hole until 1558.*

11 *William Caxton set up his first printing press in London. His first dated book (1477), illustrated here, was* The Dictes and Sayings of the Philosophers. *By his death in 1491 he had printed almost 100 books, including works by Chaucer, Gower, Lydgate and Malory's* Morte d'Arthur. *He did not, however, print any work by a living author – except his own translations!*

Ere endeth the book named the dictes or sayngis of the philosophers enprynted/by me Wyllm Caxton at Westmestre the yere of our lord.M.cccc. Lxxvij/Whiche to ok is late translated out of/frensh into englyssh.by y noble e puissant lord Antoine Erle of Ryuers lord of Scales e of the/Isle of Wyght. Defendour and directour of the siege Apstolique.for our holy Fader the Pope in this Royame of england and gouernour of my lord prince of Wales.and It is so that at suche tyme as se had accomplisshid this said Werke it liked hym to sende it to me in certayn quayers to ou[er]see/Whiche forthwyth I sawe e fonde therin many grete notable.and Wyse sayenges of/the philozophres. Actor:

12 *This illustration of 'The Apothecary' comes from Caxton's* Game and Play of Chess *printed in the 1480s. Chess was known in the East since antiquity, and made its way to the West in the tenth century. The rules have hardly changed since Caxton's day, although the names of some of the pieces have. Medieval ivory chess pieces have been found on various archaeological sites.*

13 Richard III (d.1485) was a king who divided the nation when he lost the throne at the battle of Bosworth. While many scholars believe he was responsible for the murder of his nephews, popular opinion asserts that he was innocent. Tudor propaganda, such as this bench end at Christchurch Priory (Dorset) showing the Tudor-invented deformation of his back,

chipped away at his reputation. Shakespeare followed the Tudor version of the story and modern audiences have become familiar with increasingly extravagantly disabled representations of this most controversial figure.

14 The reclusive, scholarly and strict order of Carthusians enjoyed great popularity in the later Middle Ages and bore the proud motto 'never reformed because never deformed'. Members refused to subscribe to Henry VIII's first Act of Succession, which declared a child by Anne Boleyn to be his rightful heir. They were horribly tortured before being hanged and disembowelled in London at Tyburn, it was said with the king in disguise, watching.

15 Title page to the Book of Common Prayer (1549). Twelve-year-old Edward VI sits in the council, which settled the issue of the prayer book. Much is a direct translation from the Latin that preceded it. It is a historical document in itself – marriage vows 'till death do us part', for example, meant something very different when life expectancy at birth was thirty years or so rather than the seventy or eighty it is today.

16 Title page of Acts of Parliament (1585). Elizabethan parliaments are rightly famous because of the surviving records of their proceedings, but the queen used parliament very infrequently: to settle the religious question, to rework the poor law, to forward the execution of Mary Queen of Scots etc. Her speeches to parliament were both appropriate and stirring.

17 Queen Elizabeth at the opening of Parliament. Lords sit, Commons stand for the ceremony. Parliaments usually met in the former royal chapel of St Stephen, Westminster from which the canons had been ejected at the Reformation. Note the Lords occupying facing seating as the canons would have done. It was into the crypt below that Guy Fawkes placed gunpowder aiming to destroy parliament. When the palace burnt down in 1834, the architect of its replacement mirrored the ancient canonical arrangement bequeathing the nation adversarial face-to-face politics.

18 Inigo Jones (Hollar, 1649), in his late seventies. Although we now know that it was Cardinal Wolsey and not Jones who brought Renaissance architecture and design to England, Jones remains a hugely important figure at the court of Charles I where he put together the breathtaking masques which were performed. He laid out Covent Garden and Lincoln's Inn Fields, and designed the Queen's House, Greenwich in the 1630s.

19 London, Westminster and Southwark (1543) in Anthony van Wynegaerde's panorama. The four areas: city, royal palace, abbey and transpontine suburb were distinct. London Bridge is seen crowded with shops in a lucrative location. It also provided a convenient latrine for the city prompting the quip 'he is a fool who sails under London Bridge'!

S PAULES CHURCH

20 Portrait of Queen Elizabeth c.1585 by William Rogers. We know that Elizabeth's reign ended in comparative success. For much of it she was beleaguered: in the mid-1580s challenged by Mary Queen of Scots, threatened with Spanish invasion and managing a stream of marriage schemes. Her lavish, bejewelled clothes, helped maintain her image in those dark days.

21 Visscher's panorama of London was published in Amsterdam, 1606. Here we see Old St Paul's, which was destroyed in the Great Fire of 1666. Among the treasures lost at St Paul's in the fire was the shrine of St Erkenwald, which had survived the Reformation. Erkenwald, a late seventh-century bishop of the East Saxons, whose diocese was centred on London was clearly held in much affection by the people of his adopted city, although virtually nothing is known about his life.

22 James I and his wife, Anne of Denmark, whom he married in 1589. It was the atrocious weather which affected her journey across to Scotland and the implication of the involvement of witches in it that inspired Shakespeare's witch scenes in Macbeth.

23 English troops campaigning in Ireland during the sixteenth century. Protestant England feared Catholic Ireland would be used as a 'back door' by European Catholic powers. Signs of Irish rebellion were confronted with great force. The mainland authorities instigated a policy of Protestant 'plantation' areas in Ireland, of which the plantation of Ulster (1608–11), largely populated by Scots, was the most effective.

24 Trial of Archbishop Laud in the House of Lords (1644). As with Strafford, the king was unable to save Laud and he was executed on a flimsy act of attainder, when treason charges failed. The walls are hung with James I's famous Mortlake tapestries, which illustrated engagements of the English fleet with the Spanish Armada (1588). Although the originals were burnt in the fire of 1834, their designs had already been recorded and published by John Pine in 1739.

25 Print of a Van Dyck painting of Charles I, reproduced by Hollar at the time of the king's execution in 1649. It shows the king with his major London palaces. In 1649 Westminster was occupied by the Long Parliament, while the king's great banqueting hall of 1619 had provided the backdrop for his execution in January that year.

26 A coin of the final year of Cromwell's Commonwealth period, showing him as a Roman emperor, but with the crowned arms of the British Isles on the reverse. Although he refused the crown, he was a king in all but name, as recognised by the succession of his son, Richard.

27 Dutch satire of Cromwell dismissing parliament (1653). There was a striking contrast between Elizabeth's rare use of parliament, and the Stuarts and the Protector's continuous use of the institution, essential to feed their financial needs, but often recalcitrant not only in respect of providing money, but also in agreeing conflicting religious and social legislation and, of course, in refusing dissolution.

28 Charles II (1630–85) returned to a tumultuous welcome in England, in 1660. He was always aware of the fate of his father and worked hard to avoid going on his 'travels' again. There was some retribution, the exhuming and hanging of Oliver Cromwell's remains, and pursuit of some of the regicides, but on the whole Charles was pragmatic and tolerant.

29 George Monck (1608–70), duke of Albemarle, was a key figure in the Restoration of the monarchy. He was an outstanding general in the Civil War, fighting for both Royalists and Parliamentarians. He restored order and governed in Scotland for Cromwell. With Edward Hyde, earl of Clarendon, he engineered the Restoration and both men defended a middle way in religion, to the exclusion of radical Catholics and Protestants, such as Quakers.

30 Great Fire of London (1666) from Southwark. It was a terrifying accident, which many contemporaries thought an act of terrorism by the Dutch, whose coastal towns had been torched by the English navy the previous year. The heart of the city was destroyed including Old St Paul's Cathedral, but the suburbs largely escaped belying the popular misconception that the fire brought plague to an end. The Great Plague (1665) was worst in the suburbs.

31 James II (1633–1701) made no secret of his Catholicism. Under his brother he was a brave soldier and an efficient organiser of the navy, but was forced to resign because of his religion. Once king he advanced Catholics to office both centrally and in the localities, and established a standing army to overawe London. The resulting antagonism led to his deposition and exile in 1688.

32 London by Hollar (1647). In 1500 the capital had about 40,000 inhabitants, by 1700 it had 575,000 making it the largest city in Europe. The destruction caused by the Great Fire provided an opportunity, partly realised, to rebuild the city centre in a style befitting its growing size and importance.

33 William and Mary were faced with supporters of James II in both Scotland and Ireland. Here we see William landing in Ireland where he fought the battle of the Boyne on 1 July 1690. Complex politics meant that Protestant Williamites fought Catholic Jacobites, while the Pope supported the Protestants! Two kings fighting for the throne of England in Ireland, contributed to the fame and posterity of the battle.

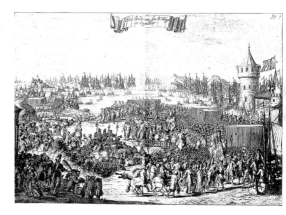

34 The Comforts of Bath *by Thomas Rowlandson (1756–1827) was more directly satirical than work by his predecessor Hogarth. Where royalty led, to Bath and Cheltenham, the lower orders soon followed in pursuit of 'the waters'. As the baths became noisy and overcrowded, royalty moved on to popularise sea-bathing.*

35 William Hogarth was a sharp observer of the contemporary mid-eighteenth-century scene, from a moralistic point of view. Abolition of censorship enabled satire to be more open and fierce in England than elsewhere in Europe. Here he captures a prime English pastime: drinking. Beer Street highlights that English characteristic of drinking which permeates the whole history of the nation from prehistory to present day.

36 Eighteenth-century elections were rumbustious affairs, with candidates luring voters by any means to hand, from funding drinking bouts to exchanging kisses with aristocratic ladies for votes.

37 Vauxhall Gardens were a pleasure ground south of the Thames, now destroyed by urban sprawl. They were notorious for the range – some said, the depravity – of the entertainment offered. They formed part of that whole area along the south bank of the Thames, which had been a haven for social outcasts, theatres, etc. since the Middle Ages and no doubt earlier.

38 Christ Church, Oxford, Henley Four (1913). The tragic fate of these young men sadly reflects the devastation the war reaped on the nation's youth as a whole. Right: George Hellyer (seated, Hampshire Regiment) died of wounds at Gallipoli after rapid promotion to captain as his comrades died fighting uphill against the Turks. Rupert Nunn (standing, Royal Horse Artillery) fought and survived the war and was the first British officer into Berlin at the end of the Second World War, where he was to be seen single sculling on the Tegelersee. Left: R.W. Lush (seated, 3rd London General Hospital Corps) and J.G.G. Leadbetter (Lanarkshire Yeomanry) also survived the Great War.

39 Field Marshal Douglas Haig (Brasenose, Oxford) was a cavalryman who commanded on the Western Front during some of the bloodiest battles of the First World War. Having seen the Germans sweep towards the sea, his ambition was to 'break through' the trenches and drive the Germans back again. This was not accomplished until 1918. Often criticised for failing to win the war more rapidly, Haig in the end triumphed whereas the militaristic Germans, who were defeated, had no better plan.

40 *Adolf Hitler had imperial pretensions, which came to include the conquest of England. This postcard of 1935 shows the* Reichskanzler *in imperial profile. It was published two years after* Mein Kampf (My Struggle) *his 'astonishing book'* (News Chronicle) *in which he had proposed that, in order to realise his ambition of a German empire in Europe (turning back history to the Anglo-Saxon past) 'no sacrifice would have been too great in order to gain England's alliance. It would have meant renunciation of colonies and the importance on the sea, and refraining from interference with British industry by our competition'. But the new Anglo-Saxon alliance was to be with America, not Germany.*

41 *The Battle of Britain 1940 raged in the summer skies over that most English landscape, the Sussex Downs. This Heinkel 111 bomber was shot down, crash landing in Pagham Harbour (West Sussex) where it is seen here, watched over by the Home Guard.*

Popular religion lost its entertainment value in the face of the broadening raft of leisure opportunities. Ever since Luther's day sermons had been satirised as potentially boring and sleep-inducing as they took centre stage in reformed religion. Hogarth captures The Sleeping Congregation *brilliantly.*

Pleasure gardens flourished in cities like London and Bath. Venues such as Marylebone Gardens afforded opportunities for the gentry to enjoy, entertain and be seen in the new leisured age.

The State Lottery (1739). The increasing expense, especially of foreign wars, and the long-term damage caused by the civil war led to a wide range of schemes to raise tax. In the Middle Ages taxation was not as inevitable as death: in the eighteenth century it was. Taxes tried out included the lottery, but also hearth taxes, poll taxes, tax on windows, wigs and much more besides.

The population needed improved food supplies: the necessity encouraged and funded improvements in farming such as the seed drills associated with Jethro Tull in the 1720s and 1730s, and the rotation of wheat/turnips/barley/clover pursued by Viscount Townshend in Norfolk a decade later. However, such oft-quoted developments were isolated and not immediately significant. The Norfolk rotation, for example, was successful more because of the good soil and temperate weather. What is apparent from landscape studies of this period is that very much more land was under cultivation than in the 1600s. Poor harvests occurred in the 1720s and c.1740, and remained a threat throughout the century. Real agricultural improvements did not occur until around 1800. Meanwhile, improved strains of sheep and cattle were developed by selective breeding. They grazed areas of land which were increasingly enclosed and divided into fields – which made selective breeding easier to control by keeping animals separate, and changed the appearance of the agricultural landscape. Some breeding results were spectacular, for example the prize cow weighing 1,741lbs astonished Shropshire people at New Marton 1749. Such a prodigious improvement in stock accounts for the tables groaning with sides of beef in Georgian England. At the same time an estimated 13 million sheep – twice the human population of the country – grazed the fields and hills much as they had in the Middle Ages. Rising livestock prices brought prosperity to farmers, not least in the highland areas, and helped to lay the foundations of agricultural improvement – and to pay for fine Georgian country houses.

Landowners became increasingly wealthy not only in mainland Britain but also in Ireland, where Protestant landownership grew exceptionally from 40 per cent at the beginning of the Civil War in 1641 to 86 per cent in 1703. By 1778 only 4 per cent of land in Ireland was owned by the Irish. Attempts to thwart this process were rendered ineffectual by the Dependency of Ireland Act passed at Westminster in 1719 which built on Poynings law. Thenceforward, not only was any law made in the Irish parliament illegal until it was agreed in London but any Westminster legislation was to be immediately effective in Ireland! In addition to these strictures, Catholic landlords were obliged to divide their estates between their children, with obvious consequences for the size of landholdings.

Religion remained very much an issue in the reign of Queen Anne and became more so as the reign proceeded without an heir. It was for the sake of the Protestant succession that the xenophobic English were prepared to accept the German king George I. However, religion proved to be less of an overt issue as the threat of Catholicism was contained and minimised: such a comment is, of course relative. Modern-day Northern Ireland with its wild sectarianism has been aptly described as a fossil of eighteenth-century England. The sectarian anti-Catholic festivals of the Hanoverian Protestant succession (1 August) and Guy Fawkes (5 November) were celebrated with great gusto and included attacks on Catholic property from village to capital. Despite this the England of Robert Walpole, oligarchic though it was, was seen as essentially free compared to continental Europe dominated by absolute monarchy hand-in-hand with the Catholic Church. The Protestant 'Glorious Revolution' was perceived through eighteenth-century eyes to have been a sound solution to the war and divisions of England in the Civil War and its aftermath. Men ceased to kill one another for religion's sake: the Church of England, compromise though it was, was sufficiently broad for most to subscribe to it and sufficiently weak to allow the existence of nonconformity, the beginnings of Methodism and scientific enquiry. People increasingly realised that if there was a choice about *where* one went to church, there was a choice as to *whether* one went to church. Congregations declined and unbelief grew.

The growth of literacy contributed to the decline of superstition – although Alexander Pope could still claim that as a child he had been cured of scrofula, the 'king's evil', by the touch of Queen Anne. It has been neatly demonstrated that the decline of belief in witchcraft coincided with the rise of newspapers. Consultation with a witch about lost possessions was rendered unnecessary by the availability of 'Lost and Found' columns in papers. News became a prime commodity and the

The first edition of The London Chronicle *(1757) with a leading article by Samuel Johnson. The compiler of the* Dictionary *(1755) was very well known by this time not only in literary circles but by the public at large. Newspapers became central to public awareness and political debate, and have even been credited with causing (through 'Lost and Found' columns) the decline of witchcraft.*

press began to flourish, fanned by growing literacy. The spells cast by the newsmen upon their credulous readers could be at least as subversive as those of witches upon the illiterate, and remain so today. However, for many poorer people, cunning-men and cunningwomen still had much to offer, especially for health problems of people and animals alike.

In the world of journalism the Whig Joseph Addison contributed to Richard Steele the essayist's foundation, *Tatler*, and co-founded the *Spectator* with Steele who was also editor of *The London Gazette* from 1707–10. On the Tory side the gloomy Dean Jonathan Swift, an Anglo-Irish clergyman, wrote satires from early in the century, first in London, then in Dublin, where he produced *Gulliver's Travels* in 1726.

Gulliver was a wide-ranging satire which included attacks on the political parties, who were characterised as high heels and low heels, and contained references to the ruinous South Sea Bubble. Bitter though it was, it did not descend to the depths of his pamphlet of 1729 which suggested that Irish parents would solve the problem of their large families by providing children as food for the rich!

At the same period Daniel Defoe, spy for both Whigs and Tories, travelled extensively assembling data which he eventually published in 1724–27 as his *Tour through the Whole Island of Great Britain*. It provided remarkable insights into the places, both historic and contemporary, and people he saw, although it was journalistic and obscure in places. A failed businessman, he was an early exponent of the novel – held by Marxists to be the bourgeois art form – with *Robinson Crusoe* (1719) and *Moll Flanders* (1722). His *Journal of the Plague Year* (1722) was inspired by a sudden recurrence of plague on the continent at that time and, although purporting to be an account of London in 1665, was largely fictitious.

Terms such as the 'age of Reason' and the 'Enlightenment' apply more to continental Europe than to England. However, the dominance of the Whig party following the accession of George I in 1714 allowed the idea of a cultural renaissance to make headway. Lord Shaftesbury's notion that 'Princes and great men' should take a lead in art and architecture was an inspiration. Classical Palladian building had been effectively produced by Inigo Jones before 1650: Hanoverian England provided further impetus. In 1715 Colen Campbell designed, at Wanstead, the first Palladian country house in opposition to Baroque building. Lord Burlington, inspired by visiting Italy in 1715 and 1719, added new dimensions to this artistic renaissance and reformation. In the first place he was, like Vanbrugh, quintessentially an English architectural amateur who out-performed professionals such as Campbell. Second, his creation of Chiswick Villa in 1725, one of the many such villas in Thames-side villages, was an artistic tour de force in its combination of classical elements. After 1720, in partnership with William Kent, Burlington began work on the gardens at Chiswick creating naturalistic vistas.

Proponents of the 'foreign' Palladian style such as Burlington fell foul of disgruntled out-of-favour Tories. William Hogarth (plate 35) in early drawings from before 1725 satirised people queuing for Italian opera, in his opinion a frivolous art-form and one which debased English works by Shakespeare and his contemporaries. Significantly, the entrance to Burlington's town house in Piccadilly can be seen in the background of this drawing. John Gay's *Beggar's Opera* (1728) was a parody of the kind of Italian opera on offer in England at that time, much of it from the pen of the German-born George Frederic Handel whom the English in time took to their hearts. Handel arrived in London in Queen Anne's reign and stayed until his death in 1759. As an outsider he was quick to see the tastes of his audiences. Contrived Italian opera was *not* to their taste – it was in a foreign language for a start, verging on Catholic Latin. Handel found a way to please them, setting Protestant English texts to grand music, so they could understand it, subscribe the religious message, enjoy it and not feel alienated by it. At the height of his powers in the 1730s he made an astonishing £1,500 in a single benefit night concert – a sharp contrast to the 8d a day earned by soldiers at that time. When George II stood for the 'Hallelujah' chorus of Handel's *Messiah*, the audience followed. As well as being an imitation of the king and in honour of splendid music, the occurrence was an indication of the uncertainties about social behaviour in a changing society. That many English continue today to stand reinforces the notion of arcane social practices which they love, without asking about their origins. George certainly liked the works of his countryman and commissioned the well-known *Music for the Royal Fireworks* in the same way as the *Water Music* had been commissioned by George I. Although a giant, Handel was not the only popular composer at work in England. In 1740, a year before *Messiah* was heard, Thomas Arne's *Alfred* was staged: this included James Thomson's *Rule Britannia*, in its original form exhortatory – 'Britannia rule the waves', but by 1900 audiences had subverted the text to 'Britannia rules the waves', which, by then, she appeared to do!

Alexander Pope, a Catholic, was a Tory who used his literary ability to attack the Whig government in particular, during the first decade or so of George II's reign. Pope's Augustan satire aimed to show how far short of classical ideals Hanoverian government fell. In this sense both Burlington and his Tory opponents, for all their hatred of things foreign, found themselves drawn to a common source of civilisation: that of Renaissance Italy and its predecessor, Imperial Rome. Interest in the classical past was tempered by a sustained interest in the past of England itself. Among the great antiquarians of the eighteenth century was William Stukeley. Stukeley trained and practised as a doctor, before becoming the first secretary of the newly founded Society of Antiquaries of London in 1718. He visited and reflected on monuments far and wide in England, publishing some of his findings in his *Itinerarium Curiosum* (1723). But while he could muse on sites such as Avebury or Stonehenge, or classes of monuments such as long barrows, he had no way of dating them closely. Thus he went significantly off the archaeological rails, believing that long barrows were the burial places of 'arch druids', when in fact they dated back thousands of years before the druids were recorded by the Romans either side of the life of Christ. From 1753 when the British Museum and British Library were founded the collections of Sir Hans Sloane, another antiquarian doctor, in the central repository provided a focus for the antiquities of Britain, and, as it turned out, for those of the rest of world as well.

The Latin language, with its order and structure, was dying out even in conservative areas of record-keeping such as the law in the 1700s. In addition there was opposition to the Latin Catholic Mass – reinforcing the English phobia about foreign languages. English, Latin's ubiquitous replacement, attracted its own law-givers and codifiers of whom Samuel Johnson is the best known. Johnson's dictionary, first issued in 1755, sought to produce standard spellings in English for the first time. Paradoxically, this achievement would make English more like Latin. Johnson was happy to admit in the introduction to his dictionary that even lexicographers could not hope to embalm a language – but thereby provided succeeding generations with the joint headaches of struggling with standard spellings, as well as anxieties about decline in standards of English. The preparation of a dictionary of the language of the imperial conquerors-to-be may be seen as an act of considerable foresight!

Musing on ancient Rome was an apt pastime for a nation, as we know, on the brink of empire. In far-flung outposts of British influence, Newfoundland and India, events developed which were to have significant outcomes for the nation. In

Canada, well-organised and well-supported French forces took the initiative in the early 1750s despite being numerically inferior to their counterpart English settlers. In India, Robert Clive had already successfully repulsed the attacks of the comparatively economically feeble French Company which was, however, well-supported with military might. French interests in India dated back to the sixteenth century; England had received Bombay from Portugal as part of Catherine of Braganza's dowry in 1662. The development of these conflicting interests was, almost inevitably, going to lead to war.

The Seven Years War (1756–63) was accepted by the people as, once again, the struggle of Protestantism against Catholicism: Protestant Britain and Prussia against Catholic Austria and France. There were successes in Europe, some preserved in pub-sign dedications, for example to 'The King of Prussia' and the dashing 'Marquis of Granby'. But more substantial triumphs were in lands far away: in India where Clive turned East India Company rule to British rule in Bengal after the battle of Plassey in 1757. In the New World fine French royal troops were dislodged from the heights of Quebec by the heroic Wolfe while, in a cameo of the era, Scottish Highland regiments and American Colonials drove the French from their Fort Duquesne which was renamed Pittsburgh. Thus the mastermind behind all these campaigns in Europe and further afield, William Pitt the elder, was honoured. European war had undoubtedly distracted French attention from the outposts of their power. The advantage had been thrust home with a mixture of good fortune, good planning and great bravery.

When George II died in 1760, the country was perhaps at the peak of international esteem, if not power. The Whig peace had secured economic and social stability at home. Pitt's victories had seen great strides abroad. The first British empire was secure. George II's funeral, which brings this period to a close, was to one observer, Horace Walpole, farcical. The solemnity observed outside Westminster Abbey, with every seventh footguard bearing a torch and horseguards parading, was in striking contrast to events inside the abbey. There the yeomen cried out for help as they staggered under the immense weight of the coffin. The duke of Newcastle, revived from sobbing with smelling salts by the archbishop, made a rapid recovery and ran about spying with his glass on who was (and who was not) present, eventually coming to rest on the velvet train of the duke of Cumberland, thus avoiding the chill of marble! So ended the first half of the century of Hanoverian rule in a mixture of public show and private shambles.

Horace Walpole looked to the future with enthusiasm. The young George III seemed promising material for the English displaying:

> extreme good nature which breaks out on all occasions. He doesn't stand… with his eyes fixed royally on the ground dropping bits of German news: he walks about and speaks to everyone. All his speeches are obliging. If they offer as well behind the scenes, as upon the stage, it will be a very complete reign.

Walpole might well have reflected on the contrasts in the funeral he had just witnessed. The early years of George III's reign were to prove disastrous in both public and private affairs. However, in the golden glow of success in 1760, the antics of the funeral were tolerable and amusing: under adverse circumstances such events could have been embarrassing and humiliating. That lay in the future.

7
Revolutions,
1760–1792

The Author... takes the liberty of laying before the public his
idea of a *parochial history*, which he thinks, ought to consist of
natural productions and occurrences, as well as antiquities.

Gilbert White, *Selborne*, 1789

While Gilbert White observed and mused upon the antiquities, climate and natural history of his country parish in
his classic *Natural History of Selborne* (1789), the king of
France was being executed. Nearby the teenage Jane Austen
was attempting a history of England in Steventon. Such was
the calm of front-line southern England in the age of revolutions, for revolutions in the American colonies and in
France were respectively completed and initiated in this
period. Other sea-changes were afoot, the Industrial
Revolution began to make tangible progress. Edinburgh
came into its own as an intellectual centre for this was –
among other things – the age of Adam Smith (1723–90),
lecturer at Edinburgh University, philosopher and champion of free trade. Meanwhile James Watt dramatically

improved the efficiency of the steam engine in the work-shops of Glasgow University, but it was at Birmingham, with Matthew Boulton, that Watt perfected his steam engine in 1775.

Musically Austrians and Germans continued to dominate. However, London was an essential port of call on their itineraries. Mozart and Haydn both visited. Indeed, Mozart considered settling in England in the late 1780s and Haydn celebrated the award of a Doctorate at Oxford in 1791 with a performance of a new symphony. It was in England that Haydn experienced a minor revolution in musical perform-ance: he encountered for the first time chamber music performed before a paying audience.

King George III and Queen Charlotte were interested in music, the arts and also in science. The king collected scien-tific instruments and created the perfectly proportioned observatory at Richmond to house some of his telescopes. He gathered clocks and especially books, as well as comm-issioning and purchasing pictures. Notably in 1762 he purchased a collection of over forty paintings by Giovanni Antonio Canal – Canaletto – whose Venetian and Thames scenes were thoroughly appropriate to the nascent age of inland waterways. The duke of Bridgewater's Worsley canal opened in 1761 taking coal directly from the mines to the consumers in Manchester and so halved the price of coal there. This made plain the canals' possibilities.

The Royal Academy was founded in 1768. The renowned portrait painter Joshua Reynolds, who had studied in Italy, was its first president. Religious art remained unfashionable with English patrons: Reynolds circumvented this problem by painting his subjects dressed as biblical figures, such as the

As George III's reign progressed and revolutions pressed in on him and his mental health failed, this much-maligned, but in fact intellectual and erudite king became more introverted. He always collected Gillray's caricatures and this one is said to have amused the king and his family greatly.

Virgin Mary. Although the king was patron of the academy neither he nor the queen liked Reynolds. They 'could not endure the presence of him; he was poison to their sight.' Reynolds, for his part, produced undistinguished work for the royal household and was more at home in the intellectual company of Dr Johnson, the actor-manager, David Garrick and Richard Sheridan, numbering them all among the many subjects of his portraits which totalled over 2,000 paintings.

The royal family set a pace in family life which was to be sustained down to, if not during, our own century. George III had fifteen children. The royal family burst out of its small residence at Kew and moved to Buckingham House (later Palace). This was purchased for £28,000 after 1762 – less than a quarter of the money George had spent on his library during the course of his reign. The value of the bricks and mortar possessed by élites in historic times was far surpassed by the value of the contents.

So far as comfort was concerned, the king's parts of the house were furnished modestly by comparison with Queen Charlotte's suite. For example, George had no carpets because he thought such floor coverings unhealthy. Buckingham House, like Kew, was really a country place on the edge of London. Plans for a grand palace at Richmond came to nought, despite aristocratic criticism of the antiquated St James's Palace with its Tudor gateway and seventeenth-century accommodation. This was considered hardly an appropriate setting for the monarch of the greatest tracts of land on earth. It compared very unfavourably with Blenheim and Castle Howard, Chatsworth and Stowe, the great houses of the Whig aristocracy. The failure of the Richmond palace scheme reinforces the view that George was a man who found himself increasingly unable to manage grand projects – and that included saving the American colonies.

However, the king had an eye for detail: that was why he liked Canaletto's topographical minutiae. So it is not surprising that one of George III's enduring legacies is the State Coach, completed in 1762, a triumphal rococo celebration of the national regions, loaded with symbolism of military victories in the then ongoing Seven Years War (1756–63) and encrusted with evocations of the imperial insignia of Rome. If George had managed to mastermind a palace, what a creation it could have been! It would have outshone the likes of Blenheim, dismissed by Voltaire, that French embodiment of the Enlightenment, as ' a great heap of stone, without charm or taste.'

Politically the Whigs dominated until 1770. Then Lord North's administration sustained Tory government for twelve years. Thereafter William Pitt the younger ran a second Tory administration from 1782 to 1801. This Pitt was the youngest prime minister and with his rival Whig leader, Charles James Fox, helped to define the Whig and Tory parties more clearly. Despite being out of power for much of the period, the Whigs set the fashions, especially Georgiana Duchess of Devonshire, the arch-Whig of Chatsworth in Derbyshire. Outstanding both of intellect and beauty, she exchanged kisses for promises of votes from Londoners in the hotly contested 1784 election (plate 36). Where Georgiana led the fashion conscious followed, abandoning hooped dresses to looking pregnant when the duchess was pregnant and reading up her treatise on the hitherto unfashionable skill of breastfeeding.

On the urban scene spas continued to flourish, the Royal Crescent at Bath was built from 1767 to *c*.1775, while coastal towns, especially Brighton, became popular. Whig followers of fashion abhorred the countryside (they even painted their cows to make the countryside appear more sophisticated). They inspired the notion of the season in London which corresponded with the sojourn of royalty there from autumn to spring. Among the entertainers of the season was a revival of British drama by Goldsmith, Sheridan and others. A famous generation of actors led by David Garrick, a manager of the Drury Lane Theatre from 1747 to 1776, led a thespian flowering. In 1776 Richard Sheridan acquired Garrick's share of the Drury Lane Theatre following the success of his play *The Rivals* in the previous year. *The School for Scandal* and other plays followed from 1777. In the provinces groups of actors toured regularly and a Shakespeare festival was instituted by

The Laſt Time of the Company's performing this Seaſon.

At the Theatre Royal in Drury-Lane,

This preſent MONDAY, June 10, 1776,

The WONDER.

Don Felix by Mr. GARRICK,
Col. Briton by Mr. SMITH,
Don Lopez by Mr BADDELEY,
Don Pedro by Mr. PARSONS,
Liſſardo by Mr. KING,
Frederick by Mr. PACKER,
Gibby by Mr. MOODY,
Iſabella by Miſs HOPKINS,
Flora by Mrs. WRIGHTEN,
Inis by Mrs. BRADSHAW,
Violante by Mrs. YATES.
End of Aŏ I. The Grand GARLAND DANCE,
By Signor GIORGI, Mrs. SUTTON,
And Mr. SLINGSBY.
To which will be added a Muſical Entertainment, call'd

The WATERMAN.

The PRINCIPAL CHARACTERS by
Mr. BANNISTER,
Mr. DAVIES,
And Mr. DODD,
Mrs. WRIGHTEN,
And Mrs. JEWELL.
To conclude with the Grand Scene of The RECATTA.
Ladies are deſired to ſend their Servants a little after 5 to keep Places, to preſent Confuſion.
The Doors will be opened at HALF after FIVE o'Clock.
To begin at HALF after SIX o'Clock.   Vivant Rex & Regina.
The Profits of this Night being appropriated to the Benefit of
The Theatrical Fund, the Uſual Addreſs upon that Occaſion
Will be ſpoken by Mr. GARRICK, before the Play.

An advertisement for The Wonder *(1776). Garrick was a towering figure in theatre, and his Theatre Royal, Drury Lane's popularity can be seen in the small print of this bill – servants being sent early to reserve seats. The performance was part of the Summer Season when gentry came to the capital for a riot of entertainment taking advantage of good weather for travel and waiting for the annual harvest.*

Garrick at Stratford. King George confided to the diarist Fanny Burney that he was not an enthusiast for Shakespeare, while admitting that it was unfashionable to criticise the bard. Fanny Burney, who obtained a position as keeper of the queen's robes in 1786, had made a name for herself with her first novel *Evelina* (1778). This work contains certain references to visits to Vauxhall Gardens (plate 37), a focus of pleasure for both polite, and exceedingly impolite, elements of London society at the time.

Merriment was tempered by problems but heightened by triumphs. Successes in the Seven Years War as well as in India and in Canada brought rewards. The Treaty of Paris of 1763 acknowledged Britain as the supreme world power. But pride comes before a fall. The American Revolution of 1776 brought national disaster but freedom for those colonies. The failure of the redcoats to subdue the American colonists was a severe blow. Lines of communication to the New World stretched 3,000 miles and at home there was confusion and complacency about America. The tension between an expectation that the colonists should pay taxes to Britain and the inability of the British for their own part to provide protection against native Americans and French forces, were crucial.

Economically England began to develop. In industry in 1779, Abraham Darby III, ironfounder, with 'Iron' John Wilkinson among the shareholders, built the Iron Bridge over the Severn at Coalbrookdale. Iron barges and even Wilkinson's own iron coffin confirmed the possibilities of the medium. Sir Richard Arkwright's water-powered spinning frame was patented in 1769 and had raised sufficient fears about future employment to lead to riots and vandalism by anxious workers in his factories. Overall industrial growth was slow and

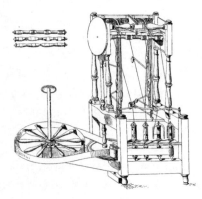

(Sir) Richard Arkwright patented his water-powered 'Spinning Jenny' in 1769 – this picture is taken from the original patent at the London Patent Office. It transformed working practices dramatically, so that by the inventor's death there were an estimated 20,000 of his machines at work in England: a real technological leap.

regionalised. If there was an industrial revolution it was identifiable by the relative rise of the north and Midlands, and decline of the south. Birmingham grew from 24,000 in 1750 to 71,000 in 1801. Its position between the south, which had become largely a hinterland for London, and the north proved beneficial. Thus it is not surprising that James Watt moved to Birmingham to work with Matthew Boulton. It was Boulton who secured from parliament in 1773 a separate assay office in Birmingham for silver, a sure sign of the city's prominence. Further north Liverpool grew from 34,000 to 78,000 in the last quarter of the century and Manchester from 43,000 to 75,000 in the last decade, while old-established regional centres such as Norwich stagnated and Worcester declined in size.

Population grew steadily and migration increased between 1750 and 1800. At the time, however, there was a fierce debate about whether population was rising or declining in mainland Britain. The cause of that significant rise now known to have taken place was not so much a declining death rate, which was marginal, but a lowering of the age of marriage, which extended women's childbearing span. The reason for the younger marriage was greater prosperity: people no longer had to put off getting married because they could not afford it.

In Ireland there was no question of demographic decline: the population was expanding rapidly. In the late 1700s there may actually have been as many Irish as there were other inhabitants of the British Isles put together – perhaps 8 million. But in 1778, 96 per cent of Ireland was in the hands of Protestant landlords. However, at the time and taken as a whole, the future for England looked promising with a swelling population, well-developed financial institutions such as banking (Sir John Soane designed the Bank of England building, 1778) and insurance, with growing agriculture and industry and highly profitable colonial trade.

The loss of the colonies in America did not prevent trade continuing there while trade increased with India and Africa. Indeed one of the debates in early post-colonial America centred around whether democracy and capitalism were inevitable bedfellows, as they seemed to be in the old country. America was free of the capitalist factories which were springing up in Britain but the supplies of goods the colonists needed had, therefore, to be bought in – often from British manufacturers. However, there were many Americans, especially in the south, whose wealth depended not on the labour of free people in factories, but on slaves – still supplied by British traders. Navigation Acts obliged traders in the colonies to bring goods to Britain for re-export, which multiplied exports many times and contributed to a growth in wealth.

The aristocracy reigned supreme in politics and society. They dominated the counties and gambled their way round the legal circuits. At first, bets were cast on the outcome of cock fights and horse races but as the century drew to a close another betting sport emerged: cricket. This developed on Broadhalfpenny Down at Hambledon in Hampshire. These local men defeated 'All England' teams. Wagers grew and fortunes were bet on the outcomes of contests. In the 1770s and 1780s Hambledon men played for colossal stakes totalling over £32,500, of which they won two thirds!

The apparent rural idyll of cricket was interrupted by events across the Channel. In 1789 revolutionary subjects of the extravagant king and queen of France captured their royal family and attempted, at first, to establish a constitutional monarchy. Isolated from the continent behind their moat, the Channel, the British watched and waited. Some, such as the Whig leader Fox were strongly in favour of the revolution. Others such as the Irishman Edmund Burke, formerly a Whig but who was so revolted by the events in France that he crossed the House to sit with Pitt, were equally fiercely against. Many British aristocrats feared for their future.

However, separation from the rest of Europe encouraged an interest in the British past. This was not new in the late eighteenth century. The Society of Antiquaries of London, founded in 1718, gained a royal charter in 1751, began publication of its journal *Archaeologia* in 1771 and acquired apartments in Somerset House in 1781. The Antiquaries encouraged depiction and recording, skills associated with William Stukeley and his contemporaries the Buck brothers who published some 500 views of antiquities.

King George showed enthusiasm for antiquity through his love of the medieval castle at Windsor, rebuilt by Edward III and home of the order of the Garter. George took an interest in his English royal heritage as exemplified in his redecoration of the state apartments. Spectacular, if fanciful, scenes were commissioned from Benjamin West, an American who had travelled in Italy and who settled at court as artist in residence after 1763. For Windsor he depicted Edward III's wars in France. Subjects included the burghers of Calais and also the crossing of the Somme prior to the battle of Crécy (1346). This was an evocation of a previous English 'empire', that in medieval France. Thus the king was at the forefront of the 'Gothick' revival, and conscious of an English imperial past.

Among his subjects, this same spirit of the past was awakening. Horace Walpole created pseudo-Gothic architecture at

Strawberry Hill, begun in 1748 and completed in 1777. It was the epitome of English 'Gothick'. The Gothic revival was a celebration of English cultural individualism in the age of revolutions. Architecturally speaking, this dated back to the parting of the ways from European Gothic when the Early English style developed in the 1200s and the national Perpendicular style of the period after 1348. Some argue that the Gothic had never gone away from England.

Not everything in art and architecture looked back to the Middle Ages. Robert Adam, Scottish architect and interior designer, visited Roman antiquities in Italy and Dalmatia seeking classical exemplars. His researches enabled him to produce neo-classical architecture and interior design of the finest quality, much of it for wealthy English patrons. At Kedleston Hall (Derbyshire) before 1765 he produced a Roman triumphal arch on the exterior and an evocation of the Pantheon at Rome is found in the large central circular room for the display of sculpture. At Harewood (Yorkshire) Adam's fine interiors were designed, as was his hallmark, to be in harmony with the exterior and such traits are also found to this day in furniture designed by his contemporary Thomas Chippendale. Similarly, English landscape gardening evolved: the park at Harewood is one of Lancelot 'Capability' Brown's best landscapes. Learning from William Kent at Stowe, Brown abandoned the formal garden in favour of highlighting, adapting and simulating the natural 'capabilities' of the landscape.

Meanwhile one dominant element of English landscapes, the Church of England, lay dormant. Its aristocratic bishops were often absent from their sees, their buildings in decay. In sharp contrast the flame of religion burned brightly in John Wesley (1703–91), the founder of Methodism. Wesley's organised Christian life was based firmly on the Bible. This inspiring man wished to remain within the Church of England but the national Church could only respond by closing church doors to Wesley, obliging him to preach in the open which brought him into contact with a broad spectrum of society who were not catered for by the traditional church. From 1784, unable to gain the co-operation of archbishops or bishops, Wesley ordained bishops and clergy himself. The necessity to provide places of worship led to the creation of chapels for Methodists and this, together with the ordination question, led to schism from the Church of England. Wesley, a child of Tory parents was an Oxford graduate, who preached a religion not *of* the poor, but *for* the poor. His autocratic leadership led his detractors to call him 'Pope John'. He was in many respects unenlightened. He was anti-intellectual and believed in witches; he was anti-aristocratic and preached the religion of envy; his marriage was unhappy yet his preaching, especially about hell, was so powerful that members of his audiences collapsed. His literal interpretation of the Bible made him anti-Semitic. He was fervently anti-Catholic. Despite all this Wesley's achievement is undeniable. His followers established Methodism as a separate sect only after his death.

As nonconformity and rationalism grew in the 1700s the established Church, if it reacted at all, was inevitably on the defensive. Intellectuals became more bold in the evaluation of ancient cultures and some proclaimed their rejection of religion altogether. Increasing interest in the past led to much historical writing. The beliefs and works of two historians illustrate the tendency to godlessness among the intelligentsia. The Scottish historian David Hume, whose *History of Great Britain* (1761) included accounts of medieval exploits and became a standard work, was an atheist. He argued that humans exist within a framework of Nature and so miracles cannot be genuine as they are against the laws of nature. By the same token there can be no 'demonstration' that God exists, as no factual evidence can be adduced in support of arguments in favour of the deity's reality. Edward Gibbon, after flirtation with Catholicism and instruction in Calvinism, became an agnostic. His *Decline and Fall of the Roman Empire* (1776–88) is an undoubted masterpiece of historical writing, although indelicate parts were not translated to shelter some of his English readers. It was at the time criticised for its unsympathetic treatment of the rise of Christianity, which he blamed for contributing to the collapse of the Roman Empire. For these men the Enlightenment was a manifestation of the possibilities of life without religion.

However, not all historians at the period were non-believers or, for that matter, men. In 1791 that 'partial, prejudiced and ignorant Historian' Jane Austen, prepared scenes from the history of England, an early essay in history by a woman, one of the aims of which was 'to abuse Elizabeth' in favour of Mary Queen of Scots! From her parsonage, the sixteen-year-old author no doubt felt well disposed towards the Church of England and praised its only martyred head, Charles I, with a vindication of whose reign her history closes.

Prior to the outbreak of war with revolutionary France in 1793 there was much that was positive in Britain to balance the lack of success in America. New lands in Australia and New Zealand were claimed by Captain James Cook. Such far-off places (and execution) provided for criminals and malcontents who opposed the largely aristocratic regime at home and fleets packed with criminals were soon setting sail for

Australia. In India, the success of Clive had been consolidated and British possessions extended. Both in India and in North America the French flag had been taken down.

Potential for division and conflict existed in Britain and intellectuals argued for and against the French Revolution, and about the use of slaves and provision for working people. Thus the Scotsman Adam Smith produced *An Enquiry into the Nature and Causes of the Wealth of Nations* (1776). Surprisingly, for some of his modern champions, he argued that employment, trade production and distribution are as much a part of a nation's wealth as its money. He advocated free trade and, like Hume, argued that tariffs on imports merely served the self-interest of merchants. Meanwhile Tom Paine's *Rights of Man* (1791–92) supported the French Revolution and opposed Edmund Burke's *Reflections* on various grounds, including that they were unhistorical. Paine's writing, in which he advocated large cuts in administrative expenditure, graduated taxation, maternity and funeral payments and much more social legislation, led to his indictment for treason and flight to France.

Literature, as ever, provides a vivid mirror of the age. Works by the Irish-born writers Laurence Sterne and Oliver Goldsmith reveal their contrasting fortunes. Goldsmith enjoyed the patronage of Dr Johnson and his circle, thus escaping the incipient poverty, and achieved some financial success: Sterne lacked patronage and died a pauper. Goldsmith's mixture of histories, novels and drama exemplify literary output in the age of Reason. The patronage of his early written work and the success of his play *She Stoops to Conquer* (1773) made him secure. His poem *The Deserted Village* (1770) expressed anxieties about industrialisation as it championed agriculture against industry and commerce in an age when 'wealth accumulates and men decay'. Laurence Sterne's private life and the morality expressed in his rambling, cosmopolitan *Tristram Shandy* caused this work and its author to be denounced by Dr Johnson, Goldsmith and the literary establishment. When Sterne died insolvent in 1768 his insane wife and his daughter were provided for by subscription of his friends. Sterne, a failed clergyman, and Goldsmith, a failed doctor, who both gravitated to London, had much in common. The contrast in their lives lay in the way society received them and this shaped their careers.

In the age of Dr Johnson and the first British empire there was a growing codification of the British experience. This was often achieved by people from the Celtic fringe who had so much to offer as architects, inventors, wordsmiths, colonial administrators or humble soldiers. This was a great age for Britain as a nation. Oliver Goldsmith and the Scotsmen David Hume and Tobias Smollett all wrote histories of Britain: the home-grown Dr Johnson codified English spelling. The Antiquaries began publishing periodicals on ancient monuments, their material and documented heritage. The Scots Adam brothers returned architecture to pure classical roots: the world of Roman Britain. The growing empire encouraged research into ancient empires and the British past. Responsibilities for colonies and the rejection of what colonists saw as an unfair relationship with the mother country lay at the heart of the troubles over American independence. At home, Hanoverians became anglicised and people from all parts of Britain poured east and south into English towns especially London. Britain reigned supreme in the world and her achievement was by no means at an end.

8

Heroes and a Villain

Nelson, Wellington and Napoleon, 1792–1815

And did those feet in ancient time
Walk upon England's mountains green?
And was the holy Lamb of God
On England's pleasant pastures seen?

William Blake, 1808

On 21 January 1793 Louis XVI of France was dispatched by guillotine, that most scientific of execution machines. Eleven days later Prime Minister Pitt, addressing the House of Commons, referred to the execution as 'that dreadful outrage against religion, justice and humanity which has created general indignation and abhorrence in every part of this island.' George III must have been delighted with his prime minister!

War followed. Pitt gathered a grand, somewhat ineffectual alliance (Spain, Holland, Austria, Prussia and Russia) against the French who fought with determination. From the start the figure of Napoleon came into focus: first in 1793 as an officer in his early twenties, he led republican forces to a victory at the naval base at Toulon, which had been captured by royalists aided by the British. This reverse for Britain was followed by others. Attempts to prevent imports of grain to France via Brest were only partially successful; attacks on the French West Indies cost 100,000 lives, with little to show for it. Napoleon returned to Paris where revolutionaries were confronting one another. In 1795 his artillery fired on the Paris mob, dispersing it. He was made commander of the home army and set out on the road to power. If the revolution was in disarray so was the alliance, at first one country and then another dropped out or was defeated by Napoleon, as the Austrians were 1797 at Rivoli in Italy.

The alliance against France was not without its successes: the victory over the French fleet at Cape St Vincent (1796) was noteworthy for Nelson played an active role. Not everything went Nelson's way. In 1797 despite his watch over Toulon, Napoleon's fleet escaped and sailed to Egypt. That territory was captured by Napoleon who saw it as a stepping stone to British India. On 1 August 1798 Nelson recovered his good standing with a crushing destruction of the French fleet at the battle of the Nile. This secured the Mediterranean, but Napoleon himself escaped and took an active part in the post-revolutionary struggle.

Peace was made between the warring nations at Amiens in 1802 and Napoleon had himself proclaimed emperor of France in 1804. He proved a remarkably successful general as he disposed of the Austrians at Ulm, entered Vienna in triumph and defeated an Austro-Russian army at Austerlitz, both in 1805. This left Britain isolated and if it had not been for Nelson's famous victory over a Franco-Spanish fleet off Cape Trafalgar in Southern Spain, during the same year, Britain might well have been exposed to invasion. For his

The Duke of Wellington at the time of the Peninsular War. Napoleon's invasion of Spain, which, despite assurances from its government, collapsed before the French army propelled the British into action. Wellington welded his soldiery, who he described as 'the scum of the earth' into a winning miltary force which was to drive the French northwards, pursued by Wellington's army and an ever-increasing army of hangers on alongside the troops.

part Napoleon later wrote that sea battles are easier to win than land battles, thus disparaging the achievement at Trafalgar. But, as we know, the invasion never happened.

Napoleon's attempt to isolate Britain economically and thereby destroy the trade of the 'nation of shopkeepers' at first paid dividends through a continental alliance of powers dominated by France. But there were pockets of resistance to France in Europe notably Portugal, a long-time ally of Britain. It was in the Iberian peninsula that Sir Arthur Wellesley, later duke of Wellington, first came to the fore. In August 1808 he defeated French forces at Vimiero and obtained an agreement that they should vacate Portugal, taking their weapons with them. For this perceived weakness Wellesley was replaced by Sir John Moore. Napoleon meanwhile reinstated his deposed brother Joseph on the throne of Spain, an unpopular move but one which underlined the French emperor's power. When Moore was killed at Corunna (1809), Wellesley returned to Portugal as commander and gained the title of Viscount Wellington in recognition of his success.

Meanwhile, Britain's isolation was compounded when the Americans joined the French after 1808. But the anti-British alliance was not watertight: Tsar Alexander I of Russia decided in 1810 that his country would resume trade with Britain whose industrial products were necessary to the Tsar's poorly industrialised territories. It was this that led to Napoleon's fateful decision to invade Russia and to the humiliating retreat from Moscow in 1812.

The two fronts, in the Iberian peninsula and in Russia, overstretched French lines of communication. When troops were withdrawn from Spain to replace those lost in Russia, Wellington was able to make steady progress, driving the French northwards. By the time Wellington won the battle of Toulouse in April 1814, Napoleon had already abdicated and was subsequently exiled to the island of Elba by the victorious European powers gathered at the Congress of Vienna. Napoleon escaped from Elba in the course of the negotiations at Vienna. Wellington set out to hunt the Emperor down, for Napoleon was once more enjoying some success on the battlefield.

The final battle was joined at Waterloo on 18 June 1815. The British, with some assistance from the Prussians, were triumphant and Napoleon was utterly defeated. He spent the rest of his days on the remote island of St Helena. There he wrote his *Memorial* in which he dismissed the English as 'continually at the table, almost always intoxicated and of uncommunicative disposition.' A good deal of space was necessarily devoted to explaining away the final defeat at Waterloo, which he convinced himself had been a victory! Taken as a whole the work provided the materials for French historians to create the legend of Napoleon's life. There is no denying that he was an extraordinarily successful and ambitious general and politician, even if he was not a gifted writer. He inspired great loyalty and achieved much in the field of legal codification and effective administration. His forays into Italy and Germany left no doubt in those countries that unification was a worthwhile and attainable objective.

The years from 1792 to 1815 witnessed almost continuous war in Europe. Further afield in Africa, the Americas, India and in the Pacific, European powers struggled for supremacy. Slavery was an increasing embarrassment for Britain. Attitudes to colonies and their peoples varied widely from person to person and between countries. Thus Napoleon could recommend polygamy in French colonies as a solution to the colour question: every man could have 'one white, one black, and one mulatto wife.' In far off British West Africa in the late 1790s administrators of the Royal West African Company did what they could for their slaves. Their letters show how they spent time creating England on foreign shores. They established gardens, grew potatoes, cucumbers and turnips, and joined the Scots to celebrate St Andrew's Day, with a feast, while the slave ships rode at anchor off Cape Coast Castle, now in Ghana.

But the days of slaving were numbered. It had been declared illegal in Britain in 1772. Within a decade provision was made at Freetown, Sierra Leone for slaves freed from Britain to settle there with deported prostitutes. Pitt spoke eloquently against slavery in 1792 but parliament went against him. It was not until Fox became foreign secretary after Pitt's death in 1806 that the clamour by William Wilberforce and the Clapham sect for the abolition of the slave trade was answered. A bill was passed in 1897, to Fox's great pleasure, and abolition came into force on 1 January 1808. Slavery was not, however, finally stamped out in all British colonies until 1834 and American slaves had to wait for freedom until after 1865, with the close of their civil war.

By contrast, the very evangelicalism which had proved so successful against the slave trade contributed to a sharp deterioration in relations in British India. The spirit of mutual understanding and intercourse which was a characteristic of Anglo-Indian relations in the age of Clive was replaced by the moral superiority of the British Raj. And yet, by 1815, British rule in Bengal was sustained by Chinese bullion, the profits of trade in which Bengal opium was exported to China – the Bengalis, with perspicacity on the part of British administrators, were forbidden to consume it.

Against this background, evangelical missionaries, largely unquestioning of the basis of British rule but horrified by native customs of which they had no understanding, poured into India. Warren Hastings summed up the new attitude in 1813 when he wrote that 'the Hindoo appears a being nearly limited to mere animal functions, with… no higher intellect than a dog, an elephant, or a monkey, might be supposed to be capable of attaining.' Thus the spiritual price India came to pay for British rule was high. In fairness, however, the British Raj was more just and less extortionate than native alternatives, and demanded increasing resources for administration and defence from Britain.

Whether the same justification can be offered in defence of Anglo-Irish relations at this period is doubtful. The population of Ireland towards the end of the eighteenth century may well have matched Britain's. Irish existence was precarious both in terms of food (the staple diet being potatoes) and employment.

42 The Sweet Track (Somerset) was built by Neolithic people in 3807/3806 BC according to tree-ring dating, making it the oldest trackway in Europe. This reconstruction is at the Peat Moors Visitor Centre.

43 Stonehenge (Wiltshire) was started c.2950 BC. The bluestones were brought from Wales c.2350 BC. It is England's finest Neolithic monument and the most celebrated in Europe. It remained in use in antiquity for about 1,500 years as a ceremonial centre, a focus for activities related to celestial events and as a gathering point.

44, 45 The original 'Seahenge' was found at Holme-next-to-the-sea in Norfolk and has been dated to c.3500 BC. This reconstruction was undertaken by Time Team to raise awareness of the techniques used to build the orginal monument and to show its possible appearance in antiquity. The upturned tree trunk set in the earth is reminiscent of pre-Christian notions of the 'underworld' where people went after death. Pagan Romans shared this notion.

46, 47 Frampton (Dorset). The Roman cult figure of Attis is seen here (above) with the nymph Sangar. The Christian chi-rho *symbol is seen below on this mosaic with a vigorous representation of Neptune and dolphins, a reminder that Christianity was a newcomer to a broad Roman pantheon. The Christian religion did not become institutionalised as a central imperial religion until the early AD 300s, under Constantine.*

VNIVERT EXRECMEN   SCVLTVMCVIC ERVL
TIMOBILEVENTIS   DELFINIS CINCTAD

48 Saxon houses at West Stow (Suffolk c.AD 400–700). Wooden houses such as these leave little evidence in the archaeological record, therefore, there is considerable debate about their form. At West Stow reconstructions have proved possible. Some of these early buildings were 'sunken floored', a characteristic found in the Anglo-Saxon homelands but especially in England where they appear in the east of the country and in the Isle of Wight.

49 Wroxeter (Shropshire), at one time the fourth largest town in Roman Britain, was a military base in the first century. A splendid baths complex was created here in the time of Emperor Hadrian (r. 117–138). As Roman resources dwindled after AD 400, Wroxeter fell increasingly into decline, the baths finally being levelled c.AD 500, being replaced with flimsy, wooden structures.

50 Deerhurst (Gloucestershire) Church, seventh to tenth centuries. This unspoilt church with adjacent farm and 'manorial' buildings provides an unique insight into the rural world of later Saxon England. The complexity of the carvings – the church was rebuilt after the Viking invasions, its decoration showing some Viking influence – and of the building itself cast light on Saxon beliefs and liturgy.

51 The Tower of London (after 1066). This the greatest stone castle of Norman England was built within the Roman walls of the city and was clearly designed to dominate Londoners – who had long since banished Saxon royalty beyond their walls to Westminster. The Tower faces the city to the west, not invaders coming up the Thames to the east. It challenges the citizens to defy their new masters.

52, 53 The Cistercians were reformed Benedictines who, with a number of other new monastic orders, entered England in the wake of the Conquest of 1066. Their first English house was founded in 1128. In contrast to the Benedictines who had an urban mission and wore black, Cistercians wore white and founded houses in the wilds, their monastic 'desert'. Assisted by lay-brother labourers and generous gifts from landowners they reclaimed areas such as those surrounding Rievaulx in its pretty valley and Fountains which took its name from the spring there.

54 (Left) *Effigy of Henry II (r. 1154–89) from Fontevrault, Anjou. The aptly named Angevin kings kept their focus in Anjou although they ruled England. Henry II had inherited the realm in the wake of a long civil war and, despite vicious fighting within his family, secured the succession in England. Like many medieval men he left his body to be cared for by nuns at his death.*

55 (Right) *Effigy of Richard I (r. 1189–99) from his tomb at Fontevrault (Anjou). Richard spent very little time in England during his ten-year reign. He was, however, well known on the crusading scene and in Europe. The tight administration of his father Henry II, for example in establishing the roll of the Exchequer which was kept every year from c. 1154, left the country capable of running for considerable periods without the king being present.*

56 (Left) *Effigy of Eleanor of Aquitaine (d.1204), queen of England, widow of Henry II. Eleanor had been cast off by the king of France for bearing him no sons; to Henry II she bore a string of healthy sons. This antiquarian drawing of her tomb (the tomb area at Fontevrault was used as a cowshed in the nineteenth century) shows her without the rather surprising book placed in her hands during restoration. Eleanor lived to be over eighty.*

57 (Above) *Edward the Confessor (d.1066) came in the 1200s to personify Englishness before the Norman Conquest (although in fact he had a Norman wife and infuriated contemporaries with his Norman counsellors). Canonised in 1161, he became increasingly popular thereafter. Henry III had a picture of Edward in his bedroom at Westminster, as the personification of good kingship. Edward's shrine in Westminster Abbey was hugely embellished after 1268. In this screen at Ludham (Norfolk) c.1500 Edward is shown with the pilgrim's ring, associated with one of his miracles.*

58, 59 Knights Templar barns at Cressing (Essex). The Order of the Poor Knights of the Temple of Jerusalem was founded around 1120 to protect holy sites in the early years of crusading. They benefited from the wealth of thirteenth-century England and amassed lands and property, which passed to the Hospitallers when the banker-Templars were snuffed out c.1310. The scale of the wheat barn (exterior) and barley barn (interior) bear witness to their wealth. Buildings such as these are treasure houses for detailed archaeological study.

60 The small Herefordshire parish church of Kilpeck is perhaps the
most beautiful of the twelfth century in scale and decorative schemes.
This doorway c.1135 in local stone highlights the west of England
style at that period, some elements avant garde, others deeply
traditional. The columns of the chancel arch were almost certainly
created by someone who had seen the magnificent Romanesque
pilgrim church at Compostela in Spain.

61 Chaucer is rightly referred to as the father of English literature.
He was a diplomat and civil servant under Edward III as well as
a writer. He was not, however, a people's poet but very definitely a
court poet whose work was patronised by Richard II and members
of his court. He witnessed the horrors of the Black Death, the
English triumphs over the French at Crécy and Poitiers, but by
his death in 1400 England had descended into civil war, and King
Richard had been deposed. This is the best likeness of Chaucer.

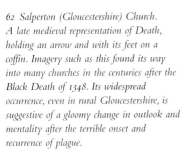

62 Salperton (Gloucestershire) Church. A late medieval representation of Death, holding an arrow and with its feet on a coffin. Imagery such as this found its way into many churches in the centuries after the Black Death of 1348. Its widespread occurrence, even in rural Gloucestershire, is suggestive of a gloomy change in outlook and mentality after the terrible onset and recurrence of plague.

63 Wharram Percy (North Yorkshire) is the best explored deserted village in England. In microcosm it represents the economic decline, check and change of the Middle Ages: growth from the tenth to the fourteenth century, in housing and in the addition of aisles to the church representing population increase and wealth. Decline post-Black Death typifies many upland settlements such as Wharram whose lords, the Percies, turned the village lands over to sheep farming as population declined and wages rose.

64 *Bodiam Castle (East Sussex). This is a classic castle of the late fourteenth century, built by Sir Edward Dalingridge after 1385. It was built 'out of pride' as an example to other local gentry, not 'out of fear' (of the French). It was clearly designed to be seen: surviving earthworks may indeed be viewing platforms. The moat, typical of unsettled times in the later Middle Ages in the aftermath of the Black Death and the Great Revolt of 1381, reminds us that although its owner proudly proclaimed his status in the neighbourhood, he took prudent measures to be safe from natives and marauding invaders alike.*

65 *Richard II (d.1400) on his tomb in Westminster Abbey. Richard's reign was unsettled and ended in civil war and his murder at Pontefract Castle. His patronage of the arts and architecture are his best memorials; these include the Wilton Diptych altar piece, his tomb, his splendid bijou-residence at Portchester Castle and the 660-ton oak roof of Westminster Palace Hall.*

66 *(Opposite) Henry IV (d.1413) usurped the throne, but the stress of holding England together led to a gradual decline into mental illness. He began his reign as a popular warrior king, of whom much was expected in the wars with France after the inaction of Richard II's reign. Henry's jowly face and corpulence as depicted on his tomb in Canterbury Cathedral capture this change from the active to the sedentary life.*

67 *Sir Thomas More by Holbein. By the early 1530s More was in his fifties and Lord Chancellor in succession to Wolsey. By turns 'merry' or 'savage and unforgiving' in the words of his modern biographer, More served Henry VII's and Henry VIII's purposes in, for example, rubbishing their Yorkist predecessor Richard III. In an echo of the Becket story of the twelfth century, More refused to acknowledge Henry VIII as head of the Church in England, and was beheaded.*

68 *Jane Seymour by Holbein. Henry VIII's third wife and mother of his heir Edward VI, was a lady-in-waiting to both his previous queens and, like Anne Boleyn, was some fifteen years younger than Henry. She died shortly after Edward was born, but Henry, at long last, had the male heir he wanted.*

69 Mary Queen of Scots as a young girl. Mary's father James V died almost immediately after her birth in 1542. She was brought up by her mother, Mary of Guise, in France to save her from the 'English' (Protestant) party, and to avoid a marriage to Edward VI. By the time she returned to Scotland – having briefly been queen of France – Protestantism was triumphing. Her life in Scotland was disastrous and she was eventually executed as a prisoner of Elizabeth I in 1587.

70 Appuldurcombe House (Isle of Wight c.1700–10). This was the grandest post-Restoration house on the island, built by the Worsleys who had been elevated by Henry VIII. He visited Appuldurcombe in 1538. It is illustrated by Colen Campbell in his Vitruvius Britannicus. The house demonstrates how the ideas of Vanbrugh and Hawksmoor spread slowly to the provinces – it shows no signs of the new eighteenth-century fashions. The grounds were later said to have been laid out by Capability Brown. It is now a ruin, having suffered bomb damage in the Second World War.

71 *George Cruikshank was the leading cartoonist of his day. Here he depicts the tragedy of the slaughter at Peterloo (1819) 'the Massacre of Peterloo or the Britons strike home'. The Hussars killed a dozen protesters and injured 400 others.*

72 *Walter Hancock's steam carriages, which ran silently and smokelessly from Stratford (East London) to Paddington and the Bank in the 1830s. They also took passengers to the coast at Brighton, and were used between Cheltenham and Gloucester.*

Gillray's caricature of an Irish Chieftain at Wexford in 1798. The fearsome suppression of the Irish in 1798, when a staggering 30,000 were killed, has resonances in Anglo-Irish relations to this day. The mainlanders were determined that there should be no 'back door' entry to Britain for the French at a time of great uncertainty, following the end of the French monarchy, and overreacted against the Irish threat.

As a result of American independence, Ireland was badly affected by loss of trade, notably in flax seed. But the necessity for the militia to defend the American colonies, and thus to leave Ireland, had contributed to a more placatory line by the government on the mainland who were fearful of Irish insurrection. In the 1780s Pitt freed trade and made the British Isles one fiscal unit.

In the 1790s, war with France raised fears of Irish rebellion once more. Catholics were given the vote but denied seats in the Irish parliament: promises of Catholic emancipation were made in 1795 and then withdrawn. This caused deep disappointment in Ireland. Anxious Protestant landlords in the south and Orangemen in the north turned on Catholics. The crunch came in 1797–98. British fortunes were at their lowest ebb. Devoid of allies on the Continent, virtually bankrupt, with a mutinous navy and a French invasion set for Ireland, the government in London was also confronted by an Irish uprising. French support for the Irish did not materialise and in 1798

30,000 Irish people were slaughtered in suppressions of risings in Ulster and Wexford. With resistance broken progress was possible, religious toleration was granted and an Act of Union was implemented in 1801. The abolition of the Irish parliament allowed the creation of a unified legislative body for Britain. This was not, however, the answer to the Irish question. Evangelical Protestantism of the kind preached by John Wesley was offensive to Catholics. Deep divisions remained in Ireland, a land largely of Catholics ruled by a tiny Protestant minority. Feelings between the two groups were scarcely different to those in England at the time of Guy Fawkes and the Gunpowder Plot two centuries earlier.

In 1798, while national fortunes were low, William Wordsworth (1770–1850) published his *Lyrical Ballads* which contained his 'Lines written above Tintern Abbey'. The Romantic movement, to which Wordsworth made a telling contribution, was beginning to flourish spearheaded by young and idealistic men. Wordsworth, who had favoured the French revolution, like many of his contemporaries found himself in a dilemma with defeat by the French staring his nation in the face. Indeed, at the end of 1798 he went abroad to Germany with his friend Samuel Coleridge Taylor but Wordsworth became increasingly conservative as he grew older. His younger contemporary George Gordon, Lord Byron (1788–1824) benefited from the war in that he inherited the barony in 1798 following the death of the previous heir fighting in Corsica.

The Romantics laid aside the self-effacing classicism of the kind in which Napoleon cloaked his character in his *Memorial*, in favour of emotion and passion. At the same time narrow intellectualism gave way to a wider view: criticism to imagination; wit to humour. Romantics such as Byron and Wordsworth, John Keats (1795–1821) and Percy Shelley (1792–1822) were at root, radicals. Shelley was sent down from Oxford in 1811 for circulating a pamphlet on atheism. The 'wider view' included foreign travel, broader experience and involvement in the politics of the day. It is no coincidence that Keats died in Rome, Byron in Greece and Shelley was drowned near La Spezia in Italy while sailing back from a meeting with Byron. The Romantics' works offer many insights into Britain at the turn of the century, not least because they came from a variety of backgrounds. William Blake (1757–1827) poet, mystic and artist, was the son of a London hosier. Like Robert Burns (1759–96), who was the son of a cottar at Alloway (Ayrshire), Blake saw industrial mills as the work of the devil: 'Satan... the work is Eternal Death with Mills, ovens and Cauldrons'. In 1787, nearly twenty years before Blake's 'Jerusalem', Burns had scratched on a window pane at the great Carron Works iron foundry that he had been to view it, not to gain wisdom but for insight into hell! Burns was at first fervently pro-revolutionary and, as a result, almost lost his post in the Excise Office. Becoming disillusioned with events in France he joined the local militia and, surprisingly, ended his days in 1796 buried with military honours. Classical allusion in his last ballad, 'Does haughty Gaul invasion threat?', reminds us that there was more to Burns than a simplistic egalitarianism. However, as Scotland's national poet, he shares with Shakespeare that elusive worldwide acclaim, tested through succeeding centuries. He has indeed proved to be all things to all men.

Literature of the period was not all in the hands of radicals, reformed or not. Sir Walter Scott was a Tory who, like

Burns, rifled the past for material for his books. As squire of Abbotsford-on-the-Tweed, Scott toiled all night at his books in order to appear a gentleman of leisure by day. His output was prodigious: beginning with *Waverley* (1814), they appeared anonymously almost one a year until after 1827 when he acknowledged his authorship, partly in order to enjoy the financial returns necessary to pay creditors after a huge debt accrued through the bankruptcy of a publishing venture in which he was a stakeholder. Walter Scott generously praised the works of his contemporary Jane Austen. Like him, she published her books anonymously during and after the final years of the Napoleonic wars – which have no place in her work. Austen lived in comfortable circumstances in Hampshire – when not visiting Bath, Stoneleigh Abbey and elsewhere – and her works such as *Pride and Prejudice* (1813) are full of the concerns of the middle classes: social aspirations and interactions, family relationships and inheritance. Austen died in Winchester in 1817, only yards from the water meadows which were to inspire Keats to write his ode 'To Autumn' some two years afterwards. In the intervening year, 1818, a very different kind of work was produced by another female author in contrasting circumstances. This was Mary Shelley's *Frankenstein or A Modern Prometheus* written originally as a ghost story while she and her husband Percy Shelley and Byron were passing a wet summer holiday in Switzerland.

Considered a palpable monster by many of his contemporaries the Prince Regent, who became George IV in 1820, was nominally ruler of Britain and the empire from 1811 when his father, George III, became blind and incompetent. The Prince Regent was an enthusiastic Francophile despite the revolution. It was therefore appropriate that the 'Regency' style to which he lent his name should be derived from Napoleon's empire style. Both looked back to the architecture of the empires of Egypt, Greece and Rome. Buildings were furnished with heavy pieces in dark exotic woods and veneers in styles purporting to derive from ancient civilisations. The Prince Regent himself was a financial patron with considerable resources rather than an innovator in the style that bears his title. He preferred his dissipated life in the company of the likes of the dandy Beau Brummell.

Britain had a more exotic empire than that engineered in Europe by the foe Napoleon. As a result there was a tendency for the British to look elsewhere than across the Channel and to Mediterranean lands for architectural inspiration. Thus all kinds of exotic influences are found: from Chinese and Indian to Saracenic taste, all three in the Prince Regent's Brighton Pavilion and its associated buildings but copied elsewhere. To quote Nikolaus Pevsner, that best known of architectural historians, 'the fancy-dress ball of architecture is in full swing' in the decades either side of 1800: Classical, Gothic, Italianate, Exotic or Picturesque and even Old-English, as at John Nash's Blaise Castle near Bristol of 1809 which had barge boards and thatched roofs. Thus did the wealthy use peasant architectural motifs and materials at one end of the scale while, as at the Prince Regent's Carlton House in Pall Mall and at Brighton Pavilion, the whole range of styles is found. New materials were also to the fore in grand buildings, for example, the cast-iron Gothic conservatory at Carlton House (1807): both iron frames and constructions became popular in the provinces as the century progressed.

The Romantics longed for the 'purity' of past civilisations in contrast to the perceived unimaginative reason of the

eighteenth century and the increasingly unpleasant industrialisation of the turn of the century. Noble savages, Greeks,
Romans and chivalric knights seemed more appealing than
modern sceptics with their passion for stuck-on rococo decoration. This view encouraged increasingly detailed and
analytical studies of the past. This fitted well with the increasingly organised architectural profession which had begun to
mould itself with the formation in 1791 of a dining club which
developed in to the Royal Institute of British Architects.

Scholarly interest and research into previous eras tempered
the Romantic poets' adoption of sentimental, and somewhat
uncritical, attitudes to the past. The feel for the past by association, so important to the Romantics found concrete form
in ancient buildings and ruins. Around 1800 John Buckler
visited many ancient sites producing watercolours which provide unique accounts of ruins as they were at that date. In
1805 John Britton began to publish his series of drawings of
The Architectural Antiquities of Great Britain and Ireland, moving
on to cathedrals after 1814 and covering aspects of the development of the palace of Westminster as it was changed and
expanded at the same period. Antiquarians thankfully managed to record the medieval wall paintings in the brilliant
thirteenth-century Painted Chamber before they were wall-
papered over by a 'modernising' architect in 1799 and
destroyed by fire in 1834.

More significant in defining the past was Thomas
Rickman's *Attempt to Discriminate the Styles of Architecture from
the Conquest to the Reformation* (1817). This work gave us the
labels Early English, Decorated and Perpendicular. Although
much debate ensued about whether the purely descriptive
titles of Decorated and Perpendicular should be more closely

related to England, on the whole his codification has stood the test of time well enough. Architectural styles native to Ireland, Scotland and Wales were not so readily identifiable. All this codification contributed to a change in outlook from the eighteenth to the nineteenth century: reason gave way to historicism and aesthetics to copying the past.

Between 1792 and 1815, Britain continued to develop and change: war sustained industry but issues such as on the one hand increasing mechanisation and on the other, long hours, led to friction. Hatred of machines was expressed in 1811 and 1812 by Luddite 'followers' of the mythical Ned Ludd. The end of the war threw many out of work and brought many thousands of ex-servicemen into an overcrowded labour market. The exclusion of foreign corn imports after 1815 kept prices up. When a peaceful, well-drilled gathering of tens of thousands, some carrying revolutionary banners, came together at St Peter's Fields (Manchester) in 1819 the authorities, fearful of insurrection, attempted to arrest a speaker. A dozen protesters died and 400 were wounded as a result of the actions of a troop of Hussars in the so-called 'Peterloo Massacre' (plate 71).

The British had come face to face with the possibility of conquest by the French in 1797–98, yet they had seen the French Revolution through to the era of Napoleon and the restoration of an enfeebled monarchy in France after 1815. Their own monarch was insane for the last ten years of his reign; his son, the Regent, was a selfish hedonist who was a poor argument for a monarchy which provided little moral or political leadership. Britain sustained itself on its naval and military victories, often achieved by outstanding leadership despite poor conditions of service and supply. The country created its own heroes in Nelson and Wellington and its precarious position contributed to an increasing awareness of British history. Above all, the empire not only provided the raw materials for industry but also accommodated overspill population including criminals at Botany Bay and elsewhere and served as a diverse and sustaining resource.

9
Regency Profligacy and Reforming Zeal,
1815–1850

The Continent will not suffer England to be the workshop of
the world.

Disraeli, House of Commons, 1838

Owing to the insanity of George III, George, Prince of Wales,
became Regent in February 1811. The old king's plight was
demonstrated when, wearing his crown, scarlet robes and
ermine, addressing parliament, he held up a speech written out
for him, bowed and began 'My Lords and Peacocks'! He eventually died in January 1820. William Thackeray (1811–63),
contrasted some interests and companions of the Prince Regent
with those of his father. Whereas George III encouraged astron-
omy, the arts and science; the Regent kept company with
'French ballet-dancers, French cooks, horse-jockeys, buffoons,
procurers, tailors, boxers, fencing masters, china, jewel and gim-
crack merchants'! Such a motley crowd was appropriate for the
man who gave his title to Regent Street, a commercial thor-
oughfare connecting his pleasure-dome at Carlton House, Pall
Mall to the pleasure ground of Regent's Park.

The government during the Regency, and for most of George IV's reign, was predominantly Tory, led first by Spencer Perceval who, uniquely for a prime minister, was assassinated in 1812 in the House of Commons lobby by a lunatic. His successor from 1812 to 1827 was Lord Liverpool, an old-fashioned 'pigtail Tory' who acted in blind defence of the existing order. There were, however, even under his leadership, inklings that old-fashioned Toryism could give way to what we now know as Conservatism. Benjamin Disraeli, half a century later, made the Tories, as Conservatives, a popular party better suited to the increasingly democratic nature of the country.

Foreign affairs were managed by Castlereagh (1812–22) and Canning (1822–27). Castlereagh held together an international alliance against France. So unpopular was he, partly because of the repressive policies of the government, such as the massacre at Peterloo in 1819, that his burial in Westminster Abbey in 1822 was accompanied by cheers. His rival George Canning took over and *inter alia* encouraged independence movements in Greece and in South America. Thus, while Britain consolidated its own empire, the government assisted the dismemberment of the old ones of Spain and the Ottomans. Canning took over as prime minister in 1827, but died within a year.

After Canning, the duke of Wellington formed a ministry. The hero of Waterloo doggedly opposed parliamentary reform which the Tories feared would undermine their supporters' vested interests. A notable achievement during his ministry was the Roman Catholic Emancipation Act (1829). In the end, however, his government fell on the issue of parliamentary reform. Wellington was prime minister again in

Benjamin Disraeli was the saviour of the Tories. His strong features made him a prime target for cartoonists. This collection from Punch *(1844–82) shows Disraeli's many faceted character.*

It was no secret that children worked in the mines as these drawings from a government report of 1842 show. Pictures of girls and boys enslaved in this way contributed to the 'Age of Reform' which had begun with the Great Reform Act of 1832 and continued for half a century and more, encompassing Education Acts which were aimed to provide new opportunities for children.

1834 and thereafter served in Peel's administration. He lived in a mansion at Stratfield Saye (Hampshire): in common with his nomination as a duke, a gift from a grateful nation. The house was rebuilt in grand style in the 1830s and his horse, Copenhagen, is buried in the grounds. When he died in 1852 he was buried at St Paul's Cathedral, his funeral carriage being made of Napoleon's melted-down cannon. A military school, Wellington College, was founded in his memory (1853).

Reform gained momentum in 1829 but not without opposition. Changes in population distribution brought about by growth in industrial towns in the Midlands and north highlighted parliamentary over-representation of agricultural areas in the south. 'Rotten' boroughs where MPs were nominated and 'pocket' boroughs where a patron, often the government, controlled elections, provided several hundred MPs. The Whigs won the election which followed the death of George IV in 1830. In the same year, the French monarchy was once more overthrown by a revolution. This focused minds in England, including that of William IV (1830–37). However, two bills for parliamentary reform were rejected by Parliament in 1831 and 1832.

The fiercest opposition was in the House of Lords: the twenty-one bishops, who could have saved the second reform bill, voted against it. Reformists among Whig MPs countered sharply: 'we don't live in the days of barons; we live in the days of Leeds, Bradford, Halifax and Huddersfield.' Places such as Birmingham and Manchester gained representation after 1832: fifty-six small towns lost two MPs each. In Lancashire three seats grew to thirteen.

An electorate of 435,000 was increased by 217,000 or some 50 per cent in England and Wales alone. The population of Britain was some 16.5 million. Contemporaries were surprised by the comparatively small overall growth in the number of voters when the franchise was extended to include more male property owners and occupiers. There was no question of the working classes being given the vote as yet. However, modest reform staved off any incipient rebellion.

Nonetheless, efforts were made to improve some working conditions. The Factory Act of 1833 made it unlawful to employ any child under nine; those of nine to eleven were not to work for more than nine hours a day and forty-eight hours a week. However, the act was limited to textile factories. Children laboured underground until the Mines Act of 1845.

The poor were particularly vulnerable to epidemic disease. The first great outbreak of cholera occurred between 1831 and 1833. Cholera is a water-borne disease and public water supplies were commonly shared. In 1842, a report showed that eleven houses out of twelve in Newcastle-upon-Tyne were without water. At Liverpool, the two water companies paid high dividends but provided no public pumps and no stand-pipes for street cleaning. The 1842 report by Edwin Chadwick, secretary (because he was considered of too lowly birth to be appointed a commissioner) to the Poor Law Commissioners was entitled *Sanitary condition of the labouring population of Great Britain*. It defined damp, filth and overcrowding as causes of disease. It noted that improvements in drainage, water supply and street cleaning led to its decline. The average age at death for professional people and gentry given in the 1842 report for Manchester was thirty-eight, while in rural Rutland it was fifty-two. For craftsmen and labourers in Manchester it was as low as seventeen and in Rutland, thirty-eight. The report was a phenomenal success: it sold 100,000 copies mirroring the success of the contemporary fiction writer Charles Dickens, who brought to life the terrible conditions outlined in the report.

The rapidly growing population included increasing numbers of poor. Rural people rebelled in 1830 in the 'Swing' riots in southern England. A few were executed and hundreds transported to penal colonies in Australia. A key issue for the authorities was defence of property: two thirds of executions were for arson. Rebellion on a grand scale may have been prevented by the government with the promise of parliamentary reforms. However, in 1834 the Whigs, assailed by huge rises in costs, also reformed the Poor Law which had operated, with additions, since Queen Elizabeth's reign.

Outdoor relief was abandoned in favour of the establishment of Poor Law Unions and workhouses: indoor relief. Workhouses were designed to be more uncomfortable than the worst conditions outside, to encourage people to work. Families were broken up. The intention to segregate people of different status was never fulfilled. Prostitutes were placed with the destitute widows. Work included breaking rocks and, until disease stopped the practice, grinding up bones. The number of poor on relief fell from 1.26 million in 1834 to 1 million in 1850 after centralising reforms in 1847. Whether this decline was due to reforms or to improvements in employment opportunities is unknown (the horrors of the workhouse discouraged people from applying). The preserved workhouse at Southwell (Nottinghamshire), shows how appalling these buildings were.

The London Working Men's Association spawned Chartism, a grass-roots movement which articulated ideas of reform after 1836, by which time it had become apparent that the Reform Act of 1832 had not been far reaching. The People's Charter of 1838 consisted of six points which included universal male suffrage, secret ballots, abolition of the property qualification and annual elections. The Chartists had seen the middle classes gain the vote in 1832: they wished to do the same for the working classes. They gathered 1.2 million signatures but their demands were not met. The movement lost momentum in the 1840s, especially after the continental revolutions of 1848. The publication in London of the *Communist Manifesto* (1848) by Karl Marx and Frederic

The Chartists on Kennington Common, London in 1848. Spurred on by reform of parliament, they drew up a People's Charter in 1838. It went to parliament with 1.2 million signatures in 1839, but the petition was rejected as were petitions of 1842 and 1848. Some relics remain, such as Chartist cottages built with large gardens a physical reality underpinned by a vision of rural self-sufficiency.

Victoria was only eighteen when she became queen. She relied at first on the avuncular Lord Melbourne to advise and support her. In this picture, a profile captured on early coins, her demeanour is reminiscent of a previous generation – that of Jane Austen who had died in 1819.

Engels was a product of concerns about unacceptable working conditions, drawn from Engels's experience in Manchester. Mrs Gaskell's *Mary Barton*, also 1848, based on Manchester, gave a graphic fictional view of such conditions.

William IV's reign saw considerable reform before the 'hungry forties'. Reform fitted well with the good-natured sailor king. Unlike his brother George IV, William had numerous illegitimate children: ten by his mistress Mrs Dorothea Jordan. But there were no more after his marriage in 1818 to Adelaide of Saxe-Meiningen who bore him two daughters, both of whom died by 1822. Thus, on his death in 1837 the crown passed to his niece Victoria, daughter of his younger brother Edward.

Victoria's father died aged fifty-three when she was less than a year old. Her uncle William IV died aged fifty-three when she was eighteen. Victoria's age obviated the necessity for a regency: her mother, despite her known wishes to the contrary, was firmly excluded from power. Victoria trusted Lord Melbourne, the prime minister. 'The Whigs are the only safe and loyal people and radicals will also rally round their Queen to protect her from the Tories', she wrote.

The queen was warmly acclaimed at her coronation, at which she recorded Lord Melbourne gave her fatherly looks, and the crowds exceeded her expectations. The new royal pageantry we see today of guards, precision, solemnity and splendour was developed in the early part of her reign, bringing to an end the farcical exhibitions which had previously accompanied such events – such as the coronation of the Prince Regent with his wife Caroline banging at the door of Westminster Abbey. In February 1840, Victoria married Prince Albert of Saxe-Coburg-Gotha who shared the burdens of state until his premature death in 1861. Victoria, the first of their nine children, was born in November 1840. The family was at Buckingham Palace at the time of the census in the Spring of 1841. While the 'Occupation' column was left blank, a firm 'F' (i.e. Foreign) is entered against Albert and some other members of the household. Queen Victoria was formal and severe, especially over moral matters. She set a good example in her Court and family, the latter on her own admission taking precedence over the former 'provided my country is safe.' She therefore left the government of the country to the politicians, and they were happy to enjoy the freedom which accrued to servants of a constitutional monarchy. They helped the queen to realise her dreams of family bliss and seclusion. It was Sir Robert Peel, to whom the queen had taken an instant dislike, who found her the Osborne estate on the Isle of Wight in the early 1840s.

Victoria's marriage to Albert was a marriage of love and devotion. The queen took to the role of wife and mother with enthusiasm, and together they enjoyed parenting and recreation. Railways allowed them to travel far and wide from the Isle of Wight to Deeside in Scotland, a place which Albert particularly enjoyed as it reminded him of his native Germany, and was a place where he could stalk stags, a pastime which as a result of his interest became, and has remained, most popular.

The coming of the railways freed the monarchy from residence in south-east England where it had been based almost exclusively since Tudor times. The Stockton and Darlington railway drawn by Stephenson's *Locomotion* but also using horse traction, had opened in 1825. The breakthrough came in 1830 with the Liverpool and Manchester railway which depended entirely on steam traction. By the beginning of Victoria's reign the system had extended to 1,500 miles of track and continued to expand rapidly in the 1840s. Thus Osborne was accessible by train and boat, yet detached from London life.

At Osborne, Prince Albert designed the Italianate mansion. Even more remote was Balmoral on Deeside (Aberdeenshire), leased in 1848. Here the royal family delighted in Scottish life: Albert delayed dinner one night, the queen recorded, as he engaged in 'a struggle to dress in a kilt.' Albert liked Scotland as the landscape reminded him of parts of Germany.

Thus the queen was happy to settle for constitutional monarchy and family life. Plaster casts of children's chubby limbs, displayed on red velvet cushions at Osborne, together with individual sets of miniature tools for their gardens, illuminate her devotion of the growing family. In addition, her interests in painting and Albert's in architecture and stalking could be realised in their remote retreats. Both loved nature and delighted in animals. Among her earliest artistic acquisitions in 1839, was Edwin Landseer's painting of an American lion-tamer, with bloody scratches to his neck and arm, reclining beside a massive lion foreshadowing Landseer's lions at the base of Nelsons Column in Trafalgar Square. In 1842, when the queen first saw Scotland, she gave Landseer's stag-painting *The Sanctuary* to Albert. As well as animal paintings the queen purchased landscapes in 1840, again for Albert, which included the Scottish painter David Roberts's

Railways were a tremendous investment early on, but excited great opposition – one critic assuring parliament that if passengers travelled on trains above 4 miles an hour or through tunnels they would certainly die! Speculation was keen, and in 1847 – two years after this cartoon of 'The Railway Juggernaut' was published – there was financial panic. As the century progressed, railway investment and financial returns fell dramatically.

topographical views of Madrid and, more outlandishly, of Cairo. These family gifts provided ideal opportunities for patronage of painters and sculptors such as John Martin whose vast landscape *The eve of the Deluge* was also purchased.

The same subject was painted by J.M.W. Turner in 1843. His skyline of London and blazing palace of Westminster in 1834, and of the railway, *Rain, Steam and Speed* were contemporary topics and recall the fear and mystery of the elements in the industrial age. Turner's landscapes such as *Buttermere* look backward towards Wordsworth and the Naturalism of the Romantics. But it was the landscapes and country scenes painted by John Constable (d.1837) which found more ready recognition by most contemporary critics. In style, Turner painted well out of his time. French critics, who liked Constable's work, described Turner's efforts as 'little jokes' but it is clear that Turner influenced the Impressionists and found a stout defender in the influential John Ruskin's *Modern Painters* (1843–60).

Constable's *Haywain* and Turner's railway scene are vivid reminders of the contrasting rural and industrial life and landscape in the first half of the nineteenth century. Nonetheless there were profits to be made in both. The price of corn rose steeply during the Napoleonic wars, but thereafter fell, especially when the Corn Laws of 1816 banned the imports of wheat until the price in Britain was very high. Overall, farming boomed in the period leading up to the repeal of the Corn Laws in 1846. The rapid growth of towns enabled farmers to sell increased quantities of food. The railways facilitated the carrying of food to urban centres.

It was the growing cities and the experience of their residents which preoccupied leading authors of the time.

A satire on Peel's Corn Law of 1842. The repeal of the Corn laws under Peel was to split the Tory party and project them into the political wilderness.

Contrasts between poverty and wealth are readily found in the works of Charles Dickens and William Makepeace Thackeray. Dickens's own father had been imprisoned for debt so it is not surprising to find Mr Pickwick incarcerated in the Fleet prison in London, for refusal to pay financial damages. Oliver Twist, whose adventures were published in 1837–38, was born in a workhouse of unknown parents and his world of London thieves was eagerly anticipated by the reading public. *Nicholas Nickleby* likewise addressed social issues with its indictment of education at Dotheboys Hall. Ten years later, Thackeray in *Vanity Fair* (1848) also treated poverty (in which the poor eat lobsters, presumably because they were accessible to catch) and descent into hard times.

Provision of services for the burgeoning urban population and growing wealth, set against stable prices, enabled investment in a whole range of new inventions. The railway was one and soon showed the shortcomings of canals, which were prey to freezing weather and those in the south were often short of water. Other innovations at this time included steam road carriages (plate 72) which ran silently and smokelessly (according to evidence to a parliamentary Select Committee) in London, to Brighton, Cambridge and Reading, and between Cheltenham and Gloucester in the early 1830s. But in 1832, an enlightened steam carriage bill fell. It began to appear that the legislature was against these vehicles. Thereafter railways gained momentum and swallowed up the available investment monies, despite the madness of pseudo-scientific opponents such as Dr Lardner who insisted that proceeding at more than a walking pace would kill the passengers, who, if they survived the speed would undoubtedly die of suffocation in the tunnels.

Rubber was a novel commodity and an innovative industry flourished at this time pioneered by Thomas Hancock who discovered the process of vulcanisation in his private laboratory in Stoke Newington on the outskirts of London in the 1840s. This process elevated rubber from a pencil eraser to the plastic of the nineteenth century. Many products followed by 1850 including the Wellington boot, raincoats produced in partnership with Charles Macintosh in Manchester, inflatable rubber cushions for the new parliament house at Westminster, baby bouncers and much more. Military uses such as inflatable boats were demonstrated to the duke of Wellington on the Serpentine and rubber tyres for vehicles produced.

Among Hancock's friends was Michael Faraday whose work led to generation of electricity and to the production of the electric motor. Unlike Hancock, whose inventions had apparent practical applications, much of Faraday's work was

Left: *A range of rubber products from Hancock's catalogue, from his book describing his life and work (1857). The hip baths certainly look old fashioned, but the baby 'jumper' bouncer and the chest expander, might find a place in any home today.*

Below: *Charles Macintosh and Thomas Hancock's great rubber manufactory in Manchester, the epitome of industrial might in the nineteenth century. Macintosh had made waterproof raincoats; Hancock invented the process of vulcanisation of rubber which elevated the substance from a mere pencil eraser to the plastic of the nineteenth and twentieth centuries.*

theoretical. When asked about the practical use of his discoveries he replied sagely 'Of what value is a new born baby?' Certainly widespread use of electricity for lighting and heating did not follow until after his death in 1867.

Men such as Hancock and Faraday were nonconformists. They came from artisan backgrounds: Hancock's father was a Wiltshire cabinet maker, Faraday's a Surrey blacksmith. Hard work and religious devotion often drove such men forward through improvement by apprenticeship, Faraday encountered scientific texts as a bookbinder. These people formed a growing middle class with a different outlook and standards to Anglican landowners and were on account of this religion excluded from university education.

It was the admission of the middle class to parliament after the Reform Act of 1832 which contributed to the repeal in 1846 of the Corn Laws, designed to keep out foreign imports of wheat. Protectionists feared that his would ruin British agriculture and thus landed wealth. Peel decided that the Corn Laws must be repealed. As a result of repeal the Tory party split into protectionists led by Disraeli and the Peelites, a small but influential group during the following sessions of parliament. The effects on prices were initially by no means as disastrous as the protectionists had predicted.

A telling reason why Peel brought forward the reform of the Corn Laws was the Irish potato famine which began in 1845. Potato blight destroyed three out of every four acres of potatoes on which the Irish depended entirely for food. Nearly a million died: another million emigrated. The British government's response was less than wholehearted for a variety of reasons including a potato shortage in England and the

The 1840s were the period of the Irish potato famine. The 'Hungry Forties' were a period of general famine with Death 'the poor man's Friend' seen here, a welcome alternative in the popular mind.

The potato famine in Ireland was a catastrophe, reliant on a single crop, when it failed, the population was exposed as never before to starvation and death. Experts in the empire were deployed in far off India, too far away to succour the Irish whose population fell by a dramatic 25% by death and emigration, mainly to America.

fact that the government dare not be partial to Ireland. There
was a shortage of officials who had experience of famine:
those who had were far away in India. The position was exacerbated after the Corn Laws debacle in the midst of the
famine. Political uncertainty persisted until Lord John Russell
formed a ministry in 1847. By then many Irish had died and
Russell took what action he could.

Circumstances and politics thus conspired against harmony
between Ireland and Britain. Although, Ireland had been
united with the rest of Britain in 1801 there was continuing
suspicion of the Irish: attitudes on mainland Britain to
Catholicism have been compared to attitudes to Communism
in the twentieth century. By comparison with England,
Catholic emancipation apart, Ireland had enjoyed a wide parliamentary franchise in the 1820s of about 250,000. In Britain,
Catholic Ireland was a particularly difficult issue for the Tories,
the party of the Church of England. However, the logic of
their position was to join the Catholic Church and this some
of their leaders such as John Henry Newman did in 1845,
although John Keble, another leader of the Oxford Movement
which promoted the Catholic basis of the Church of England,
did not. This debate within the Church of England between
the liberal Anglo-Catholic Tractarians on the one hand with
their faith in ecclesiastical authority derived from Church
tradition, and the Bible-based evangelicals with their emphasis on personal salvation on the other hand, did much to
revitalise the Church of England.

Many in England in 1850 had experienced hardship in the
form of urban deprivation, factory work and, especially in
Ireland, famine. But conversely, much had begun which it
was hoped would bear fruit in the remainder of the century:

a transport revolution, new inventions and materials, a reformed parliament and stable agriculture, even a reinvigoration of the Church of England alongside successful and diverse nonconformity.

And what of the empire? There were opportunities for growth but as experience with Ireland had shown, relations within Britain, let alone with distant colonies, could be fraught with difficulty.

10

Victorian England and a Glorious Empire,

1850–1901

The stability of England is the security of the modern world.
(Ralph Waldo Emerson, 1856)

The age of reform had been established in 1832 with the parliamentary Reform Act and continued with the factory and mines acts, sanitary reports and the new poor law. In 1846, the Corn Laws, which had limited imports of wheat to sustain home production, were repealed. This split the Tory party and led to insecure ministries in the 1840s and 1850s. In the knowledge that reforms were in progress during the early years of her reign, Queen Victoria concentrated on family life. By 1850 seven of her nine children had been born.

The Great Exhibition of 1851, planned by Albert, displayed the arts and industries of Britain, the empire and Europe in the Crystal Palace built in Hyde Park. It celebrated the industrial, scientific and social progress of the previous half-century and looked to the future. With hindsight, the great era of liberal reforms was already largely past by 1851. Even in the railways, the most profitable lines had already been created.

The Great Exhibition fell in census year and the 1851 census included detailed ages, occupations and places of birth for the first time. The population was 21 million in Great Britain of whom 16 million lived in England, compared with 9 million in England in 1801. By 1901 England was more than 40 million out of 54 million. In 1851, the largest occupational group, towards 2 million, was engaged in agriculture. Next came more than a million domestic servants. There were half a million textile workers. In the 1891 census, the largest group was 2 million domestic servants, followed by 1.5 million mining and metal workers, with farm workers – partly no doubt as a result of the agricultural recession and the reclassification into smaller groups of agricultural workers by the census officials – down to 1.3 million. There was concurrently an industrial recession, the worst periods of which were the 1870s and 1890s. There was also a religious census in 1851. This showed that the Church of England attendance was far outnumbered by nonconformist in a ratio of two-to-one. Anglicans argued that nonconformists attended services twice on Sundays, Church of England parishioners only once. Some Anglican clergy refused to count populations at divine service. There were variations, but apparently some 70 per cent of people attended church on census Sunday. The British were now a nation of practising Christians: however, the results were sufficiently embarrassing to the Anglicans that no religious census has occurred since.

Intellectuals such as Charles Darwin challenged accepted theories about evolution hitherto based on religious precepts. His seminal work *On the Origin of Species by means of Natural Selection, or the Preservation of Favoured races in the Struggle for Life* (1859) was followed by *The Descent of Man* (1871). These works were attacked by churchmen such as Bishop William Wilberforce. Others found the notion of the survival of the fittest a justification for colonisation of the world. Religion, however, remained important in the expanding empire. God was clearly on the side of the colonial power in creating the greatest empire the world had ever seen. Whereas James I had envisaged the Anglican Church as a European Protestant religion by 1850 it was becoming instead a world religion through the empire.

Society enjoyed more diversity of worship than ever before. Within the Church of England there was a revival, not without its critics, led by the Oxford Movement on the Anglo-Catholic wing and strong Evangelicalism among low church people. Non-conformity and Catholicism flourished, the former among industrial and agricultural artisans and the poor. Early trade unionists often learnt their organisational skills as chapel officials. It has been suggested that England was saved from revolution by the channelling of the working-class into hymn-singing nonconformity. This kept them from the barricades.

Agricultural profits in the mid-nineteenth century were a bonus to the Church of England which ploughed wealth back into the building of comfortable accommodation for clergy, now bound to dwell in their parishes, while individual landowners endowed many Gothic revival churches. Architects such as William Butterfield, G.G. Scott and G.E. Street were active in the Gothic revival heyday of 1840–70: but they destroyed authentic medieval features faster than ever before. Their ecclesiastical revolution sought to return church design to the 'purity' of the 1200s and 1300s: all later work was to be expunged. After 1875, as the economy struggled, the great church-building boom declined. Acknowledging the dangers and spiralling aesthetic losses at the hands of modernisers, William Morris encouraged the foundation of the Society for the Protection of Ancient Buildings in 1877.

Education went hand-in-hand with religion. The Church of England retained the universities of Oxford and Cambridge which trained Anglican clergy, concentrating on the teaching of classics. Nonconformists could become members of the university at Cambridge, but in the early 1850s had no access to degrees or scholarships. Cambridge was then the more enlightened; until 1871 at Oxford it was not possible to join the university without subscribing to the Anglican Thirty-Nine Articles.

The 1851 Exhibition underlined the need for technical education and wider access to education. The Crimean War, 1854–55, revealed administrative incompetence deriving from ignorance. The soldiers, however, were roundly praised for fighting bravely, despite inadequate equipment and clothing. Florence Nightingale with her nurses worked at the military hospital in Scutari alleviating sick and wounded soldiers' suffering. Lady Butler's painting *The Roll Call* recalled the Crimea and dwelt on the soldiers' experience. In 1874 it appeared, to overwhelming public interest and acclaim, at the Royal Academy during army reforms by Edward Cardwell, resulting from lessons learnt in the Crimea. Cardwell attacked the crux of army weakness: the purchase of commissions and promotions. With the support of enlightened aristocrats like Lord Northbrook and with a royal warrant, abolition of purchase was unwillingly agreed. From it flowed promotion on merit and reorganisation of the War Office to take over old local territorial rights of appointment of officers of the militia.

The cavalry and artillery were untouched. Military skill, through practical and intellectual training, was introduced for the infantry: in other words an appropriately educated military caste. The navy by contrast continued in its well-ordered ways, divided by ship and officer group, with respect for space on board ship. It may be that shipboard experience, a key to empire, provided the basic model for English politeness, such a characteristic of the nation in the nineteenth century.

A new standard was set for public school education by Thomas Arnold at Rugby who aimed, by religious and moral training, to develop an administrative class to run the empire. Numbers of new public schools were founded, beginning with Cheltenham in 1841, which developed an ethos of 'muscular Christianity' as Disraeli termed it. Nathaniel Woodard's schools which began with Lancing, in Sussex, stressed Anglicanism and encouraged middle-class pupils to steer clear of the practical skills of industry and trade towards a mental training appropriate to the professions.

And what of women's education and rights? The Brontë sisters deceived their publisher by assuming men's names in correspondence, having written passionate and emotional and therefore unwomanly works of fiction in the 1840s. *Jane Eyre* and *Wuthering Heights* would not have been published without such subterfuge. Queen's College, London was founded in 1848 but it was not until the early 1870s that Girton and Newnham were established for women in Cambridge. However, their chaperoned students were not allowed to receive degrees. Acceptance at Oxbridge was slow. It took one world war to persuade Oxford to give degrees to women. It took two world wars to persuade Cambridge to do likewise. Meanwhile Elizabeth Garrett Anderson had matriculated at St Andrews in 1862. Refused admission to examinations by British medical colleges, she took her MD in Paris in 1870 and became the first female medical practitioner in Britain. Florence Nightingale introduced competitive examinations for nurses in the 1860s. At secondary level, Cheltenham Ladies' College was founded in 1854 with the doughty evangelical Dorothea Beale as headmistress from 1858. Organised education for women contributed to the regiments of those fighting for women's suffrage. Lydia Becker championed female suffrage by determined correspondence with MPs in the 1860s and 1870s. The citadel of equal voting rights was not to be stormed until 1928 and even after the Second World War some nagging disabilities remained. In sport the longest race in the 1952 Olympics for women was still only 200 yards!

A steady increase in state funding of general education began almost by accident in the 1830s when over-budgeting left a financial surplus which was diverted to education. Notwithstanding this and the efforts of the church, educational supply could not keep pace with demand, especially in rapidly growing cities. A debate continued long after 1850 about what should be taught to the mass of children in elementary schools. It was agreed that reading, a basic Protestant tenet associated with Bible reading, and mathematics were important. Should children be taught to write? The danger that correspondence might lead to sedition was worrying.

Sir James Kay-Shuttleworth (d.1877) introduced a system of government school inspectors to disseminate good practice rapidly. The inspectorate included Matthew Arnold (d.1888), the poet and Arnold of Rugby's son. Kay-Shuttleworth stressed the necessity for the training of teachers. Unable to secure government funds for a training college, he founded it at his own expense in Battersea. The churches began to establish teacher-training colleges before 1840. The Paris Exhibition of 1900 provided a test of educational progress, especially in technical subjects. It was plain that Britain had fallen behind other nations such as France and Germany. Reasons included the campaign to discourage middle-class children from industry and commerce, the requirement that the best administrators go abroad into the empire (the examinations for entry to the Indian Civil Service were more rigorous than those for the home Civil Service) and the economic downturn of the later 1800s which had left the industrial machinery of Britain short of investment capital.

The importation of cheap food, especially wheat from the great plains of America and Canada, coupled with the repeal of the Corn Laws, had caused a devastating agricultural depression after 1873. Worse still, in industry, British pre-eminence in the middle of the century had disappeared. The United States and Germany were among countries whose steel production far outstripped that of Britain.

Why were other nations overtaking Britain before 1900? The unification of the United States at the end of the Civil War (1865) and of Germany (1870–71) created larger units of output. The great innovative period in Britain had largely ended. Until after 1860 the railway systems of the world were supplied by Britain using British rails and rolling stock. The development of independent heavy industries in emerging economies destroyed these markets.

Britain developed her empire, but not all could agree on its value. Benjamin Disraeli, the Conservative leader, was an enthusiast, William Ewart Gladstone for the Liberals, less so.

Some saw the empire as a source of cheap raw materials for industry. Others, such as the London Missionary Society, sponsors of David Livingstone who reached the Victoria Falls in 1855, saw it as an opportunity for Christian mission. Rudyard Kipling's work highlighted the missionary spirit as a key element in imperialism, dwelling on the right of the British 'Chosen People' to rule 'lesser breeds'. Militarily the empire was difficult to defend as the defection of the American colonies had shown. Joseph Chamberlain, Colonial Secretary in the 1890s, championed the empire. He master-minded the confederation of states in Australia and pressed, unsuccessfully, for imperial preference in world trade after 1900. The necessity to defend India against Russia led to the Afghan Wars (1878–90). The Suez Canal (1869) was in the neutral zone from 1888, thus the Cape had to be secured to ensure safe passage to India. This led to the Zulu War (1879) and the Boer Wars of 1881–82 and 1899–1902. Such wars were costly and supply lines were long. For its part, Britain had to invest in the colonies. This deflected capital away from home.

Nonetheless there were developments in social policy and in the political franchise after 1850. In politics the second Reform Act drafted by the liberals, but seen through in 1867 by Disraeli, almost doubled the electorate to something under 2 million. This reform probably marginally favoured the Conservatives but the Liberals under Gladstone won the election and put through a Secret Ballot Act in 1872. They extended the vote to farm labourers in 1884 and in 1885 restricted each constituency to a single MP. Disraeli's Public Health Act of 1875 addressed many of Chadwick's concerns in his 1842 report.

The backgrounds and careers of Gladstone and Disraeli exemplify the diversity of nineteenth-century English society, the fluidity of English politics and the way in which prime ministers acted on the national and world stage. Gladstone, son of a slave-trader, was originally a Tory and in 1832 made a speech against the abolition of slavery. He resigned over a grant to the Catholic College at Maynooth, Ireland in 1845 but later, when leader of the Liberals, encouraged educational provision by an act of 1870. He made strenuous efforts after 1886 to solve the Irish question by offering land reform, which did not prove to be a solution, and later Home Rule. He failed to get Home Rule through parliament in 1886 and 1894. Disraeli, son of an Anglicised Jew was brought up as a Christian, and established a reputation as a brilliant novelist. He started as a radical MP in 1837, but became a Tory. He presided on the one hand over a Tory administration which put through a social welfare act giving protection to trade unions, and on the other saw the queen elevated to empress, extended the empire's power and communications with the purchase of the Suez Canal and the annexation of the Transvaal. In 1878 he brought back 'peace with honour' from the Congress of Berlin which headed off a potential European war.

After the Liberals were split by Joseph Chamberlain in 1886 over Home Rule, it was only a matter of time before Conservative administrations were elected. Lord Salisbury was prime minister from 1895 to 1902. Thus at the end of the nineteenth century a member of the aristocracy still led the country. Salisbury was a descendant of Lord Burghley and of Robert Cecil, Burghley's son, the first earl of Salisbury, respectively first ministers of Elizabeth and James I. The prime minister ran the empire from Hatfield House, now equipped with a special railway station, as his famous ancestor had run the country from there in Shakespeare's time. Indeed as the House of Lords fought a rearguard action to save hereditary peers in the 1990s it was another Cecil Lord Cranborne, who led for the Conservatives. It was a sign of the changed times that Cranborne was rewarded by the meritocratic William Hague with a summary sacking from his party post.

Socialism grew in the later nineteenth century. A group of academics formed the Fabian Society in 1884 devising a programme to attain socialism by political means. They had little working-class support. However, Keir Hardie, a Scottish miner who had graduated via the temperance platform to trade unionism, was elected to parliament for West Ham (London) as the first Labour MP, 1892–95. He became chairman of the Independent Labour Party in 1893 and of the Labour Party, formed in 1900, in which year two Labour MPs were returned. The Fabians included Sidney and Beatrice Webb who had assisted Charles Booth in extensive surveys of poverty in London. Sidney Webb, on the London County Council, was a pioneer of municipal socialism. The early development of socialism was masked by imperial considerations which diverted attention from the rapid growth of trade union membership. Funds which might have gone towards the establishment of pensions, mooted at the time, were absorbed in the South African War.

The Taff Vale case of 1901 resulted in the Amalgamated Society of Railway Servants (an apt name for a union representing the greatest industry staffed exclusively from the working classes ever established in Britain) being made to pay £32,000 to its railway company employers, thereby disabling trade unions. However, it hugely stimulated membership and so resulted in funding more MPs who took parliamentary seats in by-elections. Trade unionism aimed to secure better working conditions for artisans and the labourers at a period when intense foreign competition, coupled with population growth, was driving both agricultural and industrial wages, and working conditions downwards.

Some of the inspiration for labour to organise was drawn from the guilds of the Middle Ages. John Ruskin (1819–1900), whose Guild of St George (which revived the patron saint in the cause of good craftsmanship) and other social welfare schemes occupied his last years, was an inspiration to William Morris (1834–96) and saw a clear link between art, morality and social justice. Morris was involved in the foundation of socialist groups in the 1880s, precursors of the Independent Labour Party.

Medievalism had captivated painters since 1850, notably the pre-Raphaelite Brotherhood, initially led by William Holman Hunt, John Everett Millais and Dante Gabriel Rossetti. Their early work was generally adversely criticised. However, Ruskin in his *Modern Painters* (1843–60) defended the Brotherhood's work. The pre-Raphaelite Brotherhood's emphasis on artistic styles dating from before 1500, when Raphael began painting, coincided with the interests of William Morris, whose enthusiasm for the Middle Ages found expression in designs marketed by his firm Morris and Company. Rossetti painted a number of portraits of Jane, Morris's beautiful wife, to whom he bequeathed in his will the paintings in his studio. The Arts and Crafts movement, inspired by Morris, resonated well with political, industrial and social movements of the later 1880s. There was, however, no agreed agenda in the arts. Differences often resulted from varied religious standpoints. Ruskin was evangelical and thus out of tune with the Anglo-Catholic Tractarians' view of religion and architecture. He was, like Morris, opposed to drastic restoration of buildings in Gothic style. Ruskin attacked A.W.N. Pugin, who championed the Gothic revival before 1850 and who had become a Catholic.

Knowledge was for these men essential and Ruskin's Working Men's College was founded in 1854. Likewise, Gladstone argued, on the basis of workers' use of libraries, for the award of the vote in 1867. Arnold Toynbee, a populariser of the term 'industrial revolution' and like Ruskin an Oxford academic, laboured for social reform and adult education. Toynbee Hall, Whitechapel, was built in his memory. In 1865, William Booth had founded the Salvation Army and had established its first citadel also in Whitechapel, notorious for poverty and degradation. The Salvationists dealt with people below the level at which education was a primary necessity and thus performed a complementary function of that of Toynbee Hall, staffed by young university men. In Whitechapel, the Jack the Ripper murders took place in 1888 and memorable impressions of late Victorian London are found in Arthur Conan Doyle's Sherlock Holmes stories which first appeared in 1887.

The dark side of life experienced by her subjects was also felt by Queen Victoria. The loss of Prince Albert in 1861, to typhoid, cast the queen into mourning for more than a decade. Indeed her withdrawal from public life made her increasingly unpopular. The creation of the third republic in France following defeat in the Franco-Prussian War in 1871 may have contributed to this feeling in Britain. Sensing trouble because of the queen's continuing reclusivity, Disraeli persuaded her to accept proclamation as empress of India in 1876. Her rising popularity was enhanced by the Jubilee in 1887 and the Diamond Jubilee in 1897. Her death in 1901 ended the sixty-four-year rule of a much revered monarch.

In the world of archaeology Victoria's reign had seen significant advances and changes. On the eve of her accession the Dane C.J. Thomsen had laid out the Danish National Museum on the principles of his 'Three Age System' in 1836. The Stone, Bronze and Iron Age system has remained current, although refined and dated by advances in science. The British Museum, founded in 1753 moved to its present colonnaded building in 1847. The empire provided opportunities for English archaeologists to roam far and wide, while also stimulating research for the ancient material origins of modern success. Augustus, later General Pitt Rivers, 'the father of scientific archaeology' was early in the field, inspired by Darwin's *Origin of Species* (1859), working on prehistoric and Romano-British sites especially Cranborne Chase in Dorset. Pitt Rivers's recording and technical skills in archaeology were unprecedented and it was entirely appropriate that he was appointed as the first Inspector of Ancient Monuments following the passing of the first Ancient Monuments Protection Act in 1882. His contemporary Sir John Evans published on stone and bronze implements of Great Britain in the 1860s and 1870s, and his son Arthur purchased Knossos (Crete) in 1896 and began to uncover the 'Minoan' civilisation there in 1899. In the same decade Howard Carter, later present at the opening of Tutankhamen's tomb, was establishing his credentials as a draughtsman and excavator in Egypt, investigating another ancient civilisation. It was

Heinrich Schliemann (d.1890) excavated Troy in 1873. This was of great interest to the English as Brutus, the legendary founder of their race, had fled from Troy to England, then uninhabited 'except for a few giants' according to Geoffrey of Monmouth in the twelfth century. Schliemann's work coincided with the unification of Germany and with close examination of links between Anglo-Saxon England and Germans on the continent; he was made warmly welcome in London and is seen here adressing the Society of Antiquaries of London in their apartments at Burlington House, Piccadilly, where the Antiquaries still meet today.

visiting the British Museum which inspired the work of Sir Flinders Petrie who began by publishing on Stonehenge in 1880 before moving on to work in Egypt where he surveyed the Great Pyramid and experimented with new archaeological techniques of excavation. The work of these great archaeologists at the height of the empire did much not only to elucidate the past of their own country, but also to lay the foundations of archaeology abroad. The profits of the Great Exhibition of 1851 had been put to a variety of purposes which included the funding of the Victoria and Albert Museum, the Natural History and Science Museums at South Kensington. British Schools were founded in Athens, Rome and Jerusalem, and the Great Exhibition fund continues to support these institutions today.

Victoria's reign was in many ways the golden age of the collector as her own collections bear witness. The growth of the great museums, especially in London, was a feature of her reign and the extent of British power, not only within the empire but also throughout the world brought unbelievable treasure to our shores. The great legislative programmes of the 1800s which had begun with the political reforms of the 1830s and the reforms of the poor law continued throughout her reign to include the beginnings of the protection of material heritage in the 1880s.

The last quarter of the century was dominated by the search for roots of this great empire which bestrode the world. Archaeological and historical materials were ransacked, and the search was facilitated by the pursuit of folk-traditions, the term folklore having been coined in 1846. Among senior historians and geographers the 'pure' German basis prevailed, dating to the fifth century. This Anglo-Saxon 'answer' to

English origins was one reason for the growth of interest in folk music and folk dance in the later nineteenth century not least to challenge this German focus. The composers Parry (English), Stanford (Irish) and Mackenzie (Scots) all based in England, drew on folk songs of their native lands in their compositions. The English were the first to found a Folk-Song Society (1898). All these traditions came together in the celebration of England in A.C. Benson's 'Land of Hope and Glory, Mother of the Free... God, who made thee mighty, Make thee mightier yet' (1902 for Edward VII's coronation), music by Edward Elgar, that most English of composers. Archaeologists looked further back to stone tools and material evidence, but had not found an archaeological answer to English origins by 1900, that was for the twentieth century.

II

Bloody Tests,

1901–1945

They mingle not with their laughing comrades again;
They sit no more at familiar tables of home;
They have no lot in our labour of the day-time:
They sleep beyond England's foam.
(Laurence Binyon, 'For the Fallen' 1914)

The empire did not finish with the Queen-Empress Victoria's death. But it was proving increasingly expensive, in both lives and money. When the queen died in 1901 the population of England and Wales was 32.5 million and the Boer War (1899–1902) was in progress. This was not a war against ill-armed natives (although the *impi* had shown their potential to get the better of British soldiers in the Zulu War of 1879), but against armed South African Boer farmers, who knew the terrain and who were not afraid to use guerrilla tactics, to which the British responded with that most ill-used twentieth-century innovation, the concentration camp. As Britain discovered, even if the lesson was not learnt, that in twentieth-century wars, victory could prove as costly as defeat.

For a decade or so after the death of Victoria there was a flowering of Edwardian culture under her ageing son Edward VII. Edward had been obliged to wait a very long time before he came to the throne and had passed the time developing a number of activities which he pursued with great enthusiasm. Among these was shooting. As Prince of Wales he had visited many shoots across the country to sample their pleasures. The quality of weapons had greatly improved in the nineteenth century and owners had invested in special 'shooting landscapes', with belts of trees such as spruce, to force the birds high in the air to make better sport. Edward enhanced the stock of royal residences with the architecturally unspectacular Sandringham (Norfolk), which he bought for the shooting early in the reign. In 1911 he died and his son George V ascended the throne. These years were an apparent golden age as the empire continued to expand and to people today with hindsight the period seems other-worldly, the Indian Summer of empire before the First World War (plate 38).

However, even this golden age was not without its warnings. In January 1912 R.F. Scott and members of his team including Dr Wilson reached the South Pole on foot, only to discover that the Norwegian Amundsen had beaten them to it: the Englishmen died on the return journey, only miles from safety. Shortly afterwards in April the White Star liner *Titanic* bound from Southampton to New York on her maiden voyage and dubbed 'unsinkable' on account of her design, struck an iceberg and sank with the loss of 1,500 lives. The wreck, located after a long search in the 1990s, proved a considerable test for marine archaeologists due to its great depth on the ocean bed.

The First World War cost at least 10 million lives. The British empire pulled heroically together and many Asians and West Indians fought alongside soldiers from Australia, New Zealand, South Africa and Canada. The Irish, long a key element of the British army and despite political disputes over Home Rule, gave excellent service and countless lives in the trenches of the Western Front (plate 39) and elsewhere, with Scottish and Welsh regiments. No-one knew how to manage a war on this scale and with modern mechanised weapons. It has been argued that once the troop trains began to roll westwards from Germany to Belgium and northern France, German generals were uncertain how to reverse the process. The result was carnage beyond imagining: there is hardly a community in Britain which does not have a war memorial to the First World War. Many paid the ultimate price. Like so many events there is a simple historical starting point, the assassination of Archduke Ferdinand by the fanatical nationalist student Gavril Princip in Sarajevo in 1914, as a blow in the ejection of the imperialist Austro-Hungarians and as a step towards a Slav state. Before the end of the century the same Balkan states were to become embroiled over similar issues: ethnic groupings and conflicting religious traditions. But it is plain that the origins of, and the preparations for, the war went back much further, coupled with the fact that here was no international forum in which war could be prevented. Fighting it out on land and sea, and for the first time in the air, to the politicians of the time, seemed perfectly natural.

But the actuality was horrendous. On the first day of the battle of the Somme in 1916 there were 20,000 British casualties. In the battle as a whole there were 420,000 British casualties, 200,000 French and 450,000 German. Machine

guns, barbed wire and poison gas killed and maimed the soldiers. The hope that artillery fire would destroy German
defences proved to be misplaced, they were too well dug in
and the wire proved remarkably resilient under bombard-
ment. This contributed to the catastrophic loss of life and
injuries as infantry failed to negotiate barbed wire while
under fire. Lloyd-George, the prime minister, used a picture
of the sea of mud on the battlefield of Loos, where barbed
wire alone remained amidst the corpses, to argue for more
artillery shells to destroy wire!

In the following year, 1917, the balance changed. The sinking of the liner *Lusitania* off Ireland in 1916 with many
Americans on board, began to focus minds in America.
Destruction by the German submarines of 2 million tons of
allied (and some American) shipping in the first four months
of 1917, leaving Britain with only six weeks supply of food,
were factors which contributed to the decision of President
Wilson to enter the war against the Germans in April 1917.
The Allies were in sight of victory by the time the Americans
came in, but American optimism, tempered by proportionally
large losses among American troops on the Western Front
(the Americans had the disadvantage of being larger in stature;
they also at first, according to eyewitnesses, refused to duck in
the trenches as the British and French British did, believing
it to be cowardly), contributed to the ending of the war in
1918. Criticism of the allied generals has been fashionable in
recent years, but this may be at least partly misplaced. The
Germans as the militarist nation might have been expected
to have the answers: they plainly did not. The battlefields of
the First World War have proved an extraordinary archaeological resource. Despite the clearance after the war, in places

the mud had been so deep that whole tanks, let alone individual soldiers, could be swallowed up. Today it is possible to
locate battle sites, often accompanied by large cemeteries, and
to make physical plots of engagements by the mass of allied
and German shells and equipment still strewn across the fields
of Flanders. Building developments on former battle sites
today turn up caches of soldiers' bodies, often identifiable by
their identity tags and their regimental affliations recognisable
in their cap-badges.

Among the outcomes of the war was a triumph for
European nationalism. Many states, such as Poland, were born
or reborn out of plebiscites, designed, under President
Wilson's 'Fourteen Points', to solve the problem of nationalism. Nationalist quarrels in Europe were intermittent for a
decade or so after the First World War, but fighting did take
place, for example over Silesia in 1921; the solution in 1922
satisfied neither Czechs, nor Germans nor Poles, contributing
to later fighting. Elsewhere for the Arabs who had fought for
the allies under the enigmatic T.E. Lawrence, for Africans and
for Asians self-determination was not on the agenda. Chinese
battalions were brought in to clear the shattered remains of
men and machines from the battlefields, and many died in the
process. Almost immediately following the war influenza
raged across Europe. In Britain it killed more people in 1919
than the war had done over four years, although many 'flu
victims were children and old people rather than the young
men who had given their lives on land and sea and in the air
in the war.

In addition to all the mortality, Britain was faced with a
mountain of debt. In common with Europe its industries had
been diverted into war work, and after the war found that new

industries in America, Asia and elsewhere had taken their place. The dream of recovery by depending on payments of war-reparations by Germany was unfulfilled. The brilliant English economist J.M. Keynes pointed out that the reparations could never be paid, part of the problem being the inability of Europe (including Germany and Britain) to compete with their exports in the world market as they had done before the war. Despite other countries failing to pay back Britain, the British were determined to pay off their debts, notably to America.

This determination had repercussions on taxpayers who, in sharply deteriorating economic circumstances, were required to pay higher taxes. Businesses, already hit by declining exports, increasingly cash-strapped and facing employees demanding higher wages, began to close. Returning soldiers were promised rewards by a grateful nation. Public housing schemes, the 'homes fit for heroes' were initiated, and despite a national debate on whether such houses should have par-lours in an age of revolutions (many eventually did include such a room), some fine housing schemes were established, some of the best schemes on the edges of cities were built like villages with greens, shops and a hall. But the returning soldiers and bereaved families, felt that there were too few new homes. Men were also rewarded with the vote in 1918, if they were over twenty-one, and women over thirty, who had made such an impact with their war-work, were also enfranchised. But there was little to vote for in elections: unemployment was rarely under a million in the 1920s, and women soon found themselves squeezed out of the work-place and back into the home.

The plight of the miners was especially bad. Private mine owners no longer had the resources to keep mines up-to-date. Nationalisation of the mines was called for, an echo of the Communism and Socialism which was ablaze on the continent. But the government ducked the issue of nationalisation and the miners were forced to take lower pay in 1921. A further cut in wages in 1926 was a cause of the General Strike which began in May that year. This was the nearest the country came to the revolutions witnessed on the continent, in Russia, Germany and elsewhere, with troops on the streets of London. This was potentially a disaster for a land which enjoyed the longest tradition of parliamentary democracy and should have been a warning of trouble ahead for the new post-1918 democracies. In the emergency caused by the General Strike divisions were emphasised between labour in heavy industry, coal, iron and steel, in transport and the docks on the one hand, and white-collar workers and the middle classes on the other, who unloaded ships, drove buses and so on. Troops were called out to do much of the work. In fact unemployment was in remission in 1926, at 2 million, half a million fewer than in 1925, and this may have been among the reasons that the strike wavered and collapsed after nine days, although the miners held out until December before accepting lower wages and returning to work.

With unemployment rising once more, to around 3 million in 1929, a Labour government was voted in, but against a backdrop of a world depression, and of a weakening stock market, which led to the financial crash in the autumn of 1929. The crash ushered in a cycle of three years of financial weakness in the markets and rising unemployment. The upside was that in 1931 the American government cancelled European debt in an effort to kick-start the economies which increasingly depended on American finance. The national government which followed the resignation of Labour in 1931, although led by a Labour prime minister, was largely composed of Conservatives.

A world crisis of this magnitude inevitably made countries introspective and isolationist. The League of Nations, founded with such hopes after the First World War, faltered from the start when America, anxious about being drawn into further European crises, refused to join. In 1933 Germany, under Adolf Hitler (plate 40), and Japan also feeling slighted by the world in the terms handed out after the First World War and having defiantly embarked on their own expansionist policies, withdrew from the League. Germany began to rearm at the same time, providing employment, investing in public works such as motorways and giving the people a sense of purpose. The British were at first sharply divided over Germany. Visitors to Germany saw clean, purposeful young people smartly dressed and going singing about their daily tasks: a stark contrast with the depression and unemployment in England, where aimless groups stood smoking on street corners. Among intellectuals, however, more of the truth was known; the hounding of the Jews, and what would today be called 'ethnic cleansing'. Young German Jews who chose exile included scholars such as Nikolaus Pevsner, a lecturer at Göttingen, whose fresh eye saw the possibilities of describing *The Buildings of England*, county-by-county, giving us the magnificent 'Pevsner' series. Gerhard Bersu, Director of the German Archaeological Institute, was deprived of his position in 1935 and moved to England, where he brought continental excavation methods to the prehistoric site at Little Woodbury (Wiltshire). Half the Jewish population of Germany had abandoned their native land by the autumn of 1939. If the public were confused and divided as members of English families came to blows for and against Hitler, so too was the government. The Prime Minister Neville Chamberlain, a man of honour, took Hitler at his word when the dictator claimed that each of his acquisitions of territory was his last. This was the much-derided policy of 'appeasement' between 1937 and 1939. Chamberlain represented the older generation who had fought or suffered in the First World War. Generally speaking this group could not imagine that Hitler, formerly in the trenches himself, could go to war; the younger generation together led by Churchill and his supporters thought that only war could stop the Führer. Whatever the motives behind appeasement and 'Peace in our time', as Chamberlain proclaimed on his return from Munich in 1938, the two years of the policy provided an essential, if tardy, opportunity for Britain to rearm. Without this window, the outcome of the Second World War would have been very different.

War came on 3 September 1939, the immediate cause being the failure of the Germans to withdraw from Poland – which at the end of the war was handed over to another totalitarian state, Soviet Russia. Britain mobilised and stood up, together with the gallant empire against the horror of Hitler, although a substantial minority remained unconvinced that Germany was the real enemy, a minority which included the former king, Edward VIII. At first the Germans were very successful, driving the British back to the French coast where the heroic evacuation of thousands of troops by 'little ships' from Dunkirk was an early spark in the darkness of confronting apparently overwhelming odds. The volunteer spirit of those sailors was something the English saw as iconic in their war effort – the triumph of the amateur sailors over the highly trained German army. They certainly were very brave, but it was the Channel and stormy weather, as it had been since 6,500 BC, which provided an effective barrier to tanks and infantry. As Winston Churchill made clear, if Germans did arrive 'We shall fight them on the beaches'.

Germany attempted to subdue the English from the air. Hermann Goering, a former pilot himself and head of the Luftwaffe, sought to overwhelm British defences with wave after wave of bombers and fighters with their gleaming German engines, and their airframes creaking with bombs and bullets. At the beginning of the battle of Britain (plate 41) German planes outnumbered the British by 3,000 to 1,000: but the gap was wider than this as many of the British planes were old and worn. But on the plus side England had the advantage of radar, a new invention which could detect the Germans from isolated stations staffed by young, enthusiastic and dedicated women, before their planes arrived. This airborne threat was the darkest hour. But as war films showed, British pilots with their comfortable, casual clothes, and being vastly outnumbered, entered willingly into the combat and, despite the odds, had downed 1,700 German planes in a month when Hitler personally ordered the postponement of the 'Operation Overlord' invasion plan. Churchill immortalised the pilots in his statement that 'Never in the field of human conflict was so much owed by so many to so few'. The amateur, underdog British outlook was, and is, a particular feature of Englishness. In addition, from the air the patchwork of the English countryside looked at its best, reinforcing for the pilots in reality the England of downland, farmland and field which had been the focus of so much literature between the wars, by the likes of H.J. Massingham (e.g. *English Downland*, 1936) whose readers no doubt included the founders of the Council for the Protection of Rural England and the Ramblers Association, founded either side of 1930. In 1935 Ralph Vaughan-Williams, born in Gloucestershire, had published *National Music*, reflecting a long-standing interest in English folk-music, his *Five Tudor Portraits* added a further historical dimension to his works. His *Dona Nobis Pacem* (1936) was prophetic. But despite rural yearnings England was plainly an urban, industrial nation by the time of the Second World War, when 75 per cent of people lived in towns, but the poster campaigns such as 'Dig for Victory' were designed not only to augment dwindling food supplies, but to reinforce the sub-conscious national 'agrarian stock', which since the early twentieth century had mislaid its Germanic roots.

The Second World War has left behind a mass of interesting archaeological material, but the wartime materials are being rapidly eroded by development. However, it was possible for a prize-winning study of the pill-boxes to be carried out in recent years across southern England. Other topics investigated archaeologically have included the study of airfields (many now lost), coastal defences, and the more ephemeral 'K' type (day-time decoy) and 'Q' type (night-time decoy) airfields. Specialist groups have collected detailed data on crashed aircraft and some have been spectacularly recovered from the earth. Additionally sea wrecks have been located and surveyed, although they often remain designated war graves.

By contrast to the First World War which had been conducted far away by troops dispatched from railway stations and quays, the Second World War entered English people's lives more directly. On 10 May 1940 the new Prime Minister Winston Churchill famously offered nothing but 'blood, sweat and tears' in pursuit of 'Victory at all costs, victory in spite of all terror... for without victory there is no survival'. Radio and film brought leaders such as Churchill much closer to their people as 'Dear Winnie'. The involvement of the whole nation under their new leader occurred first through the imminent fear of invasion (people asserted that they would shoot the invaders, but on the evidence of France they might not have done so when it came to the point). Britain and the empire stood alone against the tide of Nazi military might. Second the bombing of cities wrecked the homes and lives of civilians. Hundreds of thousands were killed and injured. The German plan was to act like lightning, *blitzkrieg*. The impersonal mode of air attack brought out the best in people, the 'Dunkirk Spirit' surged upwards and the nation pulled together against the common threat and enemy. When Buckingham Palace was bombed the king and queen found a joint cause with their people as they visited shattered homes in east London.

People who lived through those stirring times warmly recall that satisfying sense of purpose: they knew precisely who the enemy was – Hitler and his axis – and made the best of things. It would be naive and simplistic to say that those dark days were entirely wonderful, however brightly the spirit of Englishness shone through. Newly recruited soldiers, for example, were formed into columns and sent to devastated areas of London to shoot looters – not their idea of serving their country at all. Night refugees from cities to avoid the bombing were not encouraged by the government who feared a breakdown in order and a sapping of the common will. Government would rather the people had remained under the bombs. Families were split up by evacuation of children to the countryside, or even (if they survived the hazardous sea-crossing, where many drowned) to Canada, America and elsewhere. Families who sought refuge in the English countryside were not always made welcome, many were turned away when they asked to be taken in. Above all, with hindsight, we know the outcome of the war. People at the time did not. For the English victory was a reaffirmation of their global power and chosen national status. For residents in German cities like Dresden, who suffered blanket bombing and who ended the war defeated and humiliated, the price they had paid along the way was assuredly much too high. By the end of the war some 400,000 British civilians and combatants were dead, and the same number of Americans; but 4 million Germans died, even more Poles, and a staggering 20 million Russians.

No-one could have predicted the carnage of the world wars of the first half of the twentieth century. The 32.5 million people of 1901 had increased to 43.75 million by 1951, war having prevented a census being taken in 1941 for the only time since censuses began in 1801, such was the disruption and uncertainty of the time. What would a Nazi invader have done with all that information on ages, relationships and in particular places of birth and subject status? Although the world had changed and the empire on which sun never set in 1901 was still largely intact, there was no doubt that the future promised very much more change even than the horrors of the wars had done.

12

Consensus and Conflict,
1945–2003

> Here is a country that fought and won a noble war, disman-
> tled a mighty empire in a generally benign and enlightened
> way, created a far-seeing welfare state – in short did nearly
> everything right – and then spent the rest of the century
> looking on itself as a chronic failure.
>
> Bill Bryson, 1995

At the end of the Second World War, England was victorious,
but in economic disarray. The cost of Churchill's 'Victory at any
price' had indeed been high, Britain was deeply mired in
American debt, and the contrast was marked between the
British economy and the American where a high standard of
living built on the war-economy had dispersed the 1930s cloud
of depression and unemployment. There is no doubt that
American equipment was simple, but often effective, as their
Ford motor cars proved in the pre-war era. American-made
lightly armed, speedy tanks, for example, contributed to defeating Rommel after British tanks, superior in specifications, had
failed to keep going in the inhospitable terrain of the desert.

The American post-war agenda was clear, in return for helping Britain out financially and with lend-lease on equipment from 1941 after Churchill's impassioned plea to Congress to 'Give us the tools and we will finish the job', the Americans wanted a *quid pro quo*. They wanted a generous slice, if not all, of British imperial markets. In 1945 the State Department (the American Foreign Office) was determined to see the end of the British empire, the weapon it deployed was the debts owed by Britain in 1945. Some far-sighted British people, such as Keynes, who found himself bearing the burden of British negotiations after the Second World War as he had after the First World War, could see the way the wind was blowing. But his Herculean efforts to retain independence and power within the Atlantic alliance were to no avail. In the end he died in 1946 before he could save his country: 'He gave his life for his country as surely as if he had fallen on the field of battle'. America, with its atomic bombs, first used to ghastly effect over Japan, was left as the most powerful nation on earth, but soon to be challenged in an arms race which saw Russia, China and other nations establish a nuclear capability. The British came to rely on a nuclear arsenal purchased from the Americans.

Churchill had indeed won the war, but returning soldiers brought an overwhelming desire for reform and change. They were deeply conscious of the largely unfulfilled promises of 'homes fit for heroes' handed down from the ruling classes after the First World War. After a second bloody war the soldiers wanted to be part of the decision-making process of change. Former prisoners, for example some of those captured at Singapore where some 100,000 British troops laid down their arms, had been humiliated with inhuman conditions by the Japanese on the Burma Railway. Others, who had been in Germany, had had a more varied experience, some young officers having continued their legal and medical training courtesy of the Red Cross while prisoners of war. Those soldiers who survived the bloody invasion of Normandy, had defeated Rommel's *Afrika Corps*, had fought their way north through Italy. Sailors who had seen their mates disappear into frozen northern waters on the Atlantic or Russian convoys, and the airmen who had contributed so much to the victory, were modest heroes who wanted change at home. Great war leader though he was, the patrician Churchill born at Blenheim Palace in 1874, was comprehensively defeated in the July 1945 election: he was probably already too old at seventy-one to see the radical change required in the country.

Clement Attlee at the head of a Labour government took power. It was Attlee, therefore, who represented Britain at the Potsdam conference with America and Russia. While no Communist, Attlee was more sympathetic to Stalin than was Churchill who had advocated joining with the Germans – another reason for anxiety among the troops who saw a new war agenda unfolding – to drive back the Communists in Europe. Stalin had all the cards in his hands: his Red Army had overrun Poland and much of Germany including Berlin which now lay deep in Russian territory, and the new American president, Harry Truman, was inexperienced and untried. So Russia, which had lost 20 million people during the war came to control eastern Europe where Communism reigned untrammelled and the scene was set for another conflict, the 'Cold War' against Communism which was to last until the penetration of the 'Iron Curtain', epitomised by the destruction in 1989 of the Berlin Wall. This mighty structure had divided east from west Berlin, soon afterwards its demolition, the Communist regimes in the Russian satellite states of eastern Europe collapsed and a measure of democratisation of Russia began under Mikhail Gorbachev.

The foundation of the Welfare State, designed to provide support for people from cradle to grave against disease, lack of education, poverty and unemployment, had been laid in the war years, set out in the proposals of the surprisingly bestselling Beveridge Report of 1942, and following the principles of Keynesian economics in which, in the great economist's experience, those who had served in the world wars should be repaid by government policies of full employment. The broadly based Beveridge recommendations were already beginning to be put into effect in 1944 when the Education ('Butler') Act, raised the school leaving age from fourteen to sixteen and provided free education beyond that age at school, college and university. Rapid implementation of Beveridge, published just as the tide of the war began to turn in the allies favour, was encouraged by the sacrifice and bravery of the people during war whether as civilians or in the armed forces. It was also enhanced by the influence of Socialism which, while diluted compared to the Communism of Russia and China, was a key influence in twentieth-century Britain and Europe.

England experienced a number of remarkable developments in the post-war years in the internal dynamics and organisation of the country. England's population in 1951 was under 41 million, (out of 50 million, including Scotland and Wales); by 1971 England was over 46 million with an excess of 1.3 million women over men (out of a total of 54 million).

The National Health Service, founded under the Labour government in 1948, has developed since to become the greatest employer in the land. A socialist agenda is seen in the nationalisation of industries such as the railways (written into the companies' original privatisation), the mines and the docks. Similarly, half a century later, the development of roads (following the Nazi *autobahns*) was a national project, initiated by the M1, begun in March 1958 to join London to northern England. Public ('Council') housing which had begun early in the century was pursued with more vigour, if with little aesthetic taste: brutal, faceless, metal window-framed blocks began to appear with increasing frequency. If housing was a social issue it was also a political one with Herbert Morrison aiming to 'build the Tories out of London' in the post-war years. Thus the house in Stoke Newington where Thomas Hancock had discovered the process of the vulcanisation of rubber, damaged by bombing during the V1 and V2 raids, was among many such properties that were swept away and replaced by blocks of London County Council housing. The post-war years were a time of austerity, with rationing continuing until the mid-1950s. But gradually economic circumstances improved, pre-war levels of exports were achieved in 1950 and in 1951. Also in 1951 the Festival of Britain celebrated (somewhat mutedly) the country's arts and sciences, and provided the first opportunity to become economically a part of Europe, but neither the Conservatives nor Labour, were interested.

Britain continued to be pulled this way and that by on the one hand American capitalism, with its attractive materialist message, its developing 'youth culture', powerful military arsenal and common language. Against this American

siren-voice was the world of European politics and economics, with more Socialist (or in case of Spain almost National
Socialist, or fascist dictatorship) totalitarian tendencies. This
conflict remains the stuff of British politics to this day. At first
the British were tied to America by its mountain of debt, but
gradually over the half-century as Europe became more united
in a variety of ways, Britain has moved closer to Europe.
Harold Macmillan, as prime minister, characterised the
Conservative rule of the late 1950s as delivering such prosperity that the British people had 'never had it so good'. Harold
Wilson in the 1960s struck a blow for British independence
from America by keeping Britain out of the ill-conceived,
destructive and ultimately disastrous Vietnam War.

In the world of post-war British politics the five-year full
election term shadowed Communist five-year plans, although
the Conservatives got off to a flying start with a string of
election victories from 1951–64. In domestic policy Keynesian
full employment was the aim, whatever the cost, and whether
the government was Conservative or Labour up to 1979. In
foreign policy the twin issues of the Empire/Commonwealth
on the one hand and the America/Europe debate on the
other dominated, with emphasis on trade underpinned by
the issue of the maintenance of an independent sterling
currency. Part of the thinking in this matter concerned the
relations with the Commonwealth, and the sustaining of a
'Sterling Area', which successive governments have perceived
as an essential element of Britain's world-power status.

While England put its affairs in order after the war, the
empire did not stand still. India under Gandhi was pressing
for independence with a concerted display of civil disobedi-
ence and obstruction of British rule. Independence was not

a new idea, it had been contemplated in the 1930s, but was delayed by the war. In August 1947 independence was achieved, hastily. Ten months ahead of the timetable set in 1946, the flag was lowered and the dominions of India (with an overwhelming Hindu population) and Pakistan (largely Muslim) came into being. The end of empire in the sub-continent as elsewhere was to begin with a bloodbath in which 500,000 Muslims, Hindus and Sikhs died – including the murdered Gandhi, a prime mover in the independence movement and advocate of peaceful opposition.

In the same year Britain, which had held a mandate in Palestine since 1918, was struggling to manage the conflicting aspirations of Arabs and Jews. At the end of the First World War the Arabs, who had fought on the British side in the hope of gaining an Arab state in Palestine, were in the ascendant, but had been thwarted in their aims by an unexpected British commitment in 1917 to establish a 'national home for the Jewish people'. In 1919 10 per cent (the very small total of 50,000) of the population of Palestine was Jewish; by 1939 29 per cent were. The events of the war in which millions of European Jews had been exterminated had significantly enhanced public sympathy in American and Western Europe for Jews. In addition their worldwide (and often wealthy) diaspora gave Jews the political upper hand. The British despaired of finding a solution and were summarily stopped by the Americans from limiting Jewish immigration. They handed in their mandate to the United Nations and marched out of Palestine. The Jews immediately declared the forma-tion of the state of Israel and survived a retaliatory invasion by neighbouring Arab states. Thus a minority of the popula-tion of Palestine, continually increased by immigration and with the power and resources to purchase and develop land, gradually and despite United Nations resolutions, cemented the state of Israel in place. Balfour's declaration in 1917 set the scene for a century of conflict and inter-Semitic violence, which continues to this day. Contemporaries in the 1940s correctly predicted that no good would come of the hasty and confused end of the Palestine mandate.

Britain realised that it could no longer hold the world together, and rapidly from the 1940s onwards Commonwealth states were granted – or as in the case of South Africa which declared a republic, seized – their independence from Britain. The loose economic confederation of the Commonwealth keeps countries in touch, brings them together in sporting events and exerts pressure more or less effectively in states where politics, or economics, take a severe downward turn. This state of affairs is seen by many cynics as a sham. However, what the British have done is to hand over their own culture and language, and in many cases their Church of England traditions to millions across the world. To see what becomes of these traditions – parliamentary democracy, for example, it is much too early to judge.

The British loosening of control in Africa brought 200 years and more of colonisation to an end: seven nations were independent by 1960 – some, such as parts of northern Nigeria had only been gently colonised on an 'if you please' basis from shortly before the First World War. Harold Macmillan's 1960 speech to the South African parliament which focused on the 'wind of change' blowing through the continent of Africa recognised change, and the potential for change. Whites in Rhodesia took power into their own hands by making a Unilateral Declaration of Independence in 1965, but that was not a long-lived experiment and a black government under the increasingly controversial Robert Mugabe took over the country when white domination ceased.

As the states of the Commonwealth gained independence, and the old Dominions such as Australia turned more to their regions and began to debate the status of the queen as a distant 'ruler', Britain began to take the idea of joining in a partnership in Europe more seriously. As Britain had rejected the idea of joining the European steel confederation in 1951, we had made no contribution to the fundamental treaty of Rome in 1957. Britain subsequently found it difficult to join, being rejected both in 1961 and 1969 before finally gaining acceptance in 1973 under the Conservative prime minister, Edward Heath. This was a timely move as the United States was in turmoil with the collapse of the Nixon regime and the end of the Vietnam War. Britain could see advantages in joining with Europe and Vietnam had demonstrated beyond doubt the potential disadvantages of joining America in a 'world policemen' role. Europe looked enticing.

However, many Britons remained unconvinced and divisions exist both in the Conservative and Labour parties to this day. Continental European nations have gradually drawn closer together especially with the development of a single currency, the Euro, which became the continental Euro-states' and the Republic of Ireland's currency in 2002 when coins and notes were first issued. In Britain in the 1970s what has become called 'euro-scepticism' was one of the reasons why Edward Heath's Conservative government lost the election.

Labour came to power in the 1960s with an expectation that after 'thirteen years of Tory misrule' the clock might be turned back to the Labour statist implementation of

Beveridge, to which the Tories had subscribed only half-heartedly on the basis that all should have an equal right to remain unequal. Both government and party depended heavily on the support of the trade unions, which in turn demanded and got concessions from the government. By the 1960s and even more so by the 1970s the age of post-war consensus was over: a new generation had emerged who had not fought in the wars and to whom it appeared that rights were infinitely more important than responsibilities.

The old Keynesian world was gone. Wages spiralled upwards, the country's productivity fell and industries such as steel and shipbuilding were far out-priced by countries across the world, including, irritatingly for the British, West Germany and Japan who had *lost* the war. Labour presided over a devaluation of the pound, a great blow to those who sought the holy grail of a sterling currency-based international economy. People were deeply suspicious that devaluation had led to significant price rises despite Prime Minister Harold Wilson's reassurances that the 'pound in your pocket' was worth the same as before. Labour was turned out in 1970 and Edward Heath succeeded with a Conservative administration. Heath, a grammar-school and Oxford meritocrat, decided to face up to the power of the trade unions whose insistence on increased wages, over-manning and restrictive practices were contributing to the strangulation of British production. Heath lost the battle and the 1974 election, and thus presided over the end of 'One Nation Conservatism'. He had brought about an odd assortment of achievements which included the nationalisation of Rolls-Royce, an icon of Britishness, and had led the country at the third attempt into the Common Market of Europe. This

European agenda was confirmed by a 67 per cent vote in favour staying in the Common Market when the anti-European Wilson government held a referendum in 1974. During this Socialistic period, from the late 1960s the Beatles emerged as part of a resurgent English popular culture which has been seen as a recapturing for the English (albeit by Anglo-Irish Liverpudlians) from a dominant American youth scene.

Harold Wilson had returned to office inheriting rapidly rising debts, unemployment and inflation of 17 per cent, and rising rapidly. For two years the government struggled with financial meltdown. Wilson, probably realising his health was deteriorating, suddenly and unexpectedly resigned as prime minister in 1976, and was replaced by James Callaghan. To counter rising wages and demands Labour raised taxes inexorably. In April 1978 those whose earnings exceeded £25,000 were taxed at 83 per cent (the prime minister earned just over £20,000), and even a salary of £750 was taxed at 22 per cent. The government was retaliating to inflated wage demands by recapturing the money through taxation, as union support for the government was predicated on the condition that there should be no legally enforceable incomes policy. However, other assets, such as rapidly rising house values gave the public a sense of security. The new prime minister's attempts to curb union demands, without an incomes policy led to strikes and a stalemate and the winter of 1978–79 saw rubbish piling on the streets and became dubbed 'the winter of discontent', with all those Shakespearean connotations of the evil (northern) king, Richard III.

Callaghan was obliged to seek a new mandate and was heavily defeated by the Conservatives under their new leader, a former Oxford University chemistry graduate and daughter of a shopkeeper in Grantham (Lincolnshire). Margaret Thatcher was the first female prime minister in Europe. Mrs Thatcher began to attack the problems around her with great vigour. She confronted the unions, extended the policy of 'monetarism' (government control of the money supply, but otherwise non-intervention in the economy, in rejection of Keynesian interventionism) which Callaghan had begun to test, introduced new taxes and declared that in her own philosophy there 'was no such thing as society'. Thatcherism was born and was, at first, not at all popular. Indeed within two years of being elected she was polled as the most unpopular prime minister ever. Her short whirl-wind reign appeared likely to end as suddenly as it had burst upon the scene.

But foreign affairs came to her rescue. In 1981 the Argentinian leader General Galtieri suddenly and unexpect-edly attacked the Falkland Islands, in the South Atlantic, formerly useful as a naval coaling station in the days of empire, and which had entered national consciousness more recently as the graveyard of Brunel's ship *Great Britain* which had been rescued and restored in Bristol. Without hesitation Mrs Thatcher's government reacted by assembling a 'task force' consisting of warships and their supply ships, and a number of commandeered merchant ships including, as a troop car-rier, the country's greatest liner the *QEII*. The nation was sharply divided over whether troops should be sent so long a distance with such extended lines of communication: parlia-ment was recalled for a Saturday sitting. However once the task force had set off the nation was obliged to wait and see. In the event, despite numbers of deaths from missile strikes and ground actions, and the loss of ships (including the

Sheffield, originally commissioned by the Argentinians them-selves) the expedition was a total success. The Falklands were recaptured, the Argentinian invasion force surrendered and Mrs Thatcher swept back to power with a much-increased parliamentary majority.

In her second and third terms this indefatigable woman continued to batter the unions, in 1984 defeating the miners under their fearlessly misguided leader Arthur Scargill, and leaving a residue of much bitterness. Mrs Thatcher's govern-ment was blessed with the windfall of North Sea oil. This was kept out of the exclusive control of the Scots who felt, with some justification, that they had a claim to it. One of the unan-swered questions about the 1980s and 1990s is 'Where did the money from North Sea oil go?' When the public records are opened after thirty years, an answer may emerge and that answer may be that it went on unemployment benefit for the millions who were kept on the dole in obeisance to Thatcherist non-intervention in the economy as monetarist policies drove industry to the wall, and to focus the country's minds on a dif-ferently structured world of work. She also pursued the policy of privatisation of nationalised industries such as coal, elec-tricity, gas and water. This was aimed to produce a new nation of small shareholders in the stock-market, as well as providing income for the government. The shares were priced at a comparatively low level and many people cashed in on their shareholdings as prices rose. Time has shown that in certain respects Thatcher's 'market economy' was misconceived: severe problems on the railways which were fragmented with no repository of overall responsibility, of the nuclear power indus-try and of electricity companies, some of the latter bought up by foreign business men with little interest in customer service in a crisis. The nation was transfixed by Thatcherism, but even senior Conservatives were taken aback by the pressing home of the sale of public assets, one presciently describing it as the 'sale of the family silver' which the nation would regret. A sharp contemporary poet wrote (in homage to T.S. Eliot whose cat-poetry had proved a huge success on the London stage as *Cats*):

> *My name is Moggie Thatcher, I'm a biter and a scratcher,*
> *I'm renowned for landing on my feline feet*
> *I'm the grocer's puss from Grantham who became the National Anthem*
> *And I like expensive cuts of public meat…*

The end of Mrs Thatcher's golden age or tyranny, depending on your viewpoint, came not at the hands of the country but at the hands some of her own party who decided that she had become an electoral liability and plotted against her to secure her downfall. Her stridency over Europe, which had brought benefits in reduced British contributions early on, but was subsequently perceived as a liability by 1990 when members of her party wanted, utterly misguidedly as it turned out, to join the European Exchange Rate Mechanism (ERM), was a key issue in her downfall and in the increasing weakness of the Conservative Party. Mrs Thatcher left Downing Street in tears.

If Mrs Thatcher represented what Napoleon had termed the '*boutiquier*' (shopkeeper) element of the English, her successor John Major who won an unprecedented fourth term of office for the Conservatives, came from a most unusual background, the son of a trapeze artist and circus performer. Major unlike his Oxford-educated predecessors had no academic pretensions and no degree, and represented an emerging breed of career politicians, rather than professionals who had come into politics. However, he combined some central English male characteristics, a love of cricket and warm beer. These core English characteristics appealed to an English electorate, especially as neither was in any associated with Americanism. Major stood for decency and fair play (although later it emerged that he was less than moral, in his private life). Major held the party together, but his 'back to basics' campaign, a kind of moral crusade to rediscover family values, was derided at the time as paternalistic towards a modern society enjoying an end-of-millennium fling. With this unwise foray onto the moral high ground, the Tories exposed themselves to the potential of scandals. First one MP and then another was brought low by a hail of allegations. MPs who tried to cover up or deny their misdemeanours were hounded by the press. Paradoxically Alan Clark, who confessed his sins both to God and to the public in his published *Diaries* was richly rewarded by book sales to the public, which helped financially to prop up his castle (from which the knights had set out to murder Becket in 1170, that first spark of the English Reformation) while the shares in the family Scottish textile firm collapsed around him as work transferred to the Far East. Was it Clark's love of animals (rather than people) which endeared him the public? Maybe to English readers it mattered little that he loved Mrs Thatcher, treated most of his political colleagues with disdain, and loathed local party officials and constituents, what really mattered was his love of animals and birds and defence of their rights.

By the 1997 election the Tories were on the skids and were defeated by 417 to 165 seats. The New Labour government, under the guitar-strumming Tony Blair, had youth and vibrancy, and wisely made no claims to moral supremacy. They continued many Tory policies, including privatisation and monetarism, and cashed in on a stock-market spiralling upwards at the end of the millennium and were rewarded by the electorate with a sufficient majority to allow, for the first time, a full second term of a Labour government. When Tony Blair was elected 'politician of the year' 2002 by the readers of the *Spectator*, edited by the Conservative MP Boris Johnson, the Scottish Nationalist, Alex Salmond commented that this accolade was not surprising as Blair was 'the best Tory Prime Minister the party has ever had'. Thus in the new millennium politics has returned to the middle ground of One Nation Conservatism of the 1950s, but the electorate has shown a decreasing interest with such consensus politics.

Despite moral crusades by politicians, and the rise of fundamentalist religious tendencies throughout the world, Britain has overall become a less cohesive religious nation in the last fifty years. Already by 1970 over half of marriages were contracted in civil Register Offices, and only 30 per cent in Church of England establishments. More recently legislation has opened up a broad variety of places where people may marry, from stately homes to historic naval ships. Vigorous religious minorities follow a plethora of religious beliefs and practices, many brought by people who have migrated from the countries of the former empire contributing to multicultural Britain in which festivals such as Chinese New Year and Divali are widely celebrated alongside New Year and Guy Fawkes on 5 November. Between 1990 and 2000 the number of children born outside a legal partnership rose from 30 to 40 per cent, showing a palpable change in attitudes towards family life.

When large areas of our cities lay exposed by enemy bombing at the end of the Second World War a unique opportunity arose for the investigation of urban archaeology. This resulted in a large amount of fieldwork by great names such as the indefatigable O.G.S. Crawford, who championed dirt archaeology and derided 'clean-booted historians'. In the cities great progress was made in the understanding of Roman urban living and dying, and for the first time Saxon towns were investigated, and found to include street plans, large stone churches and, notably in the 'burhs' of *c*.900, effective defences. These discoveries sparked a revival in interest about the Anglo-Saxons, the original English, which has been sustained since. Medieval towns were investigated at Northampton and Southampton, at York and Winchester and in 1957 a Society of Medieval Archaeology was established to save medieval layers from those who would dig straight down to Roman finds. In the countryside work which had been initiated before the war on rural settlement of all periods was continued. Great programmes of building at Heathrow and other airports, on motorways and bypasses, all contributed to a vast collection of new data on all periods. These new creations will themselves be the archaeological sites of the future: airports, electricity lines, sports stadia, hospitals, motorways schools, shops and universities. Some classes of monument were severely reduced in numbers. Social change such as a decline in servants, death-duty legislation and damage caused by requisition during two world wars took a heavy toll of country houses of which many hundreds were demolished, mostly unrecorded, in the decades after 1945. Legislation brought about the closure of many great Victorian institutions such as asylums for the mentally ill, which mostly disappeared without trace. The decline in church attendance coupled with financial troubles have left many chapels and increasing numbers of churches redundant, offering opportunities for archaeologists to record and investigate them, as they head for oblivion or for use in new ways.

The archaeology of late twentieth-century Britain has been shaped by legislation, notably planning legislation in the late 1980s which put the onus on developers to fund archaeology from excavation to post-excavation and publication on their sites. Archaeology has all but ceased to be a state enterprise, although English Heritage retains an overall body of responsibility. A key development in this period has been the emergence of television archaeology, especially the hugely popular and successful *Time Team* first broadcast in 1992, led by archaeologists Mick Aston and Carenza Lewis, with their disingenuous amateur-archaeologist link-man, Tony Robinson. The team has progressed all over the country dealing in their short weekend excavations with sites from the prehistoric to the present. Their efforts have brought archaeology into millions of homes and all on an educational budget, demonstrating that scholarly archaeologists (Mick from Bristol University, Carenza from Cambridge) can make their complex and often scientific world intelligible to a wide public. Programmes such as these have proved a showcase for archaeological techniques, not only the science of stratigraphy (layers of earthly meaning), but also of geophysics (showing anomalies below the surface caused by remains of buildings etc), dendrochronology (tree-ring dating) and even studies of DNA. One secret of their success, and that of sister programmes such as Julian Richards's *Meet the Ancestors* and *Blood of the Vikings*, is that archaeology is rarely the study of the great and the good. In the century of the common man, archaeology has hit the button in providing insights into the culture of the ordinary unnamed millions who have trodden this island before us, revealing their artefacts, buildings, cemeteries and ceramics. Techniques of archaeology are applicable not only to prehistoric sites, but also to castles and even to post-medieval sites, such as Blaenavon in Wales. This remote industrial agglomeration, high in the Welsh valleys, was recently declared a World Heritage site because of surviving remains of industrial landscapes from the eighteenth to the twentieth century. There is nothing on the same scale left in England to match that landscape, which has survived through that most gentle of processes, benign neglect.

Where next in this changing, self-renewing English society in the television age? Devolution of powers to Scottish and Welsh assemblies under Labour has begun to throw differences into relief between those who govern Wales (no longer to be called 'the Principality'), Scotland (increasingly referred to as a 'nation') and England. Preferential treatment of old people in Scotland, compared with their English counterparts and abolition of university tuition fees (unless a student comes from England) are beginning to show differences of emphasis north and south of the border. Declining income from North Sea oil and the post-millennium stockmarket crash promise less gravy in the future, especially as the natural assets of North Sea oil and gas will be at an end by 2020 when gas will have to come from further away, from Russia, for example, and oil from the strife-torn Middle East. Is there a future for coal? Thus at the beginning of the new millennium, England and Britain as a whole, face a key decision in choosing between the way of America (as 'Constable' to the America's 'Sergeant' in the hierarchy of 'world police-men') and the way of Europe. But Britain may be 'too Socialist' for the Americans, and 'too American' and capitalist for the Europeans. Sooner or later the decision must be made: a quarter of a century ago the American experience in Vietnam was a determining factor in a lurch towards Europe, will it be economics, demography or politics and foreign affairs – maybe experience as an American ally in the war in Iraq – which will force the next decision on procrastinating old Britannia?

Epilogue
England and the English

The English come from two traditions which have vied for ascendancy for 2,000 years. First there is the rural tradition of farmstead and woodland folk, dating back into prehistory, codified into law by the long-haired, heathen Anglo-Saxons from c.AD 450. Second there is the short-haired, urban tradition which coalesces in our Roman and Christian heritage. These two traditions are visible today in the English language which often has a monosyllabic Germanic word and a longer Latin with the same meaning (e.g. build; construct). They are also visible in society, with the country people marching for 'liberty' established by their Germanic forebears 1,500 years ago in clearings in the forest – and against urban values of today's descendants of the Roman tradition.

Only in the heady days of empire in the late nineteenth century did it appear that from the moment of their arrival the English were destined for imperial achievements beyond the wildest dreams of the Romans. First they exterminated the Britons on their lands in southern and eastern England, then they imposed English on the babbling Welsh-Britons.

This was but one parallel with the achievements of the ancient Rome by the 'empire of New Rome', as London appeared to be after 1850. The gibberish and linguistic collapse of the conquered Britons was a clear parallel with the experience of the Romans when confronted by incomprehensible barbarian languages as they extended their empire.

The problem with this interpretation is that there must have been a residual population of Britons in the Anglo-Saxon south and east of the country, who acquired English overlords. There must have been intermarriage and the Anglo-Saxon English subsequently submitted to Viking, Norman, Welsh, Scots and German overlords.

As the racial purity origins argument is flawed, a better analogy between the decline of the British and Roman empires, is that from the fifth century, and before, the English developed Roman institutions in their own way within a crumbling infrastructure which local resources could not sustain. This residual civilisation was owned by the inhabitants of England, and passed down to their descendants after the collapse of Roman power. It was a significant element in the development of England: the built environment of Anglo-Saxon England, of churches for example, owed much to robbed Roman ruins. Only time will tell if the British empire left a lasting legacy, both institutional and material, in those formerly pink-painted areas of the world when the dust has settled and the blood-letting is over. India is often praised as a multi-faith parliamentary democracy, today despite its bloody birth experience in 1947. There is no doubt that the legacy of empire is mixed: fledgling democracies and parliaments in the former empire may or may not stand the test of time, but have lasted now for generations in some countries;

certainly the English language it is often asserted is better spoken in Africa, the sub-continent and the West Indies than it is in England. At sport European nations and South Americans outplay the English at football. Australians and West Indians have consistently been better at cricket than the English. A judge recently commented while summing up in the case of a man who had failed to behead a statue of Mrs Thatcher with a cricket bat (he succeeded with another weapon), that he epitomised the Englishman with a cricket bat as 'a total disaster'.

The empire showed that Britain, of which the English always formed the vast majority of the population, was capable of ruling the world. The empire showed how things might be done properly and was overall, despite dark moments such as the Amritsar massacre, a resounding success. Attempts to emulate the British empire were notoriously unsuccessful – the USSR and its satellites held together by Communist ideology and brute force; or the Third Reich, fascinating in its ambitious aim, to last a 1,000 years, but which survived little more than ten! The Americans are the only super-power at present, and therefore do not need to negotiate, their take-it or leave-it style being unpalatable to many.

If the Romans imposed an imperial religion in Christianity from the fourth century, they permitted a range of other religions which shared certain characteristics – such as east-west burials in the worship of Sol, for example. At the heart of historic Englishness is the Church of England, with a similar wide-Church approach. Anglo-Catholics sustain religious 'high-church' practice which the Catholics themselves have lost. Charismatics and evangelicals are now in a majority among the laity. They study their bibles and consider themselves 'properly converted' or 'born again'. In this understated national religion extremism is anathema – as was so keenly felt by that formidable duo, Albemarle the General and Clarendon the Chancellor who restored he monarchy and with it the Church of England in 1660. That is not to say that dissent has not continued to flourish whether of the Catholic or the nonconformist variety. Curiously today it is probably the case that contemporary Roman Catholics are even more establishment than the leaders Church of England. All the current party-political leaders are Catholics or incline to Roman Catholicism. In recent years a kaleidoscope of world religions has come with migrants from former imperial territories and beyond, as well as from within the English population itself. Ancient and modern religions have developed side-by-side with the mainstream from druidism and paganism to bizarre beliefs in alien abduction and much else besides. Religious toleration is a foundation of English society and therein lies the paradox of the English. They are intolerant of foreign countries and their inhabitants, but at home they would rather be ruled by foreign dynasties from within these islands or without; they willingly submit to Irish, Jewish, Scots and Welsh politicians and business people rather than their English counterparts. When they buy from a telephonic call centre they are more likely to purchase from an Indian or a Scots voice than from an English one. Apparently then, they don't trust one another. But when drawn into conflict all this is laid aside. As football supporters they are uniquely wild; cricket has spawned the 'barmy army' who drink and sing their way round the world in the wake of their cricketing heroes. English rugby crowds, oddly considering their new-found success in this sport, are characterised by their quiet enjoyment of this most physical of sports.

If England has sustained its Church since the sixteenth century and now finds solace for gloom and ecstasy in sport, the vast majority of Ireland has sustained its more ancient Catholic beliefs. The Church in Wales is disestablished, and the Welsh maintain a high level of religious nonconformity. In England it is enough to attend Communion from time to time. Among the changes at the Reformation which particularly appealed to the English was that thenceforward they could enjoy, or at least taste, the alcoholic contents of the Communion cup. This led to the wholesale destruction of small medieval chalices, but their larger replacements are a valued class of artefacts in their own right. In Scotland the Church, in true Calvinist fashion, invites individuals to the Lord's table. If you do not get an invitation you cannot go. If England is divided from Scotland on this, by what greater gap is it divided from America, where the strong nonconformist religion has developed an overwhelming fundamentalist bent. This is based on a biblical sense of right and wrong; it is straightforward and clear to its exponents who claim God as their inspiration. How far from English muddling through and compromise. The English have learnt the art of compromise and of negotiation.

People have trodden English landscapes for over 500,000 years. Fortunately we cannot see into the future. Could another climatic catastrophe be on the way, such as the ice-ages which engulfed England and which reduced life to hunting excursions across the ice-cap? Global warming, paradoxically, could make England much colder and could swamp large areas with the waters of melting ice caps and rising seas. There is nothing new that is not old. Biological and nuclear threats, if carried out, may send people scurrying to see what happened in the era of the medieval Black Death which changed the face of medieval England, or back to the plague of Justinian which devastated sixth-century England. There is much to be discussed in the story of England by, and between, followers of rural and urban traditions but the message is clear: natural and biological disasters change the course of history.

Chronology

Date	Events	Developments
500,000 BC	Earliest human remains in Britain (Boxgrove, Sussex)	Old Stone Age: hunter gatherers eat (raw?) meat, flake stone tools; Most of Britain covered in three ice-ages
10,000–4000 BC	Land bridge with Europe swamped by water from melting ice (7000/6500 BC)	Old Stone Age: gives way to Middle Stone Age (7500 BC)
4000–2000 BC	New Stone Age monuments: Sweet Track (3807/3806 BC); Avebury, Stonehenge, Silbury after 3000 BC	Early farmers arrive and begin to build monuments.
2000–700 BC	Stone circle at Stonehenge	Bronze Age Beaker folk, round barrow burials
700 BC–AD 43	Julius Caesar investigates south-east England (55 BC); Claudius invades (AD 43)	Iron Age: Hill forts (Danebury); ports (Hengistbury). Resistance: Caractacus captured (50 BC), Boudicca's revolt (60 BC)
AD 100s	Hadrian's Wall built against Picts (painted people) after AD 122	Villa culture develops
AD 200s	Invasion of Caledonia (c.AD 208–211); rebellion of Allectus crushed (AD 290s)	Saxon Shore forts and *Classis Britannica* confront raiders
AD 300s	Constantine converts to Christianity (AD 312); Pagan Picts invade over Hadrian's Wall (AD 360)	Christianity official religion of Roman Empire
AD 400s	Romans cease assisting Britain (AD 410); Vortigern invites Angles, Saxons and Jutes (traditionally AD 449); King Arthur (c.AD 500); battle of Mount Badon	Germanic settlement of Southern and Eastern England

Chronology

Date	Events	Developments
AD 500s (AD 560–616 Ethelbert, king of Kent)	Missionaries: St Ninian, St Columba (AD 565) in Scotland; St Augustine in Kent (AD 596–597)	Plague in Britain (c.AD 530–550). End of urban culture
AD 600s (c.632–655 Penda, king of Mercia)	Paulinus in Northumbria (AD 627); Sutton Hoo ship burial (c.AD 630); Birinus in Wessex (AD 635); Synod of Whitby settles disputes between Celtic and Roman Christians (AD 663)	Early monasticism at Lindisfarne
AD 700s (c. 757–96 Offa, king of Mercia, 'Rex Anglorum')	Bede's *Ecclesiastical History* (c.731); Viking raids begin (c.790)	'Heptarchy' seven Anglo-Saxon kingdoms; Offa's Dyke built between Mercia and Wales
AD 800s (AD 802–839 Egbert, king of Wessex)	Wessex conquers Mercia (AD 829)	Viking attacks continue and settlements begin;
(AD 871–899 Alfred, king of Wessex)	Alfred captures London (AD 886)	Alfred halts Danish advances
AD 900s (AD 924–939 Athelstan, king of Wessex)	Wessex defeats Irish, Scots, Welsh and Vikings (AD 937); Edgar first king of England (AD 973);	Ecclesiastical reform from AD 960;
(AD 978–1016 Ethelred the Unready, king of Wessex)	Viking raids intensify (AD 980–1016)	Danish resurgence after AD 980
1000 (1016–35 Cnut, king of England)	Ashingdon: final British defeat	England part of Danish kingdom. Norman (Romanesque) architecture (c.1050–1200)
1050 (1042–66 Edward the Confessor, king of England)	Norman Conquest of England (1066);	Normans conquer and establish castles to control England; Raids into Scotland, Wales and Ireland; New monastic orders: Cluniac, Augustinian etc.
(1066–87 William I)	Domesday Book (1086)	
(1087–1100 William II)		

Date	Events	Developments
1100 (1100–35 Henry I)	White Ship disaster: Henry I's heir is drowned (1119)	Sons of William the Conqueror consolidate Norman rule but lack of male heir leads to civil war on Henry's death; David I (1124–53) Normanises Scotland
1150 (1135–54 Stephen)		Anarchy of Stephen's reign;
(1154–89 Henry II) (1189–99 Richard I) (1199–1216 John)	Constitutions of Clarendon: dispute with Becket begins (1164); Becket murdered (1170); Richard I has two coronations (1189, 1194)	Henry II rules from border of Scotland to the Pyrenees; Richard away crusading for almost all his reign.
1200 (1216–72 Henry III)	Magna Carta sealed by John (1215)	Early English Architecture: first Gothic (c.1200–1300); Commercial and agrarian prosperity; Salisbury Cathedral 1220–1275
1250 (1272-1307 Edward I)	Simon de Montfort rebels (1258); Treaty of Paris: Henry III makes himself feudal subordinate of French king (1259); Barons' Wars (1260s); de Montfort defeated at Evesham (1265)	Edward I subdues Wales (1280s); Scots Wars of Independence (1290s); William Wallace and Robert the Bruce (1300); Scottish alliance with France
1300 (1307–27 Edward II) (1327–77 Edward III)	Scots victory at Bannockburn (1314) English victory at Halidon Hill (1333); Crécy: Edward III defeats French Scots defeated at Neville's Cross (1346); the Black Death (1348–51)	Decorated Architecture (c.1300–1400) Hundred Years War with France (1337–1453)
1350 (1377–99 Richard II) (1399–1413 Henry IV (Bolingbroke)	Poitiers: Black Prince defeats French (1356); Poll Tax (1377–81); Great Revolt (1381); Richard II's tyranny (1390s)	Population decline from c.4–6 million to 1–2 million (1350–1450); Geoffrey Chaucer's *Canterbury Tales* (1387)

Date	Events	Developments
1400 (1413–22 Henry V)	Henry V defeats French at Agincourt (1415); Conquest of Normandy by Henry V (1415–19); Treaty of Troyes (1420); Birth of Henry VI, heir (1421);	Perpendicular Architecture (c.1400-1500);
(1422–61 Henry VI)	Joan of Arc active (1420s); Burgundians make peace with France: England isolated (1435)	English efforts in France begin to fail
1450 (1461-70 Edward IV) (1470-71 Henry VI) (1471-83 Edward IV)	English expelled from France (except Calais) (1453); First madness of Henry VI (1453); Wars of the Roses (1455–83);	Lancastrians (Henry VI) defeated by Yorkists (Edward IV, Richard III); Population down to 1–2 million
(1483-85 Richard III) (1485-1509 Henry VII)	Battle of Bosworth: Henry VII (Tudor) defeats and kills Richard III (1485)	Henry VII fends off rebellions and stabilises finance (1485–1509)
1500 (1509–47 Henry VIII) (1547–53 Edward VI)	Scots defeated at Flodden (1514); New Lay Subsidy Tax (1524); Dissolution of the Monasteries (1536–40). Execution of Anne Boleyn (1536); Act of Union with Wales (1536)	Enclosure of vacant lands for grazing; Henry VIII desperate for an heir breaks with Rome to head the Church of England; The Reformation; Religious pendulum swings from Protestant (Edward VI), with two prayer books issued (1549, 1552) to Catholic (Mary)
1550 (1553 Lady Jane Grey) (1553–58 Mary I) (1558–1603 Elizabeth I)	Mary marries Philip, heir to the Spanish throne (1554); Calais lost to France (1558); Reformation crystallises in Scotland (1559–60); Mary Queen of Scots executed (1587); Spanish Armada defeated (1588)	Religious settlement under Elizabeth is Protestant; Catholics plot against Elizabeth; Wars with Spain from 1585; Shakespeare's plays 1590–1612

Date	Events	Developments
1600 (1603–25 James VI of Scotland rules as James I)	Gunpowder Plot discovered (1605); Authorised Version of the Bible (1611); Pilgrim Fathers sail from Southampton to America (1620)	Tudor Poor Law defined (1598; 1601)
1625 (1625–49 Charles I) (1649–60 Interregnum)	Charles I rules without Parliament (1629–40); Civil War: Charles loses to Parliament (1642–49); Execution of Charles I (1649)	Population about 5 million; Religious divisions: England and Wales (Anglican); Scotland (Presbyterian); Ireland (Catholic); Scots covenant against bishops (1637); Closure of the theatres (1642)
1650 (1660–85 Charles II)	Oliver Cromwell rules (1653–58); Restoration of the monarchy (1660); Great Plague (1665); Great Fire of London (1666)	Civil War turns to Revolution with the abolition of the monarchy; Protectorate government conservative; Restoration liberal in drama and court intrigue
1675 (1685-88 James II) (1688-1702 William and Mary)	Glorious Revolution (1688); Battles of Boyne and Aughrim (1690, 1691) secure Protestantism	Continuing fear of Catholics leads to Glorious Revolution; Catholic James II deposed
1700 (1702–14 Anne) (1714–27 George I) (1727–60 George II)	Act of Settlement decrees Protestant monarchy (1701); Act of Union with Scotland (1707); Rising of Old Pretender James Stuart (1715); Robert Walpole first prime minister (1721)	War Spanish of Succession (1702–13): Britain and allies defeat France; Britain an agrarian society run for the landowners: male suffrage under 5 per cent
1725	Rising of Young Pretender, Bonnie Prince Charlie (1745); Culloden: British army defeats Jacobites (1746)	Population about 6 million

Chronology

Date	Events	Developments
1750 (1760–1820 George III)	Seven Years War (1746–63); Treaty of Paris acknowledges Britain as supreme world power (1763)	Industrial Revolution begins slowly after 1750; British expel French from North America and Clive victorious in India
1775	American Declaration of Independence (1776); War of Independence (1776–83); First convict fleet sent to Australia (1778)	Iron Bridge at Coalbrookdale, Shropshire (1779)
1800 (1820–30 George IV)	Act of Union joins Britain and Ireland (1801); Battle of Trafalgar (1805); Slave Trade abolished (1807); Waterloo: Wellington defeats Napoleon; Corn Laws tax grain imports to Britain (1815)	Napoleonic Wars: British victories prevent invasion; Unrest: Luddites attack factory machinery (1811–12); Cavalry massacre reformist crowd, Peterloo (1819)
1825 (1830–37 William IV) (1837–1901 Victoria)	Reform Bill abolishes some rotten boroughs, redistributes seats (1832); Repeal of Corn Laws (1846)	Railways: Stockton and Darlington (1825); Criminal Law reforms (1827): foundation of the Metropolitan Police (1829); Irish famine (1845–51)
1850	Great Exhibition (1851); Crimean War (1854-5); Second Reform Bills extends franchise to better-off workers (1874)	Victorian 'high farming'; Britain the workshop of the world
1875	Victoria Empress of India (1877)	Great Depression in farming and industry (1870–90s); Colonisation of Africa underway (1870–90s)

Date	Events	Developments
1900 (1901–10 Edward VI)	Boer War (1899–1902); Death of Victoria (1901);	Population under 30 million;
(1910–36 George V)	Scott Antarctic expedition and *Titanic* disasters (1912); First World War (1914–18)	Reminders of fallibility of Man against Nature; Influenza (1919); Miners' Strike (1921)
1925 (1936 Edward VIII)	General Strike (1926); Great Crash (1929–30);	
(1936–52 George VI)	Second World War (1939–45): Munich Agreement (1938)	Tides turns 1942; Beveridge Report on Welfare; Labour rule (1946–51); Independence for sub-continent (1947); Nationalisation of Railways, Electricity, etc. National Health Service founded (1948)
1950 (1952– Elizabeth II)	Festival of Britain (1951); Suez Crisis (1956); Treaty of Rome (1957); 'Wind of Change in Africa' (1960); Soviets put first man in space (1961); First man on the Moon (1969); Entry to Common Market (1973)	Population 41 million (1951); Conservative rule 1951–1964; End of post-war consensus: Cold War; Population 46 million (1971); End of Vietnam War (1973)
1975	'Winter of discontent' (1978–79); Falklands War (1981–82); Poll Tax (1989–91); End of Conservative rule (1997)	Conservative rule (1979–97); AIDS recognised (1981); North Sea oil abundant; Germany reunited (1990); Internet revolution; Monetarism and privatisation under Mrs Thatcher; 'Back to basics' (John Major, 1990s)
2000	Millennium of Christ's birth celebrated; World Trade Center attacked (2001)	Labour government pursues Conservative policies during first term; War in Afghanistan (2001); Britain/US axis strengthened; First Countryside March (2001)

Select Bibliography

The books listed here are a fraction of the many which deal with England's archaeological and historic past, some range more widely over the British Isles. The list provides a variety of personal views of England today (e.g. Bryson – an outsider, Paxman – an insider), surveys written at key points (e.g. Churchill 1930–50s; Green at height of empire etc., Trevelyan when existence of England under threat etc.). Archaeology is covered by Robinson and Aston (what it aims to do); Darvill (what happened when and who did it, Darvill, Stamper and Timby (key sites in England to 1600). The Royal Historical Society symposium on 'English Politeness' (2001) provided some insights. The work of many other historians has contributed to the text (for example, Sir Keith Thomas on the decline of magic), I thank them for their insights. Nothing covers England on its own from prehistory to the present.

Bede, *Ecclesiastical History of the English Nation* (*c*.731). The early history from a Christian standpoint.

Bryson, Bill, *Notes from a Small Island* (1995). Puzzled American divided from Britain by a common language.

Churchill, W.S., *History of the English Speaking Peoples* (1959). Materials collected in the 1930s, but interrupted by Second World War, completed and published in 1950s.

Darvill, Timothy, *The Concise Oxford Dictionary of Archaeology* (2002). Compendium of approaches, archaeologists, monuments and sites.

Darvill, Timothy, Paul Stamper and Jane Timby, *England* (2002, Oxford Archaeological Guides). Introduction and gazetteer down to 1600.

Davies, Norman, *The Isles* (1999).

Ferguson, Niall, *The Empire* (2003). Up-to-date account of the British empire.

Freeman, E.A. *The Historical Geography of Europe* (1882). Asserts the Aryan origins of Europe.

Gardiner, S.R., *A Student's History of England* (1892). Strong on Germanic origins.

Green, John Richard, *History of England* (1875)

Hills, Catherine, *Origins of the English* (2003). A brilliant interdisciplinary simplification of the complexities of transition from Roman Britain to Anglo-Saxon England.

Lee, Christopher, *This Sceptred Isle 55 BC to 1901* (1996). Radio history in tapes, cassettes and a book of printed source materials.

—, *This Sceptred Isle 1901-2000* (2000). Ditto for twentieth century.

Loyn, H.R. *The Making of the English Nation* (1991). Making the nation without Arthur.

Macfarlane, Alan, *The Origins of English Individualism* (1978). Traces back to the 1200s, uses anthropology and sociology.

Macaulay, T.B., *The History of England from the Accession of James II* (1848). Asserts Whiggish 'liberty, progress' arguments with England as top nation.

Maitland, F.W., *The Constitutional History of England* (1908). Lectures given in 1887–88 tracing English law back to *c*.600.

Marshall, H.E., *Our Island Story* (*c*.1930). Classic schoolroom history, mixing fact with fantasy. Unsympathetic to the Germans.

Milton, John, *The History of England, continu'd to the Norman Conquest* (1670). Under 'Trojan, Roman and Saxon rule'.

Paxman, Jeremy, *The English* (1998). Amusing literary character sketch of the English.

Pounds, N.J.G., *The Material Culture of England* (1994). Begins with the Iron Age.

Schama, Simon, *History of Britain* (2000). TV personal view, Romans onwards.

Robinson, Tony, and Mick Aston, *Archaeology is Rubbish* (2001). What is archaeology?

Strong, Roy, *The Story of Britain* (1996). 55BC to present, art-historical.

Taylor, Tim, and Chris Bennett, *Behind the Scenes at 'Time Team'* (2000)

Taylor, Tim, *The Ultimate 'Time Team' Companion: An Alternative History of Britain* (2001)

Taylor, Tim, et al., *Time Team's Timechester: A Family Guide to Archaeology* (2000)

Trevelyan, G.M., *Social History of England* (1944). Begins in AD 410.

List of Illustrations

The illustrations on the following pages are reproduced courtesy of Jonathan Reeve: 48, 51, 52, 54, 55, 68, 69, 76, 77, 80, 82, 85, 88 (top), 93, 101 (top), 102, 106, 107, 109 (top), 111, 112, 115, 117, 121, 125, 126 (bottom), 128, 130, 132, 135, 136, 138, 142, 144, 145, 148, 150, 155, 160, 161, 162, 165, 174, 177, 178, 189, 193, 203, 204, 208, 212, 214, 218.

The following plate numbers are also reproduced courtesy of Jonathan Reeve: 7, 11, 12, 13, 15, 16, 20, 23, 25, 27, 30, 33, 34, 35, 36, 37, 61, 71

The illustrations on the following pages are reproduced courtesy of Tempus Archive: 62, 87, 90, 96, 97, 99, 101, 109 (bottom), 118, 120, 124, 126 (top), 133, 154, 209, 211

The following plate numbers are also reproduced courtesy of Tempus Archive: 8, 9, 10, 14, 17, 18, 19, 21, 22, 24, 26, 28, 29, 31, 32, 67, 68, 69

16 Piltdown Man. Reproduced courtesy of the Sussex Archaeological Society.

18 Flint knapper. Reproduced by permission of Philip Marter.

18 Boxgrove knapping evidence. Copyright Miles Russell.

20 Street House Farm. Copyright Philip Marter.

23 Grimes Graves Flint Mines. Reproduced courtesy of Miles Russell.

23 West Kennet long barrow. Reproduced courtesy of Caroline Malone.

25 White Horse at Uffington. Reproduced by permission of Society of Antiquaries of London.

28 Bronze Age round house. Copyright Philip Marter.

33 Julius Agricola from Edward Barnard's *History of England*. Reproduced courtesy of Martin Henig.

37 Roman provinces of Southern Britain c.AD 250. Reproduced courtesy of Andrew Reynolds.

39 Roman tombstone from South Shields. Reproduced by permission of Martin Henig.

41 Simplified geology of southern Britain. Reproduced courtesy of Andrew Reynolds.

43 Early Anglo-Saxon cremation urn from Sancton. Reproduced courtesy of Andrew Reynolds.

43 An Anglo-Saxon woman. Copyright Steve Hardy.

PLATE SECTIONS

Index

The following is merely an index of people and places, to see some of the events and themes covered in the text please refer to the chronology (p.276)